Second E

MW00785214

The Wing-T from A to Z

Volume 2: Installing the System

Dennis Creehan

COACHES CHOICE™

ISBN: 1-58518-926-X
Library of Congress Control Number: 2004115571
Cover design: Jeanne Hamilton
Book layout: Jeanne Hamilton
Front cover photo: Mike Gallagher/Youngstown State, courtesy of Edinboro University
    of Pennsylvania
Diagrams: James Hunt

Coaches Choice
P.O. Box 1828
Monterey, CA 93942
www.coacheschoice.com

Dedication

I would like to dedicate this book to everyone in my family. They have all been so patient and understanding over the years as we have moved all around the country so that I could pursue my dream of coaching football. To my loving wife, Linda, who is the best dance teacher in the country and has given up four different successful dance studios as we have moved. To my sons, Kevin and Casey, who attended four different schools while I chased my coaching dream. To Kevin, the older of my two sons, who is so intelligent that he has decided to use his brain power in the world of industrial engineering rather than in the arena of coaching—even though he could be a great coach, as evidenced by the American Legion state baseball championship his team won in his first and only coaching opportunity. To the younger Casey, who actually wants to go into the field of coaching and is just hardheaded enough to be a great coach. Finally, I would also like to dedicate this book to my mother and father, Peggy and Jerry Creehan, who have been big fans of mine, no matter where I have coached. And, to my brothers and sisters, Jerry Jr., Rick, Karen, Kathy, and Kenny. Rick and Kenny have already been quite successful as baseball coaches.

Acknowledgments

Many great coaches have touched my life, and I would like to thank all of them for their leadership and guidance. My high school coaches, Dan Galbraith and Joe Nicoletti, who instilled in me the desire to play the game and taught me the fundamentals at Bethel Park (PA) High School. My college head coach, Bill McDonald, who turned Edinboro University of Pennsylvania from a 40-year loser into a champion. My college position coaches, Sam Ruvolo, Jack Hyland, and Bill Straub, who helped me to achieve more personal success than I ever thought possible for myself. Upon graduation from college, I had no idea that I would ever coach, but Jerry Mancini brought me into the profession at Keystone Oaks (PA) High School. Johnny Majors and Jackie Sherrill gave me my first taste of college football as a graduate assistant at the University of Pittsburgh. Joe Gasparella and Chuck Klausing gave me my first real college coaching position at Carnegie-Mellon University. My first full-time position in college football came from Bill McDonald, my college coach at Edinboro. Three years later, I got a lucky break and succeeded Bill when he retired. During my 12 years as a head coach, I was very fortunate to have many great assistant coaches who have gone on to become college or pro head coaches themselves: John D'Ottavio, Utah Pioneers of the PSFL; Gerry Gallagher, St. Francis (PA) and William Patterson (NJ); Budgie Hamilton, San Francisco State; Tom Herman, Gannon University (PA); Mike Kelly, Valdosta State University; Malen Luke, Defiance (OH) and Clarion University (PA); Tom Menage, Westmar University (IA); Dave Lyon, Thiel College (PA); Ron Rankin, University of South Dakota; and Blair Hrovat, Allegheny College in Pennsylvania. Finally, I would like to thank the coaches who taught me the wing-T offense: Ted Kempski of the University of Delaware and, most of all, John D'Ottavio, who is out of coaching, but who is, in my opinion, the most knowledgeable wing-T coach I have ever met.

Contents

Preface

This two-volume set of books on *The Wing-T from A to Z* was written in order to provide coaches and players at all competitive levels with a useful tool to enable them to better understand the intricacies of the wing-T offense. In this comprehensive overview of one of the game's most popular offensive schemes, the fundamentals and the nuances of the wing-T offense are presented in great detail.

The first volume in the set provides an excellent guide to understanding and developing a sound base plan for the wing-T offense. This volume features chapters on philosophy and organization, goal line attack, and movements (20 series, 30 series, 60 series, and 80 series).

The second volume in the set explains how to install and implement this innovative offensive package. The responsibilities and techniques essential to each offensive player position are identified and reviewed in a step-by-step manner. This volume also includes detailed chapters on establishing an efficient and effective plan for practicing the wing-T and developing a successful offensive game-day plan.

It is hoped that the insights and the information presented in these books will also enhance the reader's sense of appreciation for the wing-T. In my opinion, the more an individual knows about this offensive scheme, the greater the level of appreciation they will have. I can only hope that every coach and player who reads these books will enjoy them as much as I enjoyed writing them.

—Dennis Creehan

1

The Wing-T Practice Plan

In this chapter, the practice plan used to teach and drill the offense will be illustrated. This plan is unique to the wing-T and certainly has proven to be successful. The plan is named for the way practices are run and practice plans are operated. The plan is called the "racehorse philosophy." The concept of "racehorse" is even used in pre-practice meetings. In pre-practice meetings, players are expected to pay attention and stay with you. They should sit upright with their feet on the floor—not lounging all over their chairs—and they take their hats off in meetings. You want to be able to make eye contact with them. During those meetings, you go quickly. You start on time, and the coaches talk loud. They talk fast, and they repeat. The coaches must get their message across in pre-practice meetings. You go over anything new or different you will do in practice that day, and you always review videotape of practice with the players.

Racehorse Philosophy

What exactly does racehorse philosophy mean? Racehorse philosophy involves working at a pace allowing for maximum repetitions and maximum learning to take place. To successfully use this philosophy, you must do the following:
- Perform maximum repetitions
- Mass teach when possible
- Run all drills on sound

- Shift in team takeoff only
- Shotgun two huddles
- Have coaches stay in centralized locations
- Have coaches make quick corrections

These concepts are referred to when talking about racehorse philosophy. Racehorse indicates you are going to go fast. And, fast is exactly what you want to do.

You want to accomplish maximum reps with this philosophy. Many coaches make that claim. Coaches are always trying to structure their practices for maximum repetitions. The racehorse philosophy really does get maximum reps. Everything done in the structure of the practice is based on getting maximum reps. Everything within this philosophy is designed to facilitate getting maximum reps for teaching. The very style with which this philosophy is coached accomplishes this goal.

Mass teach whenever possible. Anytime you have drills being run on the practice field, every player in each group should take part in that drill at the same time, if possible. All drills are done on *sound cadence*. When doing drill work, you save time by not using long cadences. By the time practice ends, you may have wasted a lot of time by calling cadences throughout practice. On sound means the quarterback or the coach running the drill will say, "Set." On the "s" in set, the ball will be snapped and the players will take off. Sound cadence will be used in as many drills as possible. If you have a 10-minute period and want to get a lot of reps during that drill, start each rep with one command rather than a long cadence. You go on the first sound and do all your drills to get maximum reps.

Another way to guarantee maximum reps is to practice *shifting in team takeoff only*. In the wing-T offense, you run many shifts throughout the course of a game. You want to be good at shifting. However, you rarely work on shifting in team periods when practicing 11-on-11. You do not want to take those extra minutes out of team period, when you could be getting more reps. You will mix up the cadences in team period and shift if you need to see the timing of a shift along with the 11 players running a play. For the most part, 99 percent of the time, shifting will be done during team takeoff period.

You should *shotgun two huddles*. This practice means during your team periods one huddle will be going while another huddle huddles up, ready to go. As soon as the players finish the first play, the second group should be saying, "Ready, break," and then sprint up to the line of scrimmage, ready to run the next play. Most of the time, the first group, which has just run the play, will have to hustle out of the way of the second group by running off toward the sideline and then coming back around to the huddle. As they get in tune with the practice tempo, the players will understand they must get back to the huddle quickly in order to get out of the way of the next group.

It is also vital for the scout team to hustle back, which is tough on them. Having two scout teams is recommended, or having three players for every two positions, so they can rotate in and out. They will become tired at times during team periods when practicing at this pace and will need a rest.

Your coaches should *stay in a centralized location* and make the players run past them for correction. In many programs, you will see a coach chase a player into the huddle to make a correction while the player is still in the huddle. What happens is the next play gets run with another group, and the coach does not see anything in that next play because he is still correcting the player from the previous group. If you tell coaches to stay in a centralized location and have the players run past them for corrections, the coaches cannot only make the corrections, but they can watch the next play. When coaches make corrections, you do not want them to earn their doctorate by giving a dissertation on the field. The coaches should make *quick, meaningful corrections* to the players on their way by. The players can thus hear the correction and know what they did wrong; the rest of the help comes from the film analysis. Every practice should be videotaped. If possible, do so with two cameras: one for offense and one for defense. Every day, players have plenty of film to watch. Your coaches can make longer explanations or demonstrations once they see the film. On the field, in order to get maximum reps, you have the players run past the coach, who then gives a short correction on the way into the huddle. If necessary, you can stop a play to explain something and make them repeat. Stopping a play does not happen very often. It does happen at times, and you should understand that. At times, it may be better to get a play stopped, make the corrections for everybody to hear, and get the problem cleared up, thus enabling the players to continue with the rest of the practice free of errors.

When the staff gets together for practice planning, the first thing to consider is how to get maximum reps, how to stay within the racehorse philosophy. It starts with pre-practice and continues all the way through the practice. Your coaches meet to find ways to get more repetitions during practice. It is very important for coaches to make sure they are getting maximum reps and to make sure each is taking time to think about how he can get more reps in the practice plan.

Team Takeoff Period

Team takeoff period will follow loosening and kicking, which are the first two periods in practice, according to the practice plan. You begin practice each day in this manner. You put 11 people on the line of scrimmage and run a play. The offensive line's assignment is to get off the ball as fast as they can, which is a get-off drill for them. You want to see them come out low and hard for 10 yards and finish across the goal line to get reps on firing out. The backs, on the other hand, will run their play assignments in order to execute footwork. They will also sprint 10 yards across the goal line. You do this drill from the 10-yard line on in to the goal line. That way, the backs run across the goal line all the time. You will make the backs run across the goal line as many times as possible in practice. The repetition sends a psychological message: "Across the goal line, across the goal line, across the goal line." Diagram 1.1 illustrates the team takeoff period.

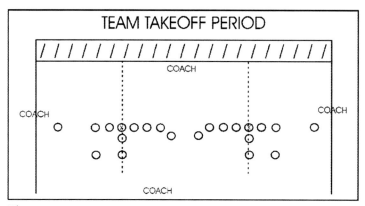

Diagram 1.1

You should have two groups going at the same time. One offensive group will be on the left hash mark, and another offensive group is on the right hash mark. Coaches will stand in centralized locations. One coach will be down at the goal line to make sure the players are firing out and crossing the goal line. Other coaches will be on the sides at the line of scrimmage, to see the team's takeoff and to note whether they are coming off the ball low. The coach running the drill will be behind the teams. He will tell the quarterback the play to be run and which quarterback will have the cadence. Both groups will go on one cadence. You can run the same plays with both groups or the mirrored play with both groups. If you are going to run 121 sweep with the group on the right hash and 929 sweep with the group on the left hash, then both units will go on the same cadence. If the coach designates that the left-side quarterback has the cadence, then the right side also listens for that cadence. Both groups fire off the line at the same time on one cadence. This period is when you will work on shifting. The coach will say, "Shift to 121," or "Shift to 929." The backs and ends will execute their shift, and then the teams run the play. One day each week, you will have the teams just fire off the ball and do team takeoff without any shifting. The next day, you will execute all the shifts to prepare for that particular week. If you are going two groups at one time, it is amazing how many reps your entire team will get. If you have a third group and, possibly, even a fourth group, then they will wait in line behind the first two groups. As soon as those two groups are done, the next two groups sprint up to the line and run the same play. Even though each team only goes every other play, they still get plenty of reps.

Because you have done all of your shifting during team takeoff, when you go to mixed group work or to team period, you do not have to work on your shifts. Times might exist when you will need to include one shift during some other part of practice, but, for the most part, shifting gets practiced in team takeoff period. Over the course of an entire practice, working on shifting during team takeoff saves time and allows for maximum reps during the other phases of the practice plan.

Shoulder Skills Period

The next drill is a shoulder skills period. Diagram 1.2 illustrates how the entire team is spaced during the shoulder skills period. This example is of mass teaching. Every player on the offensive unit is involved in this drill and working at the same time. You take the big blocking bags and align them so the bottom of the bag is intersected by one of the yard lines. One player will hold the bag while another player is down in a six- or two-point stance, ready to block the bag. The blockers are on the inside of the yard line, and the bag is directly on the line. The bags are five yards apart. If you feel you need more space, you can move them back so they are 10 yards apart.

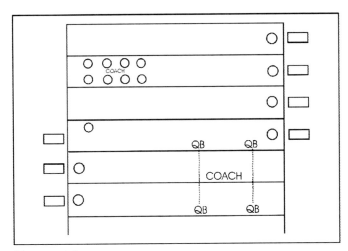

Diagram 1.2

In this drill, the coach is able to see all his players and coach them all at the same time. One bag is put out for every two players. The blockers execute the drill and trade around to become the bag holders. The players who were holding the bags then become the blockers and execute the drill themselves.

In the shoulder skills period, you start with surface, which is nothing more than a form fit drill. The second drill is strike a blow. Both of these drills start in a six-point stance. In the surface drill, you are working on how you fit into the bag. In the strike a blow drill, you strike the bag and roll your hips, keeping the bag between your legs. The third drill done every day is step and hit. When you step and hit, you are working on making sure the first step is exact. The second step is when you want contact to occur, and, on the third step, you want the body to follow through naturally. You practice this drill in progression, but you can also practice it by saying, "Set," and the entire sequence is executed. The last drill is either run and hit or hit and run. Run and hit means you will run four yards at the bag, strike the bag, drive it, and then turn it to finish the block. Hit and run is the opposite, with contact first and running after contact to emphasize leg drive. The blocker comes off, strikes the bag, which is directly on him, and then drives the bag off the line.

Everyone on the football team is doing shoulder skills at the same time. It is a very well-organized practice time period, but, more important, the players will get maximum reps in each of the drills. If a coach misses a correction, he will be able to catch it in time. A player will learn more by doing than he will by watching. The shoulder skills period is another example of mass teaching. The drill is also done on sound. You do not waste time with cadence. Again, this drill facilitates getting maximum reps in a short amount of time. You use the entire field for this drill. While the offensive line coach is working in one area, the running backs coach is working in another area. In another area of the field, the receivers coach is also doing the same drill. You have quarterbacks throwing the ball to each other with the quarterbacks coach, in order to loosen up and do their daily drills. While all the other players are doing shoulder skills, the quarterbacks will be doing arm loosening or working on the center-quarterback exchange.

Everybody on the team is taught how to execute a block. If you are the most gifted wide receiver or most talented running back, you will also get down in the dirt and get physical, just like the linemen. This method creates an unselfish offense. All skilled players will get the ball, but they must also be willing to block when their teammate gets the ball. Therefore, everyone on the team (other than quarterbacks) learns how to execute shoulder skills and does it from day one, all the way through to the end of the season.

Routine Period

The next period after shoulder skills drill is routine period. In routine, the offensive line will be lined up five yards apart. Each backup is five yards behind and five yards apart from left to right. You align them in their positions (Diagram 1.3) so the left guard is on the coach's right, but on the offense's left as they face the coach. All players in the drill are facing the coach. While the line coach is doing his drill, the running backs coach is doing his drills in another area of the field. The running backs align on lines five yards apart and are working on routine period, as well. The receivers coach has his split ends and tight ends five yards behind each other, doing the same drill as everyone else. The centers and quarterbacks are working on center-quarterback exchange. If you look over the entire field, you will observe everyone engaged in the same drill. This drill period is another where the entire team is active. Again, this method is mass teaching. Not one player is standing around watching. Everybody on the team is learning the same skills.

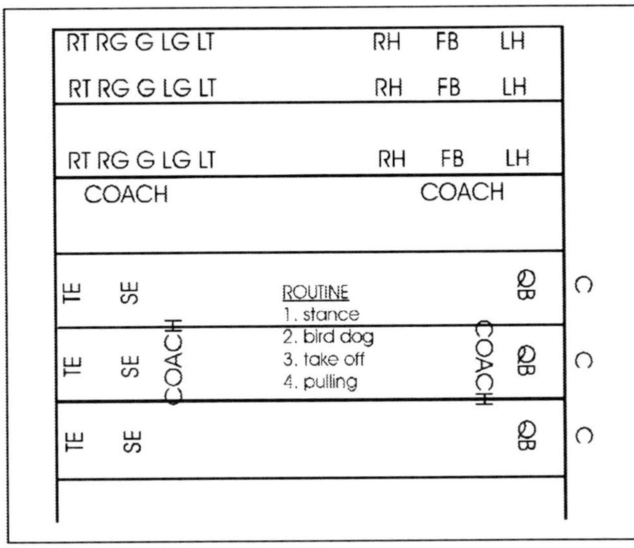

RT RG G LG LT		RH	FB	LH
RT RG G LG LT		RH	FB	LH
RT RG G LG LT		RH	FB	LH
COACH			COACH	

TE	SE		ROUTINE 1. stance	QB	○
TE	SE	COACH	2. bird dog 3. take off 4. pulling	COACH	QB	○
TE	SE			QB	○

Diagram 1.3

Four steps are done in progression during routine period. The first step is teaching the stance. After the stance is taught, you check it every day. The ends and halfbacks have different types of stances, because the ends put their inside hand down and the halfbacks also have to be comfortable with a wingback stance. The first fundamental reviewed at each position is proper stance. The coach stands in front of each group, so he can see all of his players—coaching from a centralized location. He can make a quick check of all of his players and make necessary corrections or proceed to the next drill, if everybody is performing satisfactorily.

The second phase is called bird-dog. You take one step and hold it to check the first step of whatever type of footwork being emphasized each day. You make sure the players have good opposite arm and leg action. You make sure each player's chest is down on his thigh. You make sure his butt is over his heels and that he is not overextended. These points are emphasized during bird-dog period. It is a great drill for working on the first step, which is the most important step.

The third step in the progression is takeoff. In takeoff period, the focus is on sprinting off the ball. This sprint is not long; it is only a five-yard sprint, followed by five yards of jogging to slow down. Each player will have a five-yard get-off to see if, one, he is firing out low, and, two, he is coming off the ball with the proper footwork.

When players first start taking off with a certain foot, they begin to think too much. Eventually, you want your players not to think about their feet. They must automatically know, for example, if they block with their right shoulder, then they must step with their left foot first. It has to become second nature to them. They should not have to think about it.

The last step in the progression is only for the line and the tight ends. It is an 11-step pulling drill, where they work on pulling techniques, log block techniques, and gut techniques. In these drills, you will pull to log and pull to gut. The first time you do this drill, the players walk through the drill step-by-step through all 11 steps. You do the drill by the numbers once or twice, then sprint all 11 steps. In this drill, you pull and log, or pull to wall off, or pull to gut. The purpose of this drill is to work on the footwork of both pulling and log blocking. If an offensive guard is going to pull to the right to log the defensive end, then on the fourth step (which is the point of contact), he will be on his inside foot, blocking with his inside shoulder. The fifth step must work directly up the field, while the sixth step starts back to the starting point.

The actual wing-T part of practice is made up of team takeoff, followed by shoulder skills, and, finally, routine. At the beginning of the year, these drills are longer. The shoulder skill period might be 15 minutes long, so you have plenty of time to explain and teach it. The second and third days, you may cut it down to 10 minutes; and, once the season begins, the shoulder skill period will be a five-minute period. Routine starts out being a 10-minute period and, by the end of the year, will dwindle to two or three minutes long. By that time, the players will know what to do, be able to do it well, and know how to do it quickly.

Practice Organization

The next phase of practice is the individual part of practice. It is necessary to divide the practice plan into three discrete practice plans in order for each group to work on the individual skills that relate to each position. Diagram 1.4 illustrates how the practice plan is typically divided up. The amount of time used for individual periods is up to the coaches, depending on how much time each coach needs for each of these drills.

BACKS 40'	ENDS 40'	OFFENSIVE LINE 40'
5' HAND OFFS 5' PITCH DRILLS 20' FULL BACKFIELD TECH. 10' PASSING WITH ENDS	15' BLOCKING TECH. 5' RELEASES 5' PATTERNS 5' BALL DRILLS 10' PASSING WITH BACKS	15' BLOCKING TECHNIQUE 5' SWEEPING DRILL 5' WAGGLE DRILL W/QB 10' ASSIGNMENT PERIOD 5' PASS PRO DRILLS

Diagram 1.4

Running Backs

The backs do these drills during the individual portion of their practice plan. The first thing the backs do is handoff drill (Diagram 1.5). Handoff drill is set up with four stations, with a quarterback and a fullback in one station and a quarterback and a fullback in another station. The fullbacks are working on certain plays, including the corresponding footwork. If you don't have enough quarterbacks and fullbacks to have two fullback stations, then you combine them into one. While the fullback stations are working on handoffs, the left halfbacks and a quarterback are working together on one side of the field, and a quarterback and the right halfback are working on the other side of the field. Three different running back stations are used. This drill structure enables you to get maximum reps on handoffs and on plays where the quarterback hands the ball to a back. This period lasts five minutes, and how many repetitions you can get is amazing. Five minutes does not sound like much time, but, if each station works independently of the other, each player will get enough reps to execute each play flawlessly.

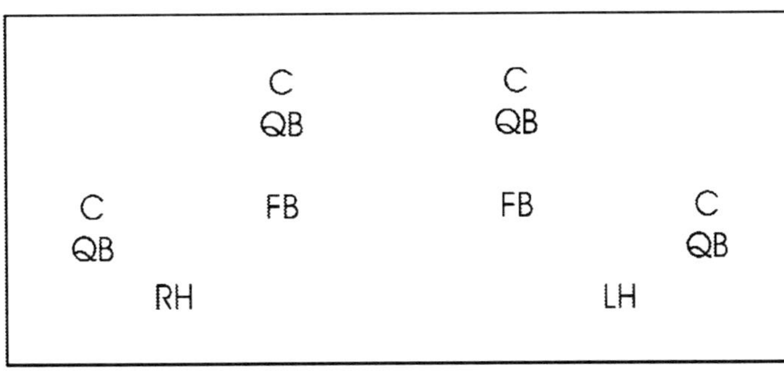

Diagram 1.5

The next drill for the running backs is called pitch drill (Diagram 1.6). During pitch drills, two groups are going at the same time. A quarterback, a fullback, and a left halfback are working on option plays to the right. Also, a quarterback, a fullback, and a right halfback are working on option plays to the left. Both groups work independently. The left-side quarterback runs option to the right and emphasizes pitching the ball. The same thing occurs with the other group of quarterbacks, fullbacks, and right halfbacks. In order to make sure that they don't run into each other, the drill is offset 10 yards upfield. By conducting one drill 10 yards upfield from the other, each drill can be run at the same time without players having to wait for the other group. You can also do this drill with both groups going at the same time, running option into the boundary. Even though you don't want to run a lot of option into the boundaries, the backs learn to take good footwork, stay in bounds, and maximize their use of the field.

Full backfield technique is the next drill (Diagram 1.7). In this drill, a full backfield, a quarterback, a fullback, a right half, and a left half are involved. If you have enough backs, you put another group back-to-back with this group, going in the opposite direction and running the same play. If you have a quarterback coach and a running back coach, you have enough coaches to work two different drill groups and get a lot of reps.

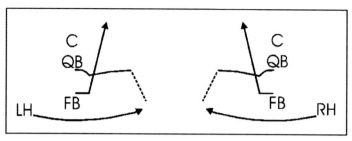

Diagram 1.6

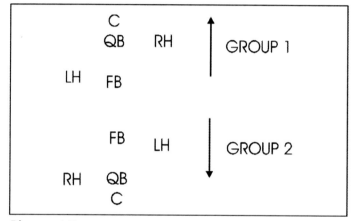

Diagram 1.7

Passing with ends is the last drill worked on during individual period with the running backs (Diagram 1.8). You also involve the ends, a quarterback, a fullback, a tight end, a split end, a left half, and a right half. You have all the backs and the ends together to work on pass patterns. They can either work on pass patterns as a total group or practice different individual cuts. You also practice getting into blocking techniques with the backs for pass protection.

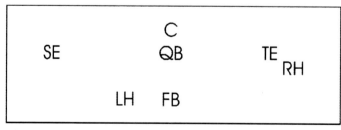

Diagram 1.8

Handoff period is no more than five minutes long. At the beginning of the year, it will be 10 minutes, but, later in the year, it will be cut down to five minutes and will stay five minutes most of the year. In the last few weeks of the season, it might be cut down to two minutes. If a coach is maximizing reps, he can still get a lot of handoffs done in just two minutes. If the coach has the drill set up quickly, gets his players there quickly, and the players know what they are doing, then he can get plenty of reps in just two or three minutes.

Pitch drill will generally last about five minutes. Usually, your coaches would like to do passing with ends for a minimum of 10 minutes. That amount will account for 20 minutes of the individual time to do those three drills. If you have planned 40 minutes for individual practice period, then use five minutes for handoffs, five minutes for pitches, 20 minutes for full backfield, and 10 minutes for passing with ends. Full backfield technique takes up the most crucial period. It is the period requiring the most time and attention to detail. The full backfield technique is the period where you correct any mistakes being made. This time period is used to perfect any plays needing perfecting. It provides you with an excellent opportunity to work the flank plays, which require the backs to block, or the flank passing plays.

Receivers

The ends have five important drills to do in individual period. They will work on these five drills every day. The position coach decides what he needs to accomplish during each drill and how much time he needs to spend with each particular drill. At the beginning of the season, he has 40 minutes of individual period. As the season wears on, it will be closer to 20 minutes or half an hour. Early in the season, a coach must use these reps as quality teaching reps.

Blocking technique period is where the ends—both spread ends and tight ends—work on the different types of blocks they will use. In the receiver section, every block is explained in detail. During blocking technique period, the coach might choose to have the tight ends work gap blocks and down blocks, while he has the split ends work on stalk blocks or crack blocks. Since each group has different blocks to work on, the coach may want to shotgun the groups. If you only have one receiver coach, then you may want to have the tight ends work a block and then the spread ends work a block, continuing to alternate in order for the coach to work with both groups at once. Another possibility is both groups could go at the same time. If you have two coaches or somebody to help the receiver coach, then you can have two groups going at the same time, independent of each other, and get more quality reps and coaching.

During release period, the receivers work their releases from the line of scrimmage against a defender who is trying to stop them from releasing. The defender trying to jam their release may be on the line of scrimmage or may be five yards off. The receivers work against all types of jams. The tight ends use different releases, while the spread ends work on the different types of releases needed on the perimeter. They can work at the same time if you have two coaches, so each group has a coach available.

Pattern drill works on the actual pass patterns the receivers run. Anything new in the week's game plan or for that day of practice is taught and reinforced during this drill. The receivers will also work on correcting patterns they need to perfect, or routes that have consistently posed problems for the players. One example might be the trap option pass, because the spread ends are having a problem with the slant route. If this case is true, then the coaches make sure the slant gets emphasis during this period. This period is usually filled by two different groups. For example, the tight ends may need work on the waggle route or their crossing route, while, at the same time, the split ends are working on the slant route or the out route. Each group can work different types of pass patterns during the same drill.

Ball drills are a part of the individual practice plan all the receivers do together. You will use many ball drills, and most wing-T teams probably use drills similar to other offenses. Some examples are distraction drills, one-hand-catch drills, drills in which the receiver must catch the ball and keep his feet in bounds, catching bad balls, jugs gun drills, and comeback drills. This drill period will usually last five minutes. If six to eight receivers are in the group, they will be able to complete two or three different drills every day during this five-minute period.

Passing with the backs is the same drill as passing with ends. The quarterbacks, fullbacks, right halfbacks, left halfbacks, tight ends, and spread ends work on patterns as a group at the same time, or sometimes they divide up in order to work on individual cuts. For example, the one set of quarterbacks might be throwing out routes to the split ends, while another set of quarterbacks is throwing waggle routes to all the tight ends.

Releases, patterns, and ball drills are each done for five minutes during every practice. At the end of the season, each might be cut down to three minutes, which forces everyone to really hustle. Our staff usually takes 10 minutes for blocking technique every day early in the season, but, by late in the year, this drill gets cut down to five minutes. Passing with backs is usually done in a 10-minute period. Those drills account for 35 minutes, with an extra five minutes for anything else the coaches feel they need more work on. Blocking technique period usually gets the most emphasis. This added emphasis helps the players understand that blocking is the most important skill they need to learn. Some of the receivers may not want to hear that, but no matter what position you play in the wing-T, players will have to block. If players are willing to block with great effort and are unselfish players, then they will be the kind of players who fit into the wing-T offense the best.

Offensive Line

Blocking technique is the number one drill any offensive line has to work on. The linemen must be good blockers. Players must excel at combination blocks as well as single blocks. Each player must understand every block, understand the techniques required, and understand how each type of block makes a contribution to winning. Offensive linemen are the ultimate team warriors in football. Football is the ultimate team game. Therefore, coaches look at offensive linemen as the ultimate team warriors in the ultimate team game. These players get very little recognition and stats. Playing offensive line is not like playing defense, where players get a certain number of tackles, sacks, pass breakups, interceptions, or other stats. An offensive lineman has no statistics, certainly none appearing in the next day's paper. If you give an offensive lineman a grade every week, he can take pride in his grades. You can also foster in them a feeling of pride in your total offense. Without them, no offense would exist. The team can have great backs, but great backs can do only so much without good blocking for them. Without strong blocking, they will not be productive. The offensive line puts most of its individual time in blocking technique period.

The pulling drills that the line does include sweep drill, with all the linemen playing guards, and waggle drill, with all the linemen also practicing as guards. Linemen also practice gut drill, guard trap drill, or several other combinations of pulling drills. Each drill is done in five-minute periods. The linemen also work together with the quarterbacks during waggle drill. This combination is very helpful for both the quarterbacks and the offensive linemen because they work together on the various pulling techniques, as well as on when to attack the flank or when to pull up, and on the timing and spacing needed to react to the different defensive reactions they face. It is a drill you should have some of your quarterbacks working on just about every day.

Following their pulling drills, the linemen have assignment period (Diagram 1.9). The assignment period is constructed similarly to an inside drill with a full offensive line. A center, a left guard, a left tackle, a right guard, and a right tackle participate. All of these positions practice all plays against the interior of a defense. The defense will use the front four and the inside linebackers. The offensive linemen will be reviewing and practicing their blocking assignments. The defensive line will send a scout team or possibly defensive starters, if your opponent uses a wing-T scheme. The number one defensive line and linebackers can then work on reacting against the blocking schemes they will see that week. An injured player, a kicker, or one of the backups will be in the backfield, indicating the direction the ball will go. This aspect is important so the defenders have a key to react to if they are keying flow. They also react to the blocking scheme they see in front of them.

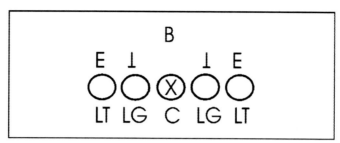

Diagram 1.9

The last drills for the linemen during individual period are pass protection (pass pro) drills. In the beginning of the season, while learning their skills, the linemen do pass protection drills against themselves, and, as the linemen become more proficient, they progress to blocking more active defensive players.

Each pulling drill takes five minutes. Pass pro drills should take no more than 10 minutes, and, as the season progresses, you will be able to finish those in five minutes. Assignment period usually takes 10 minutes, which leaves 15 minutes for blocking technique.

What has been discussed thus far is what constitutes a normal practice plan for the offensive line, the ends, and the backs during individual period. With all of these drills to do, coaches must be very thoughtful in deciding how much time is necessary for each period and exactly which drills to use each day. Each coach must have a feel for his group and know exactly which drills need working on. In blocking technique period, individual blocks and combination blocks are in every practice plan. Sweep drill and waggle drill are the primary pulling drills. Either can be replaced by guard trap drill or gut drill. Waggle drill will be done as often as possible, because the quarterbacks must get a feel for the waggle action and also because the play-action pass is key to offensive success. Assignment period will be done every day. It will either be done with the offensive coach having his extra offensive linemen hold bags, or against the defense in a live setting. Pass pro drills can be done with offensive linemen blocking against other offensive linemen, working the techniques of pass protection. They will block 1-on-1 pass protection live against defensive players during the mixed-group work period. This broad summary is of the individual period for the practice plan.

Two parts of daily practice follow individual, shoulder skills, routine, and team takeoff periods. These last two parts of practice are mixed group work and 11-on-11.

Mixed Group Period

Three different types of drills are done during mixed group period. The first drill is called four corners drill (Diagram 1.10). During this drill, the receivers, running backs, and quarterbacks are throwing 1-on-1 routes against defensive backs and linebackers in four separate sections of the field. During this drill, the defense is working on man coverage. The defensive coaches want to see how well the defensive players can cover a receiver in man coverage. The same idea holds true for the receivers and the backs. The offensive coaches want to emphasize running patterns against man coverage. Receiver technique versus man coverage plays a big part in the passing game. A key question you face is, "Can our receivers beat a coverage defender who is lined up across from them, 1-on-1, in a man-to-man setting?" The receivers are told if they cannot get open against man coverage, then they cannot play in this league. The receivers have to possess either, one, great speed or, two, great moves. Each receiver must have one of those two qualities, in addition to great hands. In order to get open, a receiver must have some good shake and bake moves and must be able to push the defense off. Certainly, it is much better if the receiver has good speed, because he can really back the defender off and sit down inside or outside, using any kind of break. If a receiver does not have great speed, then he must have shiftiness. He must be able to push a defender, work the defender in and out, get the defender to turn his shoulders, and then break.

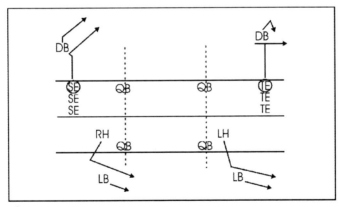

Diagram 1.10

Four Corners Drill

During four corners drill, you set up near the 50-yard line. A quarterback will be on the left hash throwing to the spread ends. On the right hash, another quarterback is throwing to the tight ends. The players decide what pass pattern they need to work on. It must be a pattern used in the offense. The coaches make sure the players are running their patterns with the proper technique. The quarterback works on his dropback mechanics and his throwing mechanics. The receiver is working on his patterns, and the defensive back is working on man coverage. Each quarterback will run his group independent of the other group.

Going in the other direction on one hash mark, you set up a quarterback throwing to the left halfbacks. Another quarterback is set up with the right halfbacks on the opposite hash. The linebackers will work against the running backs in order to work on man-to-man coverage. The quarterbacks, meanwhile, are working on throwing techniques, ball placement, and footwork. The receivers are working on specific patterns and pattern running techniques. The defensive backs and linebackers are working on coverage technique.

At the far end of the field, another drill is set up in which the fullbacks will pass protect against a set of linebackers rushing the passer (Diagram 1.11). Two outside linebackers and two inside linebackers participate. The fullbacks will step right or left and pass protect against either the outside rusher or the inside rusher. One of those two pass rushers will be the live rusher. The fullback steps to one side and pass protects against either linebacker on a blitz. Sometimes, halfbacks will be included in the drill to work on pass protection. At times, the fullbacks will be working in four corners drill, running pass patterns against the linebackers.

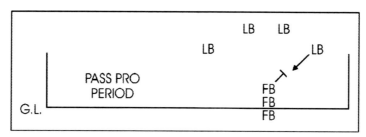

Diagram 1.11

At the other end of the field, while four corners is going on, the defensive line and the offensive line will be working on pass protection or assignments versus various types of pass rushes (Diagram 1.12).

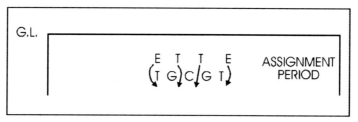

Diagram 1.12

Four corners and pass pro is one period where everybody on the field is active. Looking at this period from end to end, everybody is participating. Mass teaching is going on. In the middle of the field are the four corners. On one end of the field, an assignment period is working, and on the other end is the backfield pass protection period. All of these drills are going on at the same time. All the drills go on sound. All the coaches stay in centralized locations, and each group gets a ton of reps in just a five-minute period. Constructing this drill period in this fashion is another prime example of the racehorse philosophy. Two other mixed group periods exist — one period concentrating on runs, the other on passing.

Internal Period

During run play mixed group work, two different drills are going on at the same time. At one end of the field (Diagram 1.13), an internal drill is working on inside runs. This drill includes the offensive line and the backs. The defensive players in the drill include the nose, the defensive ends, the outside linebackers, and the inside linebackers. In this drill, the offense will run internal or inside run plays against the defense. These plays hit between the tackles or off-tackle. The tempo for the drill is live blocking. The backs will run the ball full speed. The defense tries to defeat the blocks and then tackle full go live to the ground, or to thud the backs. In this drill, coaches prefer thud, or wrapping the backs up and not taking them to the ground. Thud keeps the backs healthier over the course of a season.

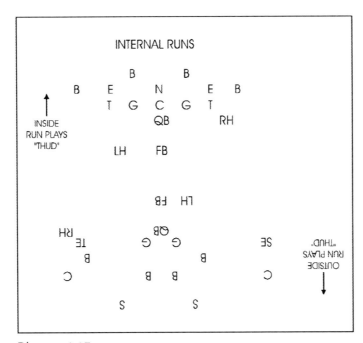

Diagram 1.13

Perimeter Period

While internal is going on, at the other end of the field, a drill called perimeter drill is happening. Perimeter drill includes the guards, all the backs, and the receivers. The defense will include the defensive backs and the linebackers. In this drill, the offense will run all the outside plays, including all the sweeps, all options, and all of the passes where the quarterback is attacking the flank with a run-pass option.

Early in the season, the offensive coaches may see all of the offensive people getting their butt whipped in these drills. It may look bad the first day and worse the second day. By the third day, the coach will feel as though it cannot possibly get any worse—then, it will start to get better.

Ten minutes is usually the amount of time given to mixed group runs, both internal and perimeter drills. Within those 10 minutes, coaches can have the guards and backs switch drills after five minutes. You can sometimes wait until the next day and then switch them. It is extremely important that the guards and the running backs get time at both drills. The ends and the quarterbacks need to be at perimeter drill. Other than the guards, the offensive linemen are usually in internal drill. Guards must work both drills. Other than one group of backs, all of the backs and receivers are at perimeter.

Mixed Group Pass

The final period in mixed group work is called mixed group work pass period. In this period, everybody on the field will be active. Again, two groups will be going at the same time. One group will be working on pass protection, and the other group will be working on pass routes (Diagram 1.14).

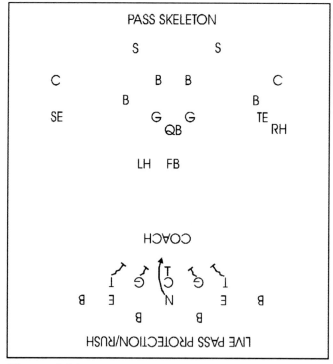

Diagram 1.14

Pass Skeleton Drill

In pass skeleton, the offense will have the quarterback, backs, and ends working passing plays against all four defensive backs and all of the linebackers. They will work pass plays against all pass defenses. The offensive coaches will ask the defense to mix in blitzes. You want them to blitz. You need to make sure the backs learn to pick up the blitz and execute their blocking assignments versus any kind of blitz. The quarterbacks also need a great deal of work on reading coverage and throwing the ball to the correct receiver.

Pass Protection Drill

While the pass skeleton drill is going on, another drill, called live pass protection, is working at the other end of the field. In this drill, a center, two guards, and two tackles will participate. They will work against the defensive line and a set of linebackers, so the linebackers can get work on pass rush with the defensive line. Only one pass rusher goes at a time. All five linemen are lined up, and a coach stands behind the drill and points to one of those defensive rushers, who knows he will be the live pass rusher. The entire defense gets in their stance. All the offense gets in their stance. When the coach gives the command, all five offensive linemen pass set at the same time. They are all getting reps on learning how to explode out of their stance and get set for pass pro. Only one of the defensive players is live when the ball is actually snapped, yet every lineman gets into a pass set. By having all linemen in their positions, a pass rush will not occur with unrealistic rush lanes. The offensive line coach will want a realistic rush and will want all defenders to work in the gaps or in the confined areas they normally do during games.

11-On-11

Only one more part of daily practice needs to be discussed, and it is called 11-on-11. It is the whole offensive team going against the whole defensive team, and you do it three different ways.

Team vs. Bags

The first method is called team vs. bags (Diagram 1.15), which means 11 players going against bags. When coaches use team vs. bags, it is a drill that can be done in T-shirts and shorts and not necessarily with all pads on. The offense can still get a lot of work done. On defense, a scout team or the number two defense are holding bags in the proper front spacing the opponent will use in the upcoming game. The big linemen will hold big bags, and the linebackers will hold hand shields. The defensive backs do not hold anything, so they will be able to cover full speed. The offense gets to block the front without having to get beat up and without having to hit live on each play. The offense will get a lot of good mental work done in this drill. The only problem is a big bag doesn't move a whole lot. Team periods will look really sharp when blocking bags. It is a great drill to do on the last two practices before a game to help promote confidence. It is not the greatest drill for blocking line stunts and movement. It does not get the players ready to play a live game at full speed. But, it is a great review drill and is a good drill for practices before the players are allowed to wear full pads. It is also a good drill to run when players are banged up and coaches need to keep them healthy, yet still working on executing assignments.

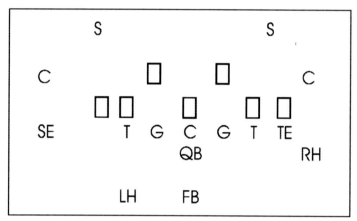

Diagram 1.15

Team vs. Scouts

Coaches can also do team versus live players. This drill is 11-on-11 and called team vs. scouts. Here, the offense will work against the scout team. All 11 offensive players will work against a scout team defense (Diagram 1.16). When the offense does team vs. scouts, the blocking is live.

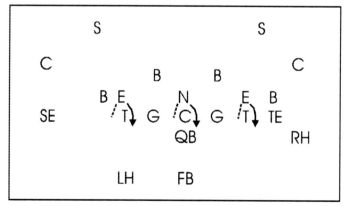

Diagram 1.16

The defense will run the kind of stunts and movements that your opponent will use against you when you play them on game day. If the opponent is a slant team, then you want the defensive line to execute slant 75 percent of the time. Everybody on the offense will block live and full speed. One thing you will never do against each other is cut block a teammate. Instead, you do cut drills on bags, or, if the defense needs to work against cuts, then you do a cut drill live against them and warn them beforehand, "This is a cut drill." No coach wants to injure his own players by allowing cutting during his practice plan. Sometimes working on cutting during team period is necessary. If so, tell the defense, so your players always know it is coming and from where, so they are prepared to protect themselves.

In team vs. scouts, the players are blocking live. The defenders are told that when they get to the ballcarrier, they should wrap him up, but without taking him to the ground (thud). Late in the season, they are even told not to touch the backs, but just to let them run by. You coach the defense to sprint to the football, tag off on the back, and not hit them at all. This format takes away a lot of the hits on the running backs, yet coaches can still see which defenders are constantly getting to the ball. They can still evaluate each blocking scheme and solve any problems. Whichever defensive player gets to the ball, even if he just tags off, will show the coaches which offensive player is having problems in that blocking scheme. If the scheme is wrong, assignments are missed, or improper technique is used, the coaches should correct it or find a way to make it work better.

Scrimmage

The last drill is 11-on-11, full speed, live scrimmage. You move the chains, make first downs, keep score, and conduct the period like a game. Coaches win no ball games or points for beating themselves up. However, during preseason and training camps, the players do need to scrimmage. They need to know what game speed feels like. Some coaches hold few scrimmages, but they make a big deal about them, as if it is game day. You keep score, draft teams in the spring, and do anything to help make the players have fun; but you should also recognize that it is game day and that they must compete. The players must get accustomed to the full-speed aspect of what a game actually feels like and to block and tackle where they have to take somebody to the ground.

Each spring, we have 15 practices and three scrimmages. The first scrimmage is a controlled, intrasquad scrimmage. The second is an intrasquad game, with teams drafted by the players. The third is an alumni game.

During preseason training camp, one controlled scrimmage is after the first week of practice. The second scrimmage is as much like a game as possible. The coaches will divide the teams up equally or play the first unit against the second unit in order for the starters to gain confidence as they finish training camp.

About five scrimmages a year are live and full speed, in which the backs are tackled to the ground. A few, if any, scrimmages happen in the normal daily practice. Occasionally, a special-situation scrimmage practicing third-and-long, or possibly goal line, becomes necessary. The varsity players who play every weekend are too important to beat up all week, especially when it does not count.

The one other type of scrimmage takes place with the freshmen who are redshirting and some of the sophomores who are not playing full time, yet who need the work. They scrimmage on at the end of the last practice of the week. The redshirts love it, since it is their game day. All of the varsity coaches are there coaching their players. The film man will also be there to film it. The coaches write up grades for the players and keep grades for each scrimmage, plus a composite of how each player grades over the course of the season. It is amazing how many times players who are not well thought of will perform over their heads in the scrimmages.

To review the wing-T practice plan, you progress from team takeoff at the beginning to shoulder skills, to routine period, to individual periods. Three categories of individual drills exist, some for the backs, some for the ends, and some for the linemen. Next are mixed group work drills and then 11-on-11 drills. That plan is how the practice breaks down. At any school in the country, practice will include working individually, working in groups, and then working as a team. Wing-T coaches are very proud of their practice plan because their players get so many repetitions—so much so that practice itself becomes a conditioner. Players hardly need to do extra conditioning after practice. The players get a lot of reps and a lot of practice on the techniques they will use in a game. Such practice builds mental toughness; it also results in character and promotes proper execution. Players must be able to think and execute when they are tired. That process is the racehorse philosophy and wing-T practice plan.

2

The Wing-T Quarterback

In this chapter, the qualities of a wing-T quarterback are discussed. Technique will also be illustrated, including the exact stance you teach the quarterback, and the hand-up technique will be shown. The hand-up technique is the center-quarterback exchange, or the snap. In addition, arm-loosening drills will be illustrated to teach your quarterbacks as you instruct them on how to throw with the proper technique. Finally, handoff drills, pitch drills, technique period, and that period in practices called passing with ends will be discussed.

Qualities of the Wing-T Quarterback

What are the qualities of a successful wing-T quarterback, and exactly what should you look for? To run the wing-T or any offense in college football, you need a fierce competitor at the quarterback position. You need the kind of person who, if he were playing checkers with his roommate, playing video games, or playing a pickup basketball game, would be irate if he lost. You want a guy who does not want to lose at anything. That trait is what is meant by a fierce competitor. It follows, then, that this fellow will not want to lose a football game when, as the starting quarterback, he is out in front of all those people.

Each quarterback is taught he must show people he is in control, and he should take control of the huddle. When the team steps into that huddle, the players in the huddle should be listening attentively. They should know with absolutely no question this quarterback, one, is in charge, two, is confident, three, knows what he is doing, and, four, has the potential to lead the team into the end zone every time he is out there.

You want the players in the huddle to have the utmost confidence in him. He must take control of the huddle. When he talks, nobody else should be talking. The quarterbacks are told, when they step in the huddle, they should call the play and the cadence only once. That way, his teammates will know they are responsible for listening closely to the quarterback. As they run from the huddle to the line of scrimmage, the rest of the players are told, "If any of you have forgotten anything, do not ask your buddy or the guy that plays next to you. You run to the quarterback, and he will tell you exactly the information that you missed in the huddle."

Another quality you should like to see in the quarterback is his taking the blame when things go wrong, especially in front of his teammates. Say a fumbled snap occurs in which the center rolled the snap back and never got it off the ground. Say it was the most horrible snap in the world. Your quarterback should turn around to the coach and say, "Coach, that's my fault. I messed up." He can grab the coach after practice and tell him exactly what went wrong. Or he can grab the center and practice with the center on the snap technique. If the quarterback is willing to take the blame in front of his teammates, he is thus showing them he is their leader and is willing to take responsibility for anything.

Another very important issue for a quarterback concerns the people he associates with when he is not on the field. The best quarterbacks are the ones who really befriend their offensive linemen. The offensive linemen are the ultimate team warriors, and football is the ultimate team game. Offensive linemen need to know their quarterback is one of them. If he is, then they will work harder to protect him. If you have a quarterback who only hangs around with the captain of the cheerleading squad, the great tailback, or a certain wide receiver, then you have a quarterback who is distancing himself from the blue-collar guys on the team. This type of quarterback will not be accepted as a leader as much as the quarterback who gets down in there with the guys in the trenches. This trait is vitally important for the quarterback.

It is also very important that the quarterback is unselfish. He is the guy who must put the team ahead of himself. He has to believe in team first. When an option is called, he must be the guy who makes the correct read and has to be willing to give the ball to the people the read dictates. The same thing holds true on a passing play. In the wing-T, where you do so much bootleg and action pass with a run-pass option built into the plays, the quarterback must unselfishly distribute the ball. If he decided to, the quarterback could keep the ball and run every time. That practice is not always best for the team. It is the same idea on the option. The quarterback keeping the ball is not always the best option. He has to believe in the team first and has to be willing to distribute the ball to the other players on the team when the defense dictates as much. The quarterback is told he must be a ball distributor.

The wing-T offense is basically built around unselfishness. The greatest team concept is that in which all skilled players take part in running the ball and pass receiving. Another selling point for the wing-T is this offense is not built around only one player. You can have great running backs, great receivers, great quarterbacks, great tight ends, great offensive linemen, and they all can be featured in the wing-T. It is a team-oriented offense, and the quarterback must be the number one team player. He must be willing to distribute the football to the players who are going to win the game. In some games, he will be the focus when he keeps the ball on the option or runs the ball on the flank pass. Often, he must deliver the ball to the correct back or receiver. He has to be a great distributor of the ball.

In any offense and at any level, you must have a quarterback who is a great decision maker. Decision making must be one of his outstanding qualities. You want a guy who can run. You want a guy who can throw. You would like to have a guy who can do both. However, a great decision maker will win for you before a guy with great talent who cannot make the correct choices. The quarterback must make the correct decisions and must make them on time. It does not matter what offense you use; the most important quality for a quarterback is decision making. He must get the ball to the correct player. It is the same thing if you are in the wishbone. Your quarterback is going to hand the ball off, or keep it, or pitch it. He must make the correct decision. A passing quarterback must certainly make correct decisions.

What gives the quarterback the ability to make the correct decision all the time? The quarterback has to have an understanding of what stops the offense. Your quarterbacks are taught the four things that will stop an offense faster than anything else:

- *Turnovers*—You look at handoffs in, accurate pitches, and throws to the correct receiver.
- *15-yard penalties*—Players should not to commit 15-yard penalties that disrupt or stall a drive. The wing-T is a ball-control offense, and, therefore, a 15-yard penalty can be destructive to a drive. It is very difficult to overcome a 15-yard penalty.
- *Poor execution*—Poor execution is the fastest way to stop an offense. A player misses a block, makes a mental error, or turns the wrong way, and you have a disaster. How can this problem be cleared up? In practice, you must be sure to repeat. You must get flawless execution out of your team. When you put in your offense, you should start at step one. You do not go to step two until step one has been done correctly. That method is the best way to avoid poor execution.

- *Poor play calling*—The quarterbacks have a lot of latitude to call plays. Most of the passing and running game is called from the line of scrimmage. The quarterback usually has two options, and he must pick the correct one. His job is not to call a perfect play, but to stay out of a bad play.

The next concept the quarterback needs to have is an understanding of what allows those first four things to happen. What allows turnovers to happen? What allows 15-yard penalties to happen? These mistakes are caused because you have not improved. If you do not improve every day in practice, eventually you will have turnovers, 15-yard penalties, and poor execution. You will have all those problems. You must improve as a football player every single day. When you do the same drill you did yesterday, do the drill better the second day. Do it better the third day. Whatever it is, be better the next time and take it to the next level.

Another reason mistakes continue to happen is that someone did not correct them. You should grade the players on film, assigning any one of five different grades, from a -2 to a +2, each week, for every play, once they step on the field. When they make a mistake, the grade is either a -1 or a -2. A -1 is a physical error: the player knew what to do, but he did not get it done. A -2 is a mental error: the player did not know what to do or gave a poor effort. When those things happen on film, if it is on the film, the coaches are responsible for it. You either coached it that way or allowed it to happen. You do not want those mistakes to go uncorrected. You need to watch all of your film, whether it is practice film or game film, and make sure the players get those mistakes corrected.

Another problem is not being mentally ready to play. If you are not mentally ready to play a football game each weekend, then you will have the kind of poor execution that stops drives. These personality traits are many of the ones to look for in a quarterback. You should really like the intense competitor aspect of his personality. You know he has to be unselfish, but, most of all, he has to be a great decision maker.

Physical Qualities

A wing-T offense can feature a great passing quarterback, even one who may not be fleet of foot. The offense, in that case, will be handoff oriented rather than option oriented. It will be pass oriented, and you as the coach must be willing to accept that. If you have a great runner who does not throw the ball well, then the offense will probably tend to be more option oriented. Either type of quarterback can be effective in your offense, but the catalyst to the wing-T is the play-action passing. The waggle off the sweep, the keep pass off the belly, and the counter bootleg off the counter play are the plays that really spark the offense. Your quarterback must be able to complete those passes, or you will have trouble moving the ball with the wing-T. Therefore, the quarterback must be enough of a thrower to complete those plays. If he can do that—and run the option—he will be just fine at quarterback. Obviously, you would love to have a guy who can both run and pass.

In terms of your quarterback's height requirements, at the college level, 6'1" is fine. However, many shorter and taller quarterbacks can also make the offense go. The athletic-type quarterback is going to do much more for your team in the long run than a slow-footed passer. Someone who has quick feet, not necessarily the greatest 40 time, but certainly quick feet and escapability, is the type of young man who will help your program more than somebody who is 6'6" and can really throw, but can't get out of his own way. Those kinds of quarterbacks have trouble, even in a passing offense, because their lack of mobility makes them a standing target. You want a quarterback who has good feet, who can handle the offense in all phases, and who can get out of trouble with quickness and agility once in awhile.

Most offenses would ask for the same qualities discussed. Of all the characteristics of a successful quarterback, decision making is the most vital.

Quarterback Drills

Stance

Both the quarterback's stance and the quarterback-center exchange, which is called hand-up, are areas often overlooked, although extremely important. The things to emphasize when teaching the quarterback's stance are, one, a narrow base, two, a slight knee bend, and, three, only wrist deep under the center.

You do not want the quarterback with his feet real wide apart, underneath the center, and squatted down low. I have seen those mistakes over and over when watching high school film. You do not want your quarterback to look like that. You would like to have your quarterback stand taller and not quite so far under the center. This action enables the quarterback to get away from the center quickly, but also does not impede the linemen in their pulling technique.

The first thing to emphasize is the width of the feet. You want four to six inches between the insides of his two ankles. You want a parallel stance, with his toes straight ahead. If you look between the ankles, you will see four to six inches of space. That space is all the farther apart you want the feet spread. You coach this way because the quarterback with the real wide stance has trouble gaining much ground on his first step. His foot will not strike as big an arc when he takes his first step away from the center. You want to be able to get away from the center quickly, to allow for the pulling which happens in the wing-T. You want to be able to get the ball to the backs as deep in the backfield as possible.

Second, the quarterback should stand tall. His waist should not have a lot of bend. You coach a slight arch in the back, with just a slight knee bend. Sometimes, in this stance, the quarterbacks appear too upright or lock-kneed. You do not want that either, but you do want the knee bend to be as slight as possible, so he can stand up tall. You want quarterbacks as tall in the saddle as you can get them.

Finally, you do not want the quarterback too low under the center. He should only be wrist deep. As the quarterback takes the ball from the center, he will only be under the center as far as his wrist and the ball will be snapped up to him. After he takes the snap, he is in perfect position to bring the ball to his belt, take a step, and gain ground away from the center. He should constantly work on a good first step that gets distance away from the center.

All the quarterbacks practice with all the centers every day. They practice every five yards on the white sideline stripe. As they line up on the white stripe, the quarterbacks straddle the white stripe so the white stripe goes right through the middle of their feet. When the centers come in, they put the ball down on the sideline. The center is over the ball, and the quarterback is behind the center. Remember, even with a short quarterback, you want him as tall in the saddle as you can get him. You do not want him to have a lot of waist bend. You do not want his feet too wide and do not want him crouched down low under the center.

Hand-Up

In the hand-up technique, which is the center snap, some important coaching points should be emphasized. The snap is taught in a three-step progression. The first step is called the fit. The second step is called a six-inch snap. The third step is the full snap.

The center is your best line athlete. You do a lot of different tests to find out who is the quickest, biggest, strongest lineman on the team, and then you combine those test results to find out who is the best big man. He is the player to play at center. You want to be strong down the middle in this offense. The center is as important as the quarterback and the fullback.

A necessary feature of the snap technique is you should be able to teach this technique to anybody. When I speak at clinics, I take somebody out of the audience who has never snapped a ball in their life and teach him quickly how to snap. It is amazing how a guy who has never snapped before can adapt to this snap technique, learn it quickly, and do it well. The best person to coach the center is the quarterback himself. He will tell the center exactly where the snap needs to be and also help the center adjust the snap.

One of the most demoralizing occurrences for an offense is the fumbling of the snap. Nothing can happen in any offense without the ball being exchanged smoothly from the center to the quarterback. You do not want to demoralize your team by having fumbled snaps. Therefore, in the practice plan, five minutes every day are devoted to what is called the hand-up period. The offensive line coach will send the centers to the quarterback coach, and the centers and the quarterbacks will work together on their snap technique. At the beginning of the season, this drill is as basic and elementary as it can be. As time goes on, you begin to have the center fire out after he snaps the ball and also have the quarterback practice any footwork he needs to work on. Sometimes, the quarterback will explode off the snap, take one step, and hold it to see if that first step is correct. Other times, the quarterback takes two steps. On other occasions, he might step through a complete play. The center-quarterback exchange period in practice can accomplish many objectives. The most important of them is the exchange between the center and the quarterback.

The first part of the three-step process to teach the snap is called the fit. You start with the center down in his stance. He should not have too wide of a base. He has to be comfortable, but does not want his feet too wide, because the wider his feet are the more he creates gaps between his shoulders and the shoulders of the next adjacent blocker. His feet should be fairly narrow. He should reach the ball out in front of him as far as he can so the defenders are farther away from the line. This maneuver will allow the offensive linemen extra space to get off the ball and execute their blocks.

When the quarterback receives the ball, he wants to receive the back end of the ball and would like to have the fat of the ball in the V of his fingers. The quarterback's right hand under the center is turned one quarter of a turn to his right. In order to learn this technique, the quarterback will point his fingers directly up to the sky. As his hand is vertical, he will make a quarter turn to the right so the V between his thumb and forefinger is now facing directly up to the sky. From there, he brings his hand down parallel to the ground, which will cause his wrist to bend. He wants his hand to assume this position just before he receives the snap from the center. He will be only wrist deep under the center.

The fit is when the quarterback holds the ball under the center where he wants to receive it, with his fingers near the passing grip and the fat of the ball in the V of his hand on the back end of the ball. The quarterback places the football under the center in the position he wants to receive it. The center then takes the ball from the quarterback and places it on the ground in reverse motion from the snap. The center is thus getting a feel from the quarterback as to where the ball should be snapped. As the quarterback puts the ball under the center, the center is getting the feel for exactly where the quarterback wants that ball snapped. The snapping motion by the center is the same motion he would use if he pulled a cord to turn on a light bulb. That pulling motion is the same motion he will use on the snap technique. The center should bring the ball straight up, without turning his wrist. He should not turn the ball sideways. The center should simply bring the ball straight up to the quarterback. These body mechanics are involved in the fit drill. The center takes the ball from the quarterback and brings the ball back to the ground, using the reverse of his snap motion. The quarterback hands the ball to the center, who takes it and brings it back to the ground. From there, the center passes the ball around behind him. The quarterback refits the ball in his hand, gives it back to the center, and they continue to do this until both the quarterback and the center feel comfortable having the ball in the right place and knowing the kind of motion to use.

The second part of teaching the snap progression is called the six-inch snap. In this drill, the center snaps the ball to the quarterback, but he starts with the ball about six inches off the ground, snaps it, and holds onto it. He does not actually give the ball to the quarterback. The center snaps the ball back and keeps control of it with the quarterback. The center takes the ball back from the quarterback to that six-inch position off the ground and then snaps it again to the quarterback. In this phase, you want the quarterback to give directions to the center. The quarterback has to know how he wants to receive the ball from the center. As the center snaps the ball, the quarterback coaches him. He is going to tell him whether the ball is too far back, too far forward, turned to the right, or turned to the left.

The final step in the progression is to snap the ball at full speed. The center will drive the ball back into the quarterback's hands. The quarterback should be able to have control of the ball with his right hand. He should not have to use his left hand at all. In fact, for all these drills, if he chooses to use just one hand to take the ball from the center, he will be building great confidence, because he will then find it much easier to eventually use both hands.

It is important to discuss what happens when the quarterback takes the ball in the wing-T. He will get the ball from the center in the same position in which he placed it under the center. When the quarterback takes the snap, the long axis of the ball will be parallel to the ground. He will be holding the ball on the back half of the ball and should have the fat of the ball in the V between his thumb and his forefinger. As he takes the ball from the center, he should rotate the ball one quarter of a turn to the right, if he's right-handed; to the left, if he's left-handed. As the ball is rotated into his second hand, it should be quickly snapped to the belt buckle. The long axis of the football will be parallel to the ground, with the quarterback's elbows in and with the back point of the ball in the belt buckle.

Arm Loosening

The next drills discussed are the quarterback arm-loosening drills, or throwing drills. The first drill the quarterbacks will work on is called quick grips. The quarterbacks have the ball on the ground and do this drill with both their right and left knees down. With the ball resting on the ground, the quarterback takes the football from the ground, without his hands starting on the ball, gets it into the passing grip as quickly as possible, and then delivers the ball to another quarterback, who will be lined up in front of him. Coaches should instruct their quarterback to take the ball from the ground and up to the passing position as quickly as possible, while using the proper passing grip, and then deliver the ball.

One of the mechanics looked for in this drill is for the quarterback to keep the nose of the football turned outward as he brings it up to the ready position. If the quarterback is holding the ball with the nose down, then his elbow will be tight to his body. Consequently, as he throws the ball, he will short arm it. If you take the nose of the ball and turn it out, the elbow comes out. The quarterback should release the ball as if somebody is standing in front of him and forcing him to release the ball up and over. This technique will extend his arm, elevate his elbow, and give him better distance on his throw. The quarterback should do this drill with both his right and left knees down. One good extension to this drill is to put two quarterbacks on opposite sides of the crossbar on a goalpost and then practice throwing over the crossbar. This extension will teach the quarterbacks to get the ball up as they release it.

The second extension is to have two quarterbacks throw the ball to each other as they practice throwing on the run. In this drill, one quarterback will run straight at the other quarterback he is playing catch with. That quarterback will be backing up to keep the spacing between them the same. What you try to accomplish in this drill is to teach the quarterback to throw on the run. You coach the quarterback to throw the ball and then follow the ball, so his throwing and his running are both going in the same direction. You do not want to have your quarterbacks run in one direction and try to throw the ball in another direction. You coach the quarterbacks to throw the ball and follow it, to chase the ball as they deliver it. As the second quarterback backs up, the first quarterback throws him the ball. Next, the second quarterback runs forward, and the first quarterback runs backward. They throw the ball as they run forward, and chase the ball and follow the ball as they deliver it.

When quarterbacks throw on the run, they should have the throwing elbow wrench to the middle of the back. You will see their shoulders turn perpendicular as they deliver the ball. You want to emphasize wrenching the elbow, so it rotates into the middle of the quarterback's back before he releases the ball. Two quarterbacks can participate in this drill at the same time. As one quarterback runs forward, his partner runs backward. They get a feel for throwing the ball at a moving target and chasing the ball. Their running motion and passing motion is all in the same direction.

The next arm-loosening drill for quarterbacks has them running in place and throwing the ball. This action gives them a feel for throwing with their feet moving. You coach the quarterback to chop his feet, run in place, and then throw the ball. The reason to do this drill is for accuracy. Sometimes, when quarterbacks start to run, they become less accurate. You want to simulate running action and then have them throw the ball to the strike point. The quarterback has a strike point on every pass play. In order to practice this, you tell him to throw the ball for the front number, the back number, the nose, or the waist. This action is called the run-in-place drill: the quarterback can run in place and throw the ball to his partner, who is a minimum of 10 yards away. He should hit a different strike point with each throw.

The next drill is the wave drill. Start the quarterback in a throwing position, as if he has already dropped back, ready to throw the football. To simulate pressure coming through the line, the coach will point in a number of directions. The quarterback is set up to throw the ball, but now he feels pressure. He has to shuffle his feet, avoid the pressure, and then be able to reset his feet to throw the football. He might have to shuffle his feet in another direction and again reset his feet to throw the football. He must slide his feet back and forth, like a wave. As he slides his feet, he throws the ball as soon as he can get set up.

The next drill is called roll-out drill. In this drill, the coach will line the quarterbacks up about 10 yards away from each other, on a yard line, as they run across the field to the other sideline. As they run across the field, they get a little bit of depth off the line, as if they are moving outside on a sprint play. Each quarterback's partner will also run down the line and get a little bit of depth. Both quarterbacks should then practice waggle and throwing to each other. As they practice this drill, they should start on one sideline and run across the field to the far sideline. They should do this all the way across the field: one quarterback throws the ball first, then the other quarterback gets the ball and throws it next. One quarterback will be moving to his right, the other quarterback will be moving to his left. As they run, they throw the ball, get it in the ready position, wrench their elbow into their back, turn their shoulders to their target, and follow the ball in the direction they are throwing.

Waggle Drill

The last throwing drill for the quarterbacks during practice is called the waggle drill. When quarterbacks do the waggle drill, all of the offensive linemen will be in the drill. Regardless of whether they play center, guard, or tackle, all linemen are taught the guard techniques for the waggle. This type of learning is called cross-training, and, in this case, all linemen learn to pull on the waggle. As a result, your best backup lineman can play any position on the line. All he has to do is brush up on his mental assignments to be able to step right in to play. This strategy keeps the five best linemen on the field.

The first play practiced in the drill is called 29 waggle, which means the quarterback fakes 29 sweep to the left and bootleg to the right. The right guard takes a flat pull step as he eyes the defensive end. As the guard log blocks the defensive end, he will work to strike with his inside shoulder while inside his foot. His next step will work up the field. He will finish the log block using the outside hand and driving it through the defensive end's outside number, bench pressing him, and finishing him back inside. This play has been set up by having the tight end release inside to see if the defensive player over him will seal inside or penetrate. If he penetrates across the line of scrimmage, run plays inside of him. If the tight end is releasing inside and the defender is jamming the tight end, he makes himself a perfect target for the log block. This log block should have contact on the fourth step. The first step should be a pull step. The second and third steps should continue in the same direction, flat down the line of scrimmage. On his fourth step, the contact should occur. On the fifth step, the guard will turn up the field and bench press the defender to the inside.

The backside guard will take a flat pull step on the first step, cross over for depth on the second step, and then flatten out down the line of scrimmage. He is looking to kick-out any penetration off the corner. If the defensive end decides to penetrate into the backfield, the first guard lets him go, the backside guard kicks him out, and the quarterback must learn to step inside the kick-out and then continue to attack the flank. If the end does not penetrate, the first guard will log him and the second guard will now lead the quarterback to the flank, looking for the next defender. Against a corner blitz, if the defensive end crashes inside, the log block takes care of him, and, as the corner comes off the edge, the second guard kicks him out. In this case, as the guard kicks him out, the quarterback will duck up inside.

The next possibility to practice involves the defensive end sealing and being logged by the first guard, with the corner dropping into coverage. The second guard will now block any defender who scrapes from the inside to the outside. The quarterback gives a go call, if he runs the ball, and the backside guard will lead him down the field and block any defender he finds.

Quarterbacks and linemen repeat this drill to both sides. They do the drill in a rapid-fire fashion, getting as many reps as possible in a five-minute period, practicing the different reactions by the defense. The first group of players will fake sweep to the left and run waggle to the right. As they start, the next group is waiting in line behind them. Two more offensive linemen run up to become the next two guards to go.

Having completed 29 waggle, the quarterbacks will now fake the sweep to the right, while the guards pull to the left. The quarterback is led by the two guards around the left end on 21 waggle. The purpose of waggle drill is to learn to react to defenders coming off the edge. The quarterback should learn to anticipate whether penetration is going to happen or whether the guards will get the flank sealed down. The quarterbacks are in waggle drill every day.

Handoff Drill

During practice, quarterbacks do four other drills: handoff, pitch, full backfield technique period, and passing with ends. Diagram 2.1 illustrates the handoff drill, which includes four stations. A center, a quarterback, and a fullback are in a middle station; a center, a quarterback, and a fullback are in another middle station; a center, a quarterback, and a right halfback are in a third station to the left; and a center, a quarterback, and a left halfback are in a fourth station to the right. At this point, in these four stations, they will work solely on the quarterback-running back exchange on selected running plays. They will get as many reps as possible in a five-minute period. It is amazing how many reps the backs will get in just a five-minute period. At the end of the season, this drill is cut down to two minutes, and you still get a lot of reps.

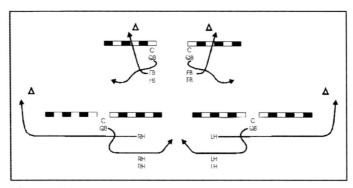

Diagram 2.1

The centers in this drill are kickers, anybody on the team who might be injured and cannot play, or somebody who is sitting out the season on a medical redshirt. The kickers make great snappers; during some parts of practice, they get bored being down at the other end of the field just kicking footballs all the time. The first thing to teach all kickers is how to be snappers. This method means the quarterback will always take the ball in exchange. As mentioned earlier, anybody can learn how to be a snapper in a very short period of time and execute at a very high percentage.

The diagram shows the four stations will be operating independent of each other. As soon as the quarterback and the running back are ready, the quarterback will snap the ball, and they will execute the play you are working on. If the fullbacks are working on the belly play, they take their footwork for the belly as the quarterback executes his handoff technique and then executes the fake he needs to perform. The ball is handed off to the running back, who bursts through the line of scrimmage full speed down the field past cones. It should be a habit for the backs to accept the handoff and burst through the line of scrimmage.

While the center, quarterback, and fullback work on belly to the right, another center, quarterback, and fullback work the same play to the left. While those groups are drilling, the halfbacks are working on the handoff planned for the day. The right halfback might work on sweep to the left. The quarterback takes the center exchange, executes his footwork, hands the ball off to the halfback, and fakes waggle. The halfback executes his sweep technique with a good cut and must burst past the cones. At the same time the right halfback is working on sweep left, the left halfback is working on sweep right. The backup players are lined up behind the starters. The halfbacks and fullbacks are going to be getting maximum reps. They will go rapid-fire and get rep after rep. The coach should tell the fullbacks to keep switching sides. As soon as they have gone on one side, they should switch back to the other side. The halfbacks stay in the same place.

The quarterbacks will rotate in this drill. They will rotate on their own after one quarter of the time through each drill. You will be amazed at how many reps on a handoff the players will get. If you have five minutes, work on two different types of handoffs in the period.

Pitch Drills

The next drill is called pitch drill. As seen in Diagram 2.2, pitch drills will involve two groups running option plays. On one hash mark is a center, a quarterback, a fullback, and a left halfback. They will be running option plays to the right. In another group is a center, a quarterback, a fullback, and a right halfback, who will be running option plays to the left. The groups are offset by 10 yards to avoid collisions. For example, if working on trap option, the fullback will take his footwork and execute his blocking assignment for the play. You use big blocking bags on the field so the fullback has to do a great job faking and also execute his block technique. The center will snap the ball to the quarterback, who will take his footwork. The left halfback is the pitchback. Another quarterback is in a read position to challenge the first quarterback. The quarterbacks should try to make it harder in practice than the defense will make it during a game. They should challenge each other during this drill. The halfback who is the pitchback should get good pitch relationship with the quarterback. Pitch relationship is five by three, meaning three yards deep and five yards in front of the quarterback, so the back can catch the ball running downhill, gaining maximum yardage. Coaches should make sure, as they catch the pitch, the backs should not turn back into the free safety and the pursuit. The backs should work a technique where they bounce from the hash mark to the numbers to the sideline. They keep trying to stay outside, away from the free safety running through the alley. While this group is working on option to the right, another group will be working on option to the left. The right halfback is the pitchback, and the quarterback executes his option technique. Another quarterback is the pitch key.

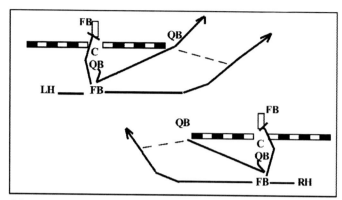

Diagram 2.2

Full Backfield Technique

Full backfield technique (Diagram 2.3) is exactly what it sounds like—all backs working together to perfect plays and techniques. You work a lot on flank runs and on flank passing in this drill. Anything that needs to be perfected is in this drill. If you are working on 21 sweep, the right halfback would execute a blocking assignment, so another right halfback is holding a bag while the halfbacks work on sweep blocks. Another fullback will be holding a bag where the fullback is assigned to block. The quarterback will take the snap, and the ballcarrier will take the ball from the quarterback as he works on his sweep cut. While this group is going in one direction, the young players will be working on the same play, going in the opposite direction. Sometimes, it will be better for the younger players to watch the older players and only have one group; but, normally, it is better to learn by doing than by watching.

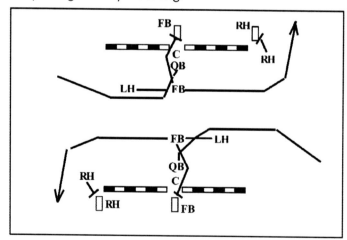

Diagram 2.3

Passing with Ends

The last drill is passing with ends. When doing passing with ends (Diagram 2.4), you will have all the ends, receivers, backs, and quarterbacks in one group. If working on waggle out, the spread end will practice his out cut and the backfield will work on waggle. The fullback will be a blocker first and a receiver second. The tight end will run the crossing route or split the middle versus two-deep coverage. The right half runs the throw back, and the left half fakes the sweep and becomes a blocker to the backside. The quarterback makes the correct decision and throws to the proper receiver. You can drill as a full group or can work on individual cuts, with one quarterback and one receiver repeating routes over and over again.

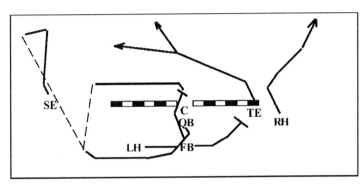

Diagram 2.4

To summarize the practice plan for the quarterbacks, the first thing they do is review their stance. They do that while working on hand-up technique with the center. They work on hand-ups every day in practice. They do arm loosening and throwing drills early in the practice to get loosened up and to review the fundamentals of throwing. Next, the quarterbacks go to handoff drills. They work individual handoffs with the halfbacks and the fullbacks. The next drill is pitch drill, where they work on option plays and especially on pitch technique. Full backfield technique follows. The quarterbacks always finish by working passing with ends, with all backs and all ends.

Play Series Techniques

The most important coaching points covered in this chapter are the quarterback's footwork on the plays he will use in the wing-T offense. Four series of plays exist, and each set of plays is fully discussed in other chapters of this book. In those chapters, each series will be diagrammed, detailing exactly who blocks whom and how to attack different defenses. Throughout the technique chapters, the footwork for each of these plays will be discussed for every position. The backfield technique chapter will demonstrate each play series for the running backs and the exact techniques used. Techniques used for the linemen and receivers will be presented in those specific sections. In this chapter, the primary focus will be on the quarterback's techniques in each series.

The 20 Series

The 20 series contains the basic plays in the wing-T offense. The first play will be the sweep play, which is the play too many coaches use to identify the wing-T offense. Too many coaches think the wing-T represents only the wing formation and the sweep play. But that play is merely one in a total system of offense. Because of its popularity, the sweep should be discussed first.

The Sweep

The first discussion about quarterback technique will be the technique taught on 21 or sweep right (Diagram 2.5). The quarterback should be in a good stance and receive the hand-up. He should use the proper stance, with his wrist deep under the center, a good arch in his back, and a slight knee bend, yet he should be upright. The quarterback's first step is to reverse pivot to the midline. On this play, it is important the quarterback pivots his back foot. His right foot, the foot he will pivot on, pivots all the way around. A cardinal sin, and a common error that can be detected on film, is when the quarterback does not pivot his back foot and does not get his shoulders completely around, thus allowing the defense to see the ball. When looking at this from the back, the ball is exposed to the defense, and a defensive player in a linebacker position will have a clear look at the football. If the quarterback reverse pivots all the way around with his back to the defense, the defense will not know where the football is. The fullback will be stepping with his right foot for the left foot of the center.

On his second step, the quarterback continues to stay on the midline. The fullback fakes over an imaginary ball. The fake occurs between the first and second steps. The quarterback will not fake with the ball to the fullback. The fullback takes his first step for the backside foot of the center and, on the second step, will fake over an imaginary ball. The close proximity of the shoulders of the quarterback and the fullback gives this the name proximity fake. The nearness and the closeness of the shoulders and the fact the fullback faked over an imaginary ball are enough for a good trap fake. The quarterback will take his first two steps on the midline. His third step begins to cross over as the handoff to the halfback takes place. The handoffs look like you're dealing cards. They are all at forearm's length only. The quarterback will not reach the ball. If the quarterback is reaching the ball, the defense will see the ball. If he keeps his elbows tight to the side of his body, then the defense will not be able to see the ball. The halfbacks will be coached to take the ball with the inside thumb down. Their footwork is to crossover step, run through the fullback's position on the second step, and receive the ball on the third step. After that, the quarterback will continue to threaten the flank, faking waggle. The halfback will run the sweep. When the quarterback hands the ball off on sweep, he will need to read the free safety as he continues to fake waggle. As a result, he will know exactly what the free safety's reaction will be when calling waggle. As the quarterback fakes waggle, his inside arm should pump hard, and his outside

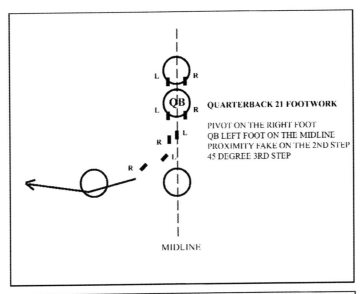

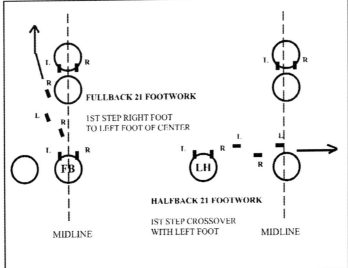

Diagram 2.5

hand, his backside hand, should be in the crotch, where the ball would be placed if he were running the waggle.

The Fullback Trap

The next play is 24 and 26, guard trap up the middle (Diagram 2.6). In this play, the footwork for the quarterback and the fullback are determined by the spacing of the defense. If it is an even spacing, with the guards covered and the center uncovered, the fullback's footwork will be exactly the same as in the sweep. He will step with his right foot on 24 guard trap. His first step is right foot for left foot of the center. If the guards are uncovered and the center is covered, the defense is an odd spacing—the first step by the fullback is now on the midline. In an even defense, the center's block will be back to the man covering the left guard, and the fullback will be cutting off that block. If it is an odd defense, the center will block the man directly on him. The fullback now steps right down the midline, where the center's block will occur. The fullback will cut off this block in either direction.

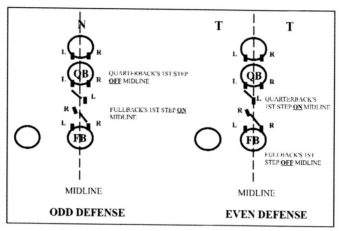

Diagram 2.6

Against even defenses, the fullback steps for the backside foot of the center, so the quarterback can stay on the midline. His first two steps will be on the midline, and his footwork is exactly the same as on the sweep. The quarterback's second step continues on the midline, and the ball is handed off on the second step. His elbows are in tight, and the ball is handed off from no farther than forearm's distance away. When the quarterback has to reach the ball to the fullback, one of them has bad footwork or bad aiming points.

Techniques against the odd defense require the fullback's first step to be on the midline; therefore, the quarterback's first step must be beyond the midline to give the fullback the midline unimpeded. On the quarterback's second step, he will handoff to the fullback. On his third step, he will begin to cross over and make an effective fake to the left halfback. He will then continue to attack the flank and fake the waggle.

It does not matter if the line is blocking the play with guard trap blocking, on blocking, or gut blocking. The line uses all those different blocking schemes, but the quarterback's footwork remains consistent. He and the fullback depend on the spacing of the defensive front. This method will give the fullback the optimum chance to option run the most important block, which is the center's block, regardless of which defense you are facing.

The Off-Tackle

The off-tackle play is 22 and 28. This play looks like the sweep (Diagram 2.7). You run this play if the third defender in the defense is a penetrating defensive end and is running up the field, making it hard to run the sweep. You try to make the play look just like the sweep, but turn up one hole short. The basic concept is to kick the penetrator out and run the ball off-tackle.

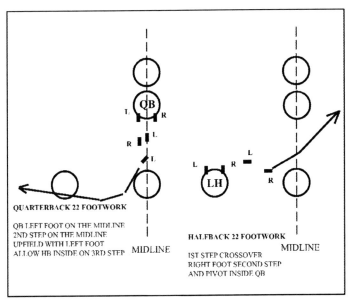

Diagram 2.7

Many coaches run 22 and 28 (the off-tackle play) like they run the sweep and hand the ball to the halfback over the top. The halfback fakes the sweep and cuts it up inside.

Coaches have found over the years this cut is tough. They have modified both the quarterback's footwork and the halfback's footwork. For the quarterback, the first two steps will reverse pivot to the midline like 21. The halfback will cross over just like 21 and take his second step just like the sweep. The left halfback, who is running 22 to the right, plants his right foot on his second step and then cuts off that right foot and turns up into the off-tackle hole. The quarterback will hand the ball off on the inside. His footwork is almost identical to that in the sweep. He will make the inside handoff on his third step. The halfback continues to the off-tackle hole, and the quarterback continues to the flank and fakes waggle.

For the first two steps, everything is exactly the same as the sweep. If the backs have taken poor footwork, the defense will recognize the play. This mistake happens when the quarterback reverse pivots too far across the midline or the halfback takes the crossover step, forgets to take the second step, and then starts running for the off-tackle hole. This error results in a play where the quarterback must reach to give the ball and the defense can see the play. Coaches should make sure this play looks just like the sweep for as long as possible. If the backs execute good footwork, meaning the quarterback stays on the midline for two steps and the halfback takes two good steps, as in the sweep, then the play will look like sweep.

The Waggle

On this play (Diagram 2.8), the quarterback will operate on the midline. The quarterback has the ball, so the fullback will step for the backside foot of the center. The quarterback owns the midline for the first two steps. The quarterback snaps the ball to his belt as he pivots—the long axis of the ball is parallel to the ground, the back point of the ball is at his belt buckle, and his elbows are in tight. With his elbows in tight, no one on the defense can see where the ball is. On the third step, the quarterback will fake the sweep with two hands. He will fake with two hands to the halfback to make the defense believe the halfback has the ball. From there, he will tuck the ball into the crease of his pants and attack the flank on the waggle. The faking halfback has a blocking assignment on the backside of the quarterback.

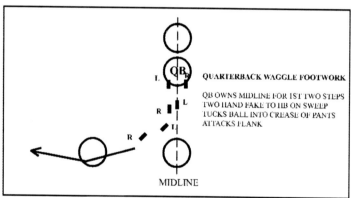

Diagram 2.8

As the quarterback runs to the flank on the waggle, different defensive adjustments may occur, forcing blocking adjustments (Diagram 2.9). The quarterback must be keyed into this. It is a must to bring the quarterbacks to waggle drill every day and is important for them to know how to react when the defense is penetrating.

As the quarterback attacks the flank on the waggle, if the defensive end comes upfield, he gets trapped or kicked out. If the quarterback tries to outrun the defensive end, the play will result in a big loss. He will give up an 8 to 10-yard loss, a sack, and a big play to the defense.

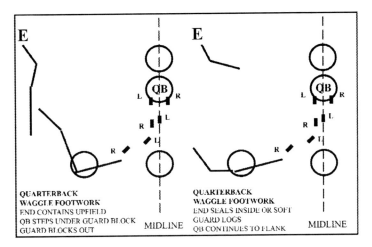

Diagram 2.9

The problem on the waggle play comes with the penetration. As the defensive end penetrates, the first guard will let him go and turn inside looking to help on any inside out pursuit. The backside guard should kick out the penetrating defensive end. The quarterback will step underneath the kick-out block and then continue to the flank, where he can either drop the ball off quickly to an open receiver or run the ball.

If the defensive end seals down inside or plays soft, then the guard should be able to get a good log block on him, and no problems exist for the quarterback. As he attacks the flank, nobody will be in his face. He should thus be able to continue outside and really threaten the flank with a run or pass option.

Waggle Solid

An alternative to waggle is waggle solid (Diagram 2.10). The quarterback is now a pure passer. The route combinations change to waggle out, waggle curl, and waggle, with the wing breaking over the center position, which is called wing at five. The split end can also run the same route, which is called waggle at five. Another adjustment is waggle switch, which means the fullback goes deep and the end is in the flat. Many different ways exist to change these patterns. Another waggle keep play is called waggle run, where the flank is blocked like a sweep play. Numerous variations exist to the waggle.

Against aggressive corners, an effective technique to use is waggle solid. This play means the quarterback will have a drop-back style of passing attack, but with 20 action. He uses the buck action, the misdirection in the backfield, and the deception of the play, but it is similar to drop-back passing. On this play, the fullback and the halfback who fake the sweep are blockers, and it is a three-man route. The fullback takes his

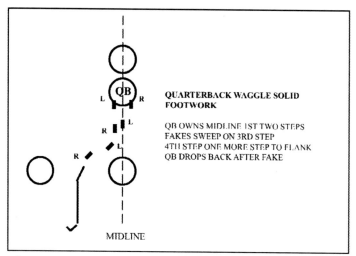

QUARTERBACK WAGGLE SOLID
FOOTWORK

QB OWNS MIDLINE 1ST TWO STEPS
FAKES SWEEP ON 3RD STEP
4TH STEP ONE MORE STEP TO FLANK
QB DROPS BACK AFTER FAKE

MIDLINE

Diagram 2.10

footwork and the quarterback still owns the midline. On the third step, the quarterback will fake sweep, take one more step to the flank, and then start to drop back. It is now a drop-back pass, as the quarterback gets his shoulders turned and sets up to throw the pass. It is very similar to pocket protection. The fullback is a blocker. He will block his area inside. The halfback who fakes the sweep will gear down and become a blocker on the backside. Only one guard pulls; everybody else is cup protecting. The line blocks the defense from inside out. The quarterback will start to the flank for one step, but then he will drop back to pass. As such, he turns his shoulders and, at this point, can throw the ball from right to left and use the whole field.

The 60 Series

The next part of the offense is the trap option package, which is called 60s. The series number is changed to 60s instead of 20s because times exist when plays must be called at the line of scrimmage and it is difficult to tell the difference between 21 sweep, 21 waggle, 21 trap option, 21 trap-option pass, and other plays which can be run using buck action.

The Wide Guard Trap

Guard trap is at the 3 or 7 hole. The quarterback can execute 20s technique or can use 60s technique. If the play is 23 guard trap, the ball will go to the fullback and the trap is at the 3 hole, which is one hole wider than a normal guard trap (Diagram 2.11). Against even defenses, instead of trapping the defensive tackle over the guard, you double-team him, take the play one hole wider, and trap the defensive end. If it is an odd, or 50, defense, the play reverts back to 24 guard trap. On 24 guard trap, the fullback will step with his right foot for the left foot of the center, showing buck action. On 23 guard trap, he will step with his right foot, but since the trap is one hole wider, his right foot will step for the right foot of the center. The quarterback reverse pivots beyond the midline enough to allow the fullback his course. On the second step, the ball is handed off. On the third step, the fullback will veer to the 3 hole but stay tight to the tackle's down block. The quarterback's handoff fake is the same as his fake on the sweep to the left halfback. For 23 guard trap, he will fake the sweep and continue to show waggle action.

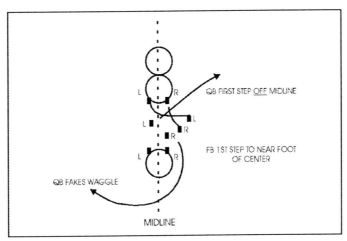

Diagram 2.11

You can also run 63 guard trap or 67 guard trap, with the quarterback faking trap option (Diagram 2.12). It will not change the fullback's footwork in any way. If the call is 63 guard trap, the fullback will step with his right foot for the right foot of the center. The difference is the quarterback is beyond the midline on the first step, giving the fullback the midline. On the second step, the ball is handed off. The quarterback will then snap his chin to his frontside shoulder, pivot off his second step, and come downhill to fake the trap option to the right. When running the trap-option series, the defense might read trap option, overpursue, and allow the fullback to run inside of them on the trap. The alternative is to run the 20 action with the quarterback faking waggle, which is 23 guard trap.

The Trap Option

On the trap option play, the quarterback owns the midline (Diagram 2.13). If the play is trap option to the right, it is called 61 trap option, or 69 trap option to the left. You will option the third defender. The quarterback will keep the ball or pitch it, depending on the reaction of the third defender, and the other defenders are blocked at the point of attack.

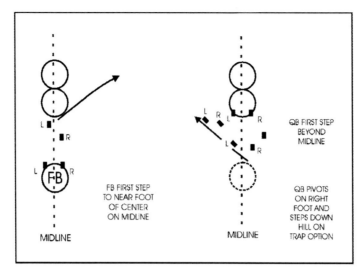

Diagram 2.12

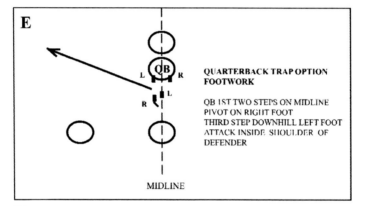

Diagram 2.13

On the trap option, the first step for the quarterback is on the midline. The backside foot must pivot. The second step is also on the midline, but, from there, the quarterback begins to change from the 20 series. At this time, his right foot should begin to pivot and his chin should snap to his shoulder. This movement gives him a clear read on the defense. At the same time, he begins to pivot his foot and his third step starts downhill, enabling him to attack the inside shoulder of the third defender playside. He will run downhill and keep or pitch the ball, depending on the third defender's reaction.

The third defender, usually the defensive end, can give him a number of different reactions (Diagram 2.14). He could come right at the quarterback. That reaction is why the chin must snap to the shoulder on the second step. As the quarterback starts downhill, if the defensive end is attacking quickly, he will not have a chance to run very far before he must pitch the ball. This reaction is the reason why the chin has to be snapped to the shoulder and the foot will start to pivot on the second step. The defensive end could also run straight across the line and take the pitch, which will make him an easy read. This read is clear cut for the quarterback to keep the ball and burst through the option alley. The quarterback will also get defenders who try to play in between the quarterback and the pitchback. The next reaction he might see is when defenders play cat-and-mouse or slow play. The defensive end will be shuffling his feet, trying to keep position on both threats. If this defender gives ground, the quarterback should make a little pitch fake to get the defender to bite and then turn up inside of him. If the defender is keeping good position on the quarterback shuffling, but not letting the quarterback out leverage him, then the quarterback should pitch the ball. The quarterback must get in his face and then pitch the ball to the halfback. You also get the defender who wants to play cat-and-mouse on the quarterback, but is responsible for the pitch. The quarterback should give him a quick pitch fake and then run up through the option alley.

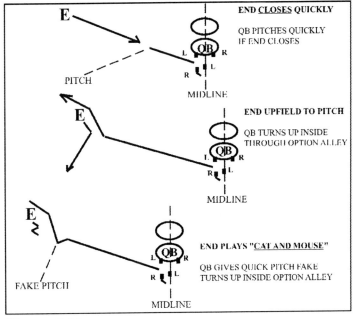

Diagram 2.14

Trap Option Pass

A natural complement to trap option is trap-option pass (Diagram 2.15). To stop the trap-option crack, the fourth defender will read trap option, come flying up to beat the crack, and be in good position to stop the trap option. With trap-option pass, a conflict exists for the fourth defender. If he comes hard on the option, the pass play is open. If he is soft on the option, the end should be able to block him with crack blocking or stalk blocking. The strong safety, #4, when too aggressive, has come hard into the backfield and opened up the slant area for the quarterback to throw the ball quickly behind him.

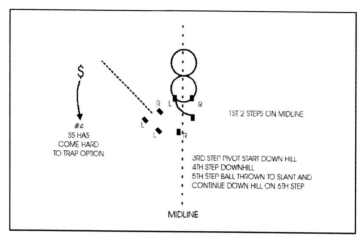

Diagram 2.15

The quarterback's first two steps will be on the midline and should resemble his action on the sweep. By this time, the halfback has crossed the backfield and has established pitch relationship. For the first two steps, the defense cannot recognize if the play is sweep or waggle. On the third step, the quarterback's chin has been snapped to his shoulder and his toes begin to pivot into the third step in order to start downhill on the trap-option course. On the third step, he will have identified the strong safety's (#4) reaction. As soon as the quarterback snaps his chin to his shoulder, his eyes need to go to the fourth defender. The fourth step continues downhill, and, on the fifth step, the ball should be thrown off his left foot, followed by his right foot. The ball is released between the fifth and sixth steps. The quarterback follows through on the same course as the ball. The ball must be placed quickly in the passing position. The quarterback has to release the ball on the sixth step. Right-handed quarterbacks are more comfortable throwing off their right foot and on their sixth step. The ball should go to the slanting receiver—or to the flaring halfback, if the corner chases the slant.

Trap-Option Reverse

Trap-option reverse is a great momentum-changing play (Diagram 2.16). You can establish flow with the trap-option series, get the defense running, and then run a reverse. You pitch the ball to the spread end coming back through the backfield from a spread position. On this play, you coach everybody to show the picture of trap option. The backside of the offense is going to look a lot like waggle, with a blocker for everybody on the defense making this play sound, regardless of what defense you face. The footwork for the quarterback should be exactly the same as on the trap option: take two steps on the midline, snap the chin, pivot the toes, and start downhill playside on the third step.

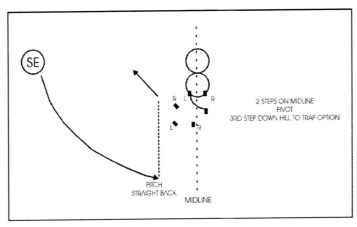

Diagram 2.16

The difference on this play is the normal pitch relationship with the halfback is five yards out in front and three yards deep. The quarterback pitches the ball out in front for the halfback to catch on the run. When running the trap option, the halfback should be receiving the pitch with his momentum going in the same direction as the quarterback. The ball needs to be pitched in front of the halfback so he can catch the pitch and make yards. When running trap-option reverse, the spread end will come back through the right halfback's diveback position. The left halfback, who was the pitchback, will get a little more depth and fake catching the pitch, but the spread end will catch the pitch with his momentum going in the opposite direction. The pitch is straight back, as opposed to being pitched out in front of the halfback. The spread end can catch the ball without slowing his momentum and run to the flank in the opposite direction, as the quarterback continues to fake trap option.

67 Counter

Within the 20 series, a counter package exists which uses 60s footwork for the quarterback. The first play is called 27 counter or 67 counter. Since the quarterback will fake the trap option, these plays are called 67 instead of 27.

The quarterback will take two steps on the midline and start downhill on his third step, as in trap option. The wingback will run back to the diveback position and receive an inside handoff. The wingback does not go in motion. Instead, he runs the same course, as if he was going in motion, but he leaves on the snap. On the third step, the wingback starts downhill and the quarterback, who is running trap-option footwork, will hand him the ball with an inside handoff. The wingback runs the 7-hole counter play, as the rest of the offense fakes the 60 trap-option package.

The 63 counter is the same play to the right side (Diagram 2.17). The quarterback will fake 69 trap option to the left and, as he comes downhill, hands the ball to the left halfback coming inside on the same course attacking the 3 hole rightside. The quarterback continues to fake trap option.

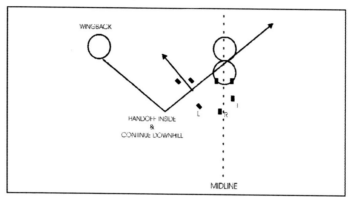

Diagram 2.17

60 Counter Sweep

Off of 60 counter action, you can run counter bootleg or counter sweep. The first of these is 61 or 69 counter sweep (Diagram 2.18). The quarterback is doing nothing more than taking 61 to the right or 69 to the left with trap-option footwork. The quarterback's first two steps are on the midline. On the second step, he snaps his chin and his toes start to pivot. He will run downhill from there. This handoff will also be inside. The wingback will take the same path he runs on 67 counter. He takes three steps, starts downhill, and receives the handoff from the quarterback. As the handoff is exchanged, the quarterback fakes counter bootleg and the halfback gets extra depth around the opposite end. The quarterback will continue to fake the trap option. The line blocks the same as 21 waggle.

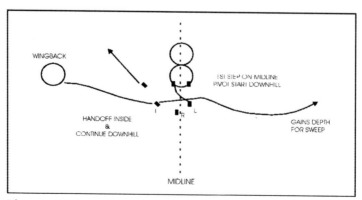

Diagram 2.18

60 Counter Bootleg

The next play in the package is 63 or 67 counter bootleg (Diagram 2.19). On this play, the backs will fake 63 and 67 counter. The quarterback takes his two steps on the midline, snaps his chin, pivots his toe, and starts downhill. He will fake the handoff to the halfback coming back inside. The quarterback will fake the handoff, then get depth, and run counter bootleg. The halfback, who is normally the pitchback on trap option, is the log blocker at the flank. The quarterback gets extra depth and will have a run-pass option at the flank.

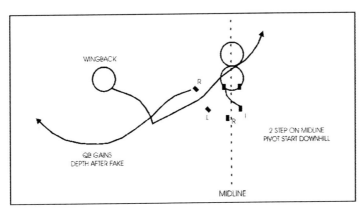

Diagram 2.19

The 30 Series

The Power Sweep

The 30 series is closely related to the 20 series. The first play in the series is the power sweep. On this play, the quarterback will execute the same footwork he uses on 20s, as will the ballcarrier. If you run 31 power sweep right (Diagram 2.20), the quarterback takes two steps on the midline and his technique is exactly as on 21. He will make the handoff exchange on his third step. The ball is handed off, at forearm's distance, to the left halfback, who will run 31 sweep. The quarterback continues to fake the waggle and attack the flank. One key question is, "Why run the 30 sweep instead of 20s?" You run the play when facing a blitzing eight-man-front defense. The defense is not reading, just trying to blitz, cause confusion, and wreak havoc in the backfield. Sometimes, the 20 blocking scheme allows penetration because of the pulling, but, in 30s, the line is blocking with fire technique and the back has a solid wall in front of him. The full flow is not a problem now, because the defense, if stunting, is not reading guards or backfield flow. The front will be well blocked, and the fullback will be the kick-out blocker instead of the frontside guard, who provides the kick-out on 21 and 29 sweep. This play is a power sweep, but the footwork for the quarterback and the ballcarrier is exactly the same as in the buck sweep (20s): take two steps on the midline, cross over on the third step, make the handoff, and fake waggle.

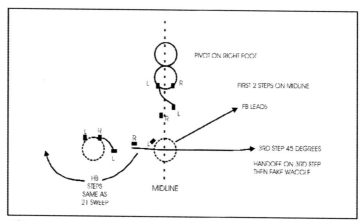

Diagram 2.20

The Power Off-Tackle

As in the 20 series, if the defensive end is a penetrator, not allowing the wing to block down on him, then a companion play exists to the sweep, which puts the end in a conflict. The 30 series play is called 32 and 38 (Diagram 2.21). On 32 and 38, the play is a direct shot off-tackle. The halfback needs to run directly to the off-tackle hole. He will take his first step using a crossover step, as the quarterback takes his first step directly at the halfback to hand the ball off. On the second step, the handoff will occur as the quarterback and the halfback have their hips open to each other. The halfback runs off-tackle, and the quarterback will do the best job he can trying to make the play look like waggle. This play is nothing more than an off-tackle, double-team down, fullback kick-out, power play.

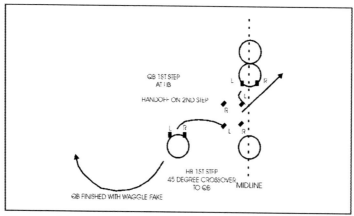

Diagram 2.21

The Blast Play

The complete 30 series is power oriented. The series employs double-team and kick-out blocking, with a direct path for the running back at the point of attack. Within the same series, a play exists called 34 blast, which is similar to 32, except the double-team is more inside. Against an odd defense with a man covering the center, the guard is uncovered, the tackle is covered, and a double-team will be on the noseguard. The tackle will turn out on the man covering him, and the fullback will run through to isolate on the frontside inside linebacker. The backside guard is responsible for the backside backer and will fire straight ahead or pull around the center to block him (Diagram 2.22).

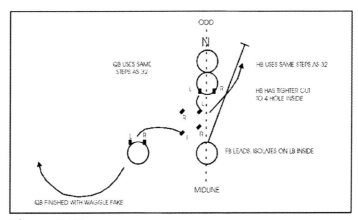

Diagram 2.22

On this play, the techniques for the quarterback and the left halfback are the same as on the off-tackle play. The quarterback will bring the ball directly to the halfback. The halfback will take a crossover step. On the second step, he receives the ball and makes a quicker cut to stay tight to the double-team. He must make sure not to overrun the hole. As the quarterback gives the ball to the halfback, he will step right to the halfback, make the handoff, and do the best he can with the waggle fake.

The Counter Crisscross

The next play, which also looks like 32, is called 37 counter crisscross (Diagram 2.23). The quarterback's footwork resembles that in 32 and 38. He will bring the ball directly to the halfback, but he will step a little bit deeper because the halfback will run a course similar to the power sweep. The halfback crosses over as he runs across the backfield, receives the handoff, and, as he approaches the opposite halfback, hands the ball off to him. The play is a handoff-to-handoff reverse, with the quarterback faking waggle. The quarterback becomes an added feature to this play. As he attacks the flank, he should draw defenders with him. If the right halfback breaks through the line of scrimmage down the field and then the defense collapses on him, he can option pitch back to the quarterback. The players have a lot of fun with this in practice. They are cautioned they can pitch to the quarterback—anytime they are up by 40 points. Otherwise, they are to keep the ball and run it upfield.

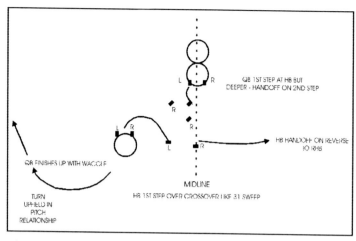

Diagram 2.23

The quarterback should be instructed to bring the ball to the halfback as quickly as possible and allow the defense to see it so they will react with the sweep fake. The line can block the counter crisscross at 3 and at 7 with three different blocking schemes. You can also run another counter crisscross back to the tight end, which is called 32 and 38 counter crisscross. On that play, the techniques for the backs will not change at all.

The Tackle Trap

The most classic counter play in the wing-T offense is the tackle trap counter, called 34 and 36 counter. This play is one of the outstanding plays in the offense, along with the bootleg off of the counter. The backfield technique will be different on this play. The call 34 counter indicates the 4 hole is the point of attack, and the word counter tells all the backs who are not receiving the handoff to run in the opposite direction, away from the point of attack. The fullback on this play will run for the outside leg of the guard and then fake over an imaginary ball, thus giving the picture of a belly. The halfback is the ballcarrier. If the halfback is in a diveback position, the fullback and the halfback show the picture of belly.

When running the belly play, the fullback runs the ball off-tackle and the halfback leads through the hole. The halfback will not jab step, but he will try to give that impression. The halfback rocks his weight, takes a lead step, a crossover step, and squares up into the hole to receive the handoff from the quarterback. The quarterback's first step is either on the midline or a little beyond the midline, depending on the defensive front spacing. If the defense is odd (Diagram 2.24), with a man covering the center, the halfback takes his footwork, receives the handoff, and runs for the near foot of the offensive center. The center will post, the right guard will lead, and the two of them will drive the nose down the line of scrimmage as flat as possible. By having the halfback run for that landmark, he can stay tight to the double-team. If the nose fights across the double-team, the halfback could cut off the backside of the double-team.

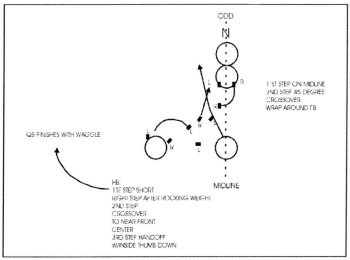

Diagram 2.24

The quarterback's first step will be on the midline. On his second step, he will wrap tight around the fullback's tail to make the handoff to the halfback. The quarterback then snaps his hands in. He will drag the hand to make it look like the counter bootleg. His left hand is in tight, and his right arm is pumping as he attacks the flank. He shows good deception by not letting the defense see where the ball is.

The halfbacks take the handoff with their inside thumb down. This play, along with the counter crisscross, are the two main reasons to coach the inside thumb down. On the counter crisscross, the halfback receives the handoff and, as he crosses the backfield, merely pushes the ball straight ahead to hand the ball off to the other halfback. This method is opposed to receiving the handoff traditionally and then having to turn the ball over in order to hand it to the other halfback. You merely push the ball to him. The second reason is the tackle trap counter play. If the halfback accepts the ball from the quarterback with his elbow up, what happens to his shoulders? His shoulders raise up. If he takes his footwork and takes the ball from the quarterback with his inside thumb down his shoulders, he will maintain a good body lean. As a result, he will have a much better chance at deception because he has great body lean and is tight to the quarterback.

You can hand the ball off to a halfback who is in a diveback position or run the same play to a halfback in three-step motion. The footwork for the quarterback is no different. It is up to the motion halfback to get the play timed up correctly and get the proper aiming point.

When running the 34 counter against an even defense (Diagram 2.25), the double-team will occur over the backside guard. The center and the left guard execute the double-team. The left guard is the post blocker, and the center is the lead blocker. On contact, they will work their butts together and drive the defender laterally down the line. The hole for the halfback is shorter or closer to the halfback. As the halfback takes his footwork, he will bend his path for the inside foot of the guard. The quarterback's first step will be six inches beyond the midline. On the second step, he wraps tight around the fullback and, on his third step, will be in position to make the handoff without having to reach to the halfback. The ball can also be handed off to a halfback coming in motion. The halfback bursts through the line, and the quarterback attacks the flank, faking counter bootleg.

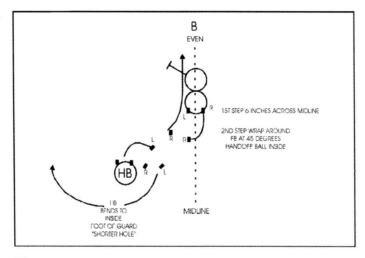

Diagram 2.25

The Counter Bootleg

The counter bootleg (Diagram 2.26) is the companion play to the tackle trap. The fullback and halfback techniques are explained in the running back chapter. The quarterback keeps the football and will attack the flank with a run-pass option. The fullback's footwork is different and depends on what kind of defense he sees and whether the tackle pulls. The halfback and the quarterback will always use short-hole technique. Whether the defense is odd or even makes no difference to the quarterback and the halfback. The halfback will bend his path to the inside foot of the guard, and the quarterback will reverse pivot beyond the midline. When pulling, the tackle must pull to the opposite guard and then break down. If the tackle pulls with speed and the halfback fakes at a short hole, a collision will not occur between the halfback and the pulling tackle. Collisions occur because one player, or both, uses poor technique. By using short-hole technique, the quarterback has also started his momentum moving faster to the flank. He will be attacking the flank with quickness. On his fourth step, the quarterback will drag his hand as he did when he handed off. The ball is hidden from the defense as he attacks the flank.

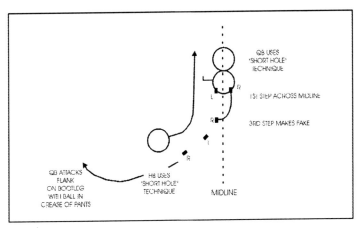

Diagram 2.26

The 80 Series

The final play series is the 80 series, and it contains important coaching points for the quarterback's footwork. The first play in the series is the fullback belly play, which is a big play in the offense. The play can be blocked with a variety of different blocking schemes. You use cross block as the number one scheme, but you also block the play with on blocking, blast blocking, isolation blocking, or fire blocking.

The Fullback Belly

The belly play has always been a great play (Diagram 2.27). The fullback will take a lead step, crossover step, and square-up step. The fullback will take the handoff in the traditional manner, with his inside elbow up and his inside thumb down. The quarterback's technique on the belly is to reverse pivot beyond the midline on the first step. The fullback has taken a lead step and, on the second step, crosses over. The quarterback's next step is toward the heels of the fullback. He will reach the ball to the fullback's far hip. On the fullback's third step, he will square up and the quarterback will give him the ball as he fakes keep pass. After the handoff is secure, the quarterback will drag his back foot out of the way to give the fullback a cutback lane and not trip him. The belly is the sprint draw play of the wing-T. The fullback will gain many yards in a variety of ways. He should be able to bend this play anywhere he sees daylight along the line of scrimmage. Long-time coaches of the wing-T have probably run into the main problem with this play, which is the quarterback has to keep his backside foot out of the way of the fullback so the fullback can cut anywhere.

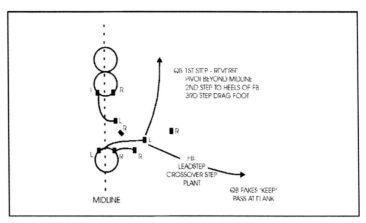

Diagram 2.27

Focusing on the quarterback, his first step is on the midline. On his second step, he will wrap tight around the fullback and start to reach the ball. On his third step, the exchange is completed. Finally, on his fourth step, the quarterback begins to fake keep pass at the flank. It is important to make the defense believe the quarterback has the ball. He must get his hands up quickly and into a ready position to throw the ball.

The Keep Pass

On the belly keep pass, the fullback takes the same footwork as usual, except his path is a little wider because of his blocking assignment (Diagram 2.28). The quarterback will have the ball instead of the fullback, since he only fakes to the fullback. The fullback's first step is still a lead step; the second step is still a crossover. The quarterback will make a short arm's-length ride and snap the ball into the ready position to throw the ball. As the quarterback comes off the fake, he brings the ball up quickly in the passing grip and in the passing position. On his fourth step, the quarterback will begin to attack the flank, ready to throw the football quickly. The quarterback should be ready to throw to the halfback in the flat as he comes off the mesh with the fullback. It is helpful to tighten the split of their playside end in order to out leverage the defense in the flat with the playside halfback.

As the quarterback reverse pivots and makes the fake, he will get the ball up into the ready position. As he attacks the flank, the ball may go back and forth or side to side. The ball is in the carriage, and for this type of shoulder action to occur is normal.

As the quarterback reverse pivots on the keep pass, his first step is slightly across the midline. On his second step, he will poke the ball quickly into the fullback's pocket. He gives a quick arm's-length ride to the fullback and snaps the ball up to the ready position as he comes off the fake. The ball remains in the carriage, and he must be

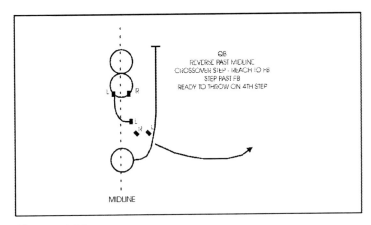

Diagram 2.28

able to quickly throw the ball to the back in the flat. If the play is run to a spread end-wingback flank, the spread end runs a fly and the halfback is in the flat. The quarterback can throw quickly to the halfback, allowing him to catch the ball and get turned up the field. If the corner in deep third coverage runs off with the split end, the halfback gets the ball. If the back breaks one tackle, he can run down the sideline for a big play. The quarterback will make his throw on his sixth step. The quarterback is taught to think, "Mesh, throw, mesh throw," and to get rid of the ball on his sixth step.

When running 89 keep pass to the left, the ball will be thrown on the fifth step. The quarterback should think, "Mesh, throw." That way, he will get the ball up on his third step, ready to throw. He should then look to dump the ball off to the halfback in the flat quickly.

It is common to call individual pass routes for the spread end in an attempt to get him the ball or to take advantage of the weakness of a certain coverage. Some examples include keep pass out, keep pass curl, keep pass post wheel, and keep pass with drag routes.

Belly Drop-Back

Very closely related to the keep pass is a play called 83 and 87 pass (Diagram 2.29). The fullback will fake 83 or 87 with lead, crossover, and square-up footwork. As he fakes through the hole, he has a blocking assignment on the inside linebacker. The halfback is in motion on 83 pass and sets up after passing the quarterback-fullback mesh to pass-block the first defender outside the right tackle's block.

For the quarterback, differences exist between this play and the keep pass. First of all, keep pass is called at the 1 hole (81), which tells the quarterback fake 83 or 87 to

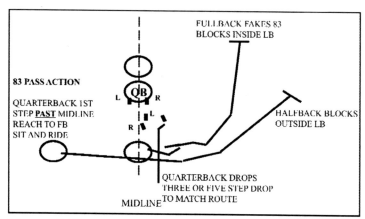

Diagram 2.29

the fullback, but then attack the flank with a run-pass option at the 1 or 9 hole. On 83 pass, the quarterback will make a more deliberate fake to the fullback, then drop back. The coaching point is to sit on the ride. After that, the quarterback snaps the ball back quickly with his hands and drops back as the fullback fakes through the line.

The quarterback should drop back three to five steps, pushing off his front foot. Crossing patterns are good at this point, since the backfield action the defense is seeing is full flow. The 87 pass is the same play to the left.

80 Counter

Closely related to 83 pass is 83 and 87 counter (Diagram 2.30). On 83 and 87 counter, the footwork for the quarterback and the fullback remains the same. The term counter means the backs who are not getting the ball run away from the play. The fullback will fake 83 to the right. He uses the same footwork as belly, but he then becomes a blocker. The quarterback will hand the ball to the wingback coming back inside. The quarterback's footwork consists of reversing pivot just beyond the midline; reaching the ball to the fullback; pulling the ball out, as in keep pass; and then handing the ball to the halfback on the inside. The halfback runs the counter off-tackle, and the quarterback continues to fake keep pass. The 87 counter occurs when they fake 83 and counter back to the left. The opposite would be 83 counter.

The Down Play

On 82 and 88 down, the fullback runs a direct path for the off-tackle hole (Diagram 2.31). The quarterback will reverse pivot flat down the line of scrimmage. The play could be blocked (82 and 88) gut. Although different blocking schemes exist, the quarterback will use the same technique on each. The quarterback will reverse pivot down the line. On his second step, he will reach the ball out. On his third step, he will

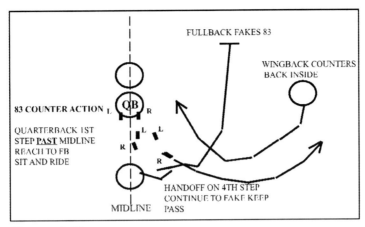

Diagram 2.30

ride the fullback into the line, hand him the ball, and shuffle with him into the line. The quarterback will then fake down option at the flank. Instead of handing the ball to the fullback and faking the belly keep pass, the companion play to 82 down is 82 down option. The quarterback will fake the option to set up 82 down option for future use. The quarterback may need to step around penetration when he rides the fullback. The ride helps establish the fullback off-tackle and also helps set up the option.

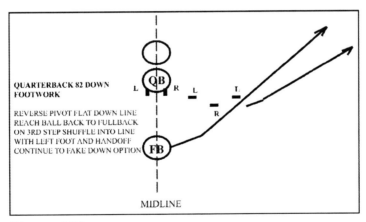

Diagram 2.31

Down Option

The 82 down option contains alternate blocking schemes, including 82 load, 82 down load, and 82 down option. An important coaching point for the quarterback is to make sure the ball is in the ready position after he comes off the mesh with the fullback. He must be ready to pitch the ball. He will use a passing grip.

On down option (Diagram 2.32), the fullback should block the free safety. Depending on the reaction he gets from the defense, the fullback might be able to go through the line and cut the safety off. But, this instance does not happen very often. Remember, this play is called because the third defender is sealing. If #3 were penetrating, you would call 82 down and run the ball off-tackle. If #3 is sealing down inside, then the fullback should block him inside, take the ball outside, and run the option. The fullback making it through the line of scrimmage to block the free safety is optimal. What normally happens is the fullback has to bounce outside the log block on the defensive end in order to block the free safety. The quarterback's footwork does not change, and he should try to make the play look like 82 down, as if the fullback is carrying the ball through the line of scrimmage. After the shuffle, the quarterback may have to step around penetration, because the log block will occur there. You coach your quarterback to step around this trash, so he can get to the fourth defender in order to option him.

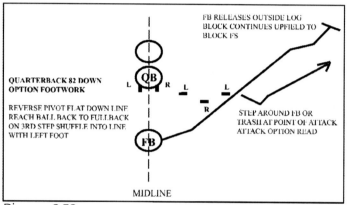

Diagram 2.32

The Quick Belly

One more belly footwork can be used and is called quick belly (Diagram 2.33). The quick belly series includes a quick short belly to the fullback, an option off the quick belly, a scissors or Sally type of play, and 81 waggle, where the backs fake 80 action and the quarterback attacks the backside flank.

In this series, the quarterback does not need as much width. The fullback takes a quick jab step, as he does on cross block, except, on his second step, he will dive for the butt of the guard. Since the quarterback does not need much width, his first step will be a jab step forward, which gets him into the line. He will then reverse pivot off the toes of his playside foot. After the quarterback reverse pivots flat, he will mesh with the fullback. On his third step, the quarterback reaches the ball back to the fullback; on his fourth step, he rides him into the line. From there, the quarterback will fake option.

The play will be blocked with fire-on-backer blocking and is a quick hitter to the fullback. To the split end-wingback flank, the play is a quick belly to the fullback with zone blocking and is a north-south play.

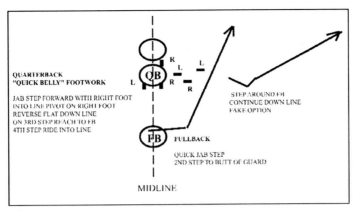

Diagram 2.33

Quick Belly Option

The quick belly will set up 81 and 89 option (Diagram 2.34). The footwork for the fullback and quarterback will be the same. The fullback will not get the ball. He will become a blocker, and the quarterback will take the ball down the line of scrimmage to option the third defender.

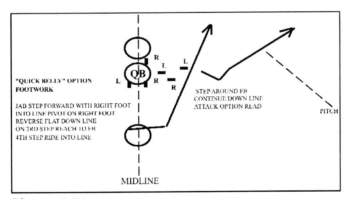

Diagram 2.34

The quarterback's technique is to jab step forward on his first step, reverse pivot on his second step, reach the ball back to the fullback on his third step, and ride the fullback to the front foot on his fourth step. The quarterback will then snap his hands in and continue down the line to option the defensive end. If you run the same play to the left, it will be called 89 option. The quarterback will jab step with his left foot, reverse pivot off that foot, reach back, ride the fullback, snap his hands back in, come downhill, attack the flank, and execute the read on the third defender. The backside halfback is in motion. He is the pitchback.

The Scissors

The next play in the series is a scissors play, which some coaches call Sally. You block the scissors a bit differently from the coaches who run Sally, but it is basically the same principle. The quarterback will use his normal footwork, except he will fake to the fullback and hand the ball to the wingback coming back inside on an inside counter. After his fake to the fullback, the quarterback's footwork will change slightly. On his fifth step, the quarterback will step back and hand the ball inside to the wingback. From there, the quarterback will fake the option play. The wingback, who is running the football, does not go in motion. His first step will be back, for depth, which will open his shoulders to the quarterback. As the quarterback reverse pivots, the wingback will start to run for the tail of the center, which is his aiming point. The quarterback will step back and give the ball to the wingback. The wingback will then turn up the field north and south. You teach the wingback to option run the center's block. This scissors play is called 84 scissors at 6 (Diagram 2.35), which means you will fake 84 and the right halfback will scissors back toward the 6 hole. The opposite is 86 scissors at 4.

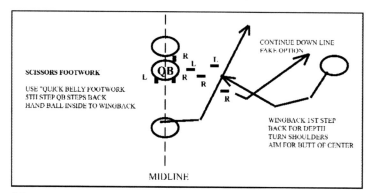

Diagram 2.35

The 80 Waggle

The last play to discuss is 81 and 89 waggle (Diagram 2.36). The best time to run this play is when the linebackers are keying the fullback. When they see the fullback start, the linebackers will fly in his direction. This play is tougher to run if the linebackers are blitzing, because the fullback in the waggle play is also responsible for blitz pickup. If the defense is blitzing inside linebackers, 81 or 89 waggle is not a good call. When playing a team that does not blitz the inside backers, but will flow with the fullback, this play can be devastating. If the play is 81 waggle, the quarterback will simply run 21 waggle.

On this play, the fullback uses different footwork. He takes a jab step, which resembles his footwork on 84, then starts to attack the butt of the guard. The fullback will fake over an imaginary ball and, on his third step, will start back to the side of the waggle. The fullback will then work to the frontside and be a receiver. The quarterback will attack the flank. For the quarterback, no difference exists between this play and 21 waggle. The 81 waggle is a great key breaker for the defense, especially if they are keying the fullback. If the call is 89 waggle, the play will go to the right, away from the 9 hole, and the fullback will fake 86. The quarterback's technique is exactly the same as on 29 waggle.

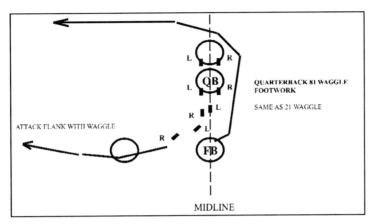

Diagram 2.36

3

The Wing-T Running Back

Qualities of Wing-T Running Backs

Before discussing the techniques of wing-T running backs, the qualities required to play those positions, along with the physical skills coaches look for, should be addressed. As with all positions in the wing-T, the running backs must be unselfish. They have to understand what their role is and that the ball will be spread to all of the skilled positions. This offense will get the ball to the spread end, the tight end, both halfbacks, and, certainly, the fullback. Everybody will share in the skill responsibilities. Coaches want players who are comfortable in this offense, but they also want the best talent possible at every position. They want players in these positions to be talented enough so the defense cannot key on just one back. If the halfbacks are having a big day, it might be because the defense is keying on the fullback, or vice versa.

The second vital quality is the backs must be willing to block. They will not block all the time, but, when their turn comes to block, they have to be willing to do it. No back will be allowed to have the attitude he is going to get the ball all the time, while everyone else's job is to block. He will not be allowed to think that way. Backs must be willing to block. Many ways exist to get halfbacks and fullbacks to block in this offense, without having to take the physical abuse from blocking all the time. Often, people on the opposing team will out-size you. As long as your talented backs are willing to make an attempt, they will find that great running backs can also become great blockers.

The next qualities to look for are the physical tools needed at each position. At the college level, the fullback needs to weigh somewhere between 205 and 225 pounds. He can be bigger, as long as he is also fast enough. Occasionally, he might be smaller, but smaller fullbacks are the exception, rather than the rule. You would like to have a fullback with powerful legs, who can run through arm tackles, but is also capable in the open field. The fullback in this offense is somewhat like the tailback in the I. He will average the most carries in a game, because he gets to run plays to both sides of the formation. By the time the season is over, the fullback will have carried the ball a full third of the time more than the halfbacks. Which backs carry the ball in the wing-T depends on how the games go and who the defense is keying on.

The halfback in this offense is a player who needs to be a minimum of 185 to 200 pounds. Those sizes are what you should try to recruit. Sometimes, smaller backs can get the job done, but, many times, the smaller players do not stay healthy for the whole season. If you have smaller running backs, it is very important to also have backups.

The halfback needs to understand his role in the offense is to rush for 500 to 1,000 yards in a season and catch from 300 to 700 yards' worth of passes. You look for halfbacks who have great hands, as well as great running skills. They will catch the ball a lot. In college football, it is critical to throw the ball efficiently. You should not throw the ball all the time, but you should throw it efficiently. You need to be able to complete passes when you decide to throw them.

The catalyst in this offense is the play-action passing game. A wing-T offense must be able to complete the keep pass play, the counter bootleg play, and the waggle play in order to experience success in the offense. If you are running trap option, you must also be able to complete trap-option pass. Those four action passes are the basic staples in this offense and are the keys to keeping the ball moving north and south. You must have a quarterback who can throw the ball accurately and must have backs and receivers who can catch it.

The first of the physical tools you want the backs to concentrate on are their running skills. They should be north-and-south runners. It is inaccurate when coaches label the wing-T as a parallel offense. The sweep is the only play in the offense ever parallel to the line of scrimmage. However, the sweep becomes north and south once the back makes the cut. It is also amazing how those same coaches say the defense will run the sweep down with speed and catch it from behind. Most humorous of all is those same teams do not catch it when they actually play against it. Remember, they have other threats to worry about and are frozen in place by the misdirection in the backfield.

Besides needing backs who are north-and-south runners, you need backs who will break tackles. You should keep a statistic called yards after contact, or YAC. This yardage is probably the most important statistic a running back has. If you gain between 100 and 150 YACs, then you will win the game, or at least have a big day offensively. Breaking tackles and being a north-south runner are two crucial qualities running backs must have, regardless of their position.

Another physical skill to look for in your running backs is the ability to catch the football. You must have backs with soft hands, who can catch the ball, turn upfield, and gain additional yards after receiving the ball.

Blocking, though, is the most crucial attribute your backs can have. You should require the backs to block. They will get plenty of opportunities to have the ball in their hands, but when the other backs have the ball, they must correctly execute their blocking.

Selling this philosophy has been very successful. The backs take great pride in their blocking. They are able to block big defenders and not be mismatched physically. You teach cut technique and always teach blocking at the hip. When blocking at the hip, a back might be outsized, but he can still get movement if he uses the proper technique.

Last, but not least, are faking skills. The wing-T is a misdirection offense. Many times exist when you run a play and then run the companion play, which looks just like it, requiring the backs to fake. Those fakes help misdirection. They create deception and force the defense to be frozen in place, unable to read the ball and unable to pursue as quickly as they would like.

These skills are considered the most important a running back can have. He has to run, catch, block, and do a great job of faking. An unselfish back will do those four things. If your backs are all willing to be unselfish, then the end result will be they all will end up with impressive statistics.

Shoulder Skills

The remainder of this chapter will deal with exactly what the wing-T running backs do on the field. You start with shoulder skills. You always start with the actual teaching of blocking. You put the backs, just like the linemen, down in a stance and teach them how to block. You do this first with bags, then with people. You teach blocking skills first.

The first fundamental to start with is shoulder skills (Diagram 3.1). By senior year, the backs have done this drill for four or five years each. At the start of every practice, you use a big heavy bag to simulate the size and bulk a defensive player will usually have. One of your players holds the bag, while another player blocks the bag. Shoulder skills include four drills in a four-part progression. The first drill is called surface. Surface drill entails fitting into the bag in order to teach blockers how they should finish when they hit. The second drill is called strike a blow, emphasizing striking a blow and rolling the hips. The third drill comes into play when you teach the footwork in conjunction with the block. This drill is called step and hit. The fourth drill teaches backs to run full speed at the bag and execute a block and is called run and hit.

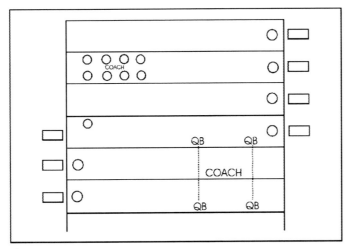

Diagram 3.1

Surface

In this drill, you emphasize the fit, or the blocking surface, that you use. The wing-T requires you teach the importance of shoulders in blocking. That method is not old fashioned or passé. You use shoulders as the primary striking point, but you also finish blocks with the hands. You are incorporating your hands into your blocks, but you are also using the hardness and the blocking surface of a shoulder. The surface of a block includes the side of the neck, the front of the shoulder, all the way down to the elbow, the front of the arm, the fist, and even the pec. That surface is what your backs will drive through on the bag when they make contact. In the old days, coaches would teach players to put their face in the numbers. But, as players made contact and put their face in the numbers, they were suffering neck injuries. In time, rules were legislated to prevent the teaching of face blocks. Blockers could no longer use the top of the head, or the face mask, as the initial striking point on a block. Many coaches still teach blocking by leading with the head. They just do not say it or print it anymore, because they do not want to be sued or have a liability problem. In the wing-T offense, coaches can sleep well at night because they know, morally, they are doing the right thing by the players. You aim for the middle of the opponent when you strike him, but, as you make contact, you slide the head so you use the blocking surface described earlier. As the backs contact the defender, they drive their shoulder, forearm, and entire blocking surface through the bag. When they block, they block through the man, not at the man. When they make contact on the bags, they try to explode through the bag.

The first thing to do is have the backs get down in a six-point stance. You want them right up to the bag, so their face mask is touching the bag. You want their knees under them and their thighs at a 90-degree angle to their lower legs. You want a nice, flat back. You want the bag to stay between the blocker's knees. If players block and tackle with the opponent between their legs, they seldom will miss.

In the surface drill, all the backs do is fit into the bag. As they fit into the bag, their head will slip to the side and their hips will go down, but their eyes will stay up. All of the drills in practice are on sound cadence (i.e., the first sound they hear). Sound cadence saves time and gives the players more reps. The command to the blocker is, "Surface, right shoulder, on sound." The coach will say, "Set," and all the blockers fit into the bag. Every two backs share a bag. If you have four blockers, then, obviously, they need two bags. You need one bag for every two blockers you have. You want all the bags to be lined up on the sideline so the bottom of the bag is intersected by the white sideline. All blockers will be facing into the bag, while the coach stands either behind or in front of his blockers, so he can watch their eyes. Either coaching location is advantageous to the coach.

You have three drills going at the same time. All blockers will execute when the coach gives the command. By doing this, your coaches are mass teaching. All the backs are learning how to do this drill at the same time. The coach will try to see everything and, at times, will not see everything, which is okay. The players will be learning by doing rather than by watching, which is always better. Sooner or later, coaches will find any technique errors that might be occurring.

To review, the first drill is called surface. Here, you will merely fit into the bag. You are not going to strike the bag, yet. You are just going to fit in. You tell the back to go at the bag and slide his head to the side. The bag is still between the back's legs, he has a strong blocking surface, and, when he simulates contact, he will place his forearm as if he were driving it through the bag along with his shoulder. The coaching points to emphasize for this technique are that the eyes should be up. The blocker must be able to see how many clouds are in the sky. Check to see if his butt is down. The midsection of his body should be into the ground. If a blocker has his hips off the ground, he has not rolled his hips, yet. Make sure each blocker is all the way down, hips into the ground. A nice squeeze between the neck and the shoulder should be on the bag. Looking at the line of blockers, the coach can check all of them quickly or one guy at a time and then reset them.

When they are in a six-point stance, the blockers' toes should be flat. They do not want their toes curled under their feet because, when they strike, their knees will lift up off the ground. By flattening their toes, the blockers' knees will not come up and their hips will roll.

The second half of the same drill is surface with the left shoulder. Make sure to emphasize both shoulders. The command will be, "Surface, left shoulder, on sound." All blockers will fit into the bag, while the coaches check for the key fundamentals. After using both shoulders, the blockers will switch. At this point, the man who just blocked will hold the bag and the man who was holding the bag will work on surface. When the second blocker is ready to go, the coach should give the same two commands and have them repeat the drill.

Strike a Blow

Phase two of the shoulder skills progression is strike a blow. When players put bags down on the sideline, the white line is intersecting the bottom of the bags. When you strike the blow, you want the blocker to knock the bag off that white line. That movement is how your coaches know if the blocker is really striking a blow.

You use the normal six-point stance, with hands and knees on the ground and toes flat to the ground. Blockers are facing the bag, with the cage of their helmet on the bag. The coach will give the command, "Strike a blow, right shoulder, on sound." This hit is live. The running back will cock back slightly to get momentum, then strike the bag and drive his blocking surface through the bag, knocking the bag off the line. The nose of the blocker will aim for the middle of the bag, then slide to the side as contact occurs, so the shoulder and the forearm is the blocking surface which makes contact. That block is moral and legal. It has hardness and is physical. As blockers finish, coaches should see the same fundamentals as in the surface drill. Blockers have their eyes up, the bag between their legs, their hips down, and a tight neck squeeze between the blocking surface and the side of their neck.

Next, you do the drill with the left shoulder. You also switch the blockers. The man who just blocked will now hold the bag. The man who held the bag will now be the blocker. These two players work daily as partners and challenge each other. If one man feels the hit was too soft, it is his job, as a good teammate, to tell his partner what he might be doing wrong. The coach, obviously, will do the same.

Step and Hit

You are now ready for the third part of the progression, which is called step and hit. In this phase of the drill, the coach should get the blockers up in a two-point stance with their forearms resting on their thighs. Measure the distance to the bag by reaching out and touching the bag. Blockers want to be about an arm's distance from the bag. The reason is they will take a short, six-inch power step and then strike the bag on the second step. They have to be back far enough so contact will occur on the second step. The blockers keep the bag between their legs as they line up.

You teach another extremely important blocking fundamental. When a blocker blocks with his right shoulder, then he must step with his left foot. When people walk and when they run, if they step with their right foot, then their left arm comes forward. Therefore, you use opposite arm and leg action when you practice this drill. If the backs strike with their right shoulder, then they take a short step with their left foot and the result will be that the second step will be the contact step. Coaches teach this drill in phases. They first do the drill one step at a time, to check the first step. If the blocker is going to block with his right shoulder, he needs to step with his left foot. What should happen on the first step is the blocker's toes should be replaced by his heels. That distance is all the first step should cover. As he steps with his left foot, he cocks his right forearm. His right shoulder blocking surface will drive through the bag. When doing this drill in steps, take the first step and hold it. Check for the chest on the thighs and the butt over the heels to prevent being overextended. Emphasize the chest on his thighs, so the blocker has the chance to block at the hip. He is not overextended, his chest is on his thighs, and he is low. He is ready for the second step. The coach will say, "Finish," or, "Two," and the blocker will explode through the bag, with his third step following through naturally. As he finishes, he should have that same fundamental blocking surface, with his eyes up and a tight neck squeeze between the bag and the blocking surface.

Next, you do the same drill with the left shoulder. The coach is behind, watching all of his blockers at the same time. You are getting a lot of reps by mass teaching. Again, the blocker should take his first step and hold it. The coach should not allow the blocker to overstride with a big step. Rather, he should replace his toes with his heel. This power step is only six inches, and, on "Two," he should explode through the bag. The third step follows naturally and is a result of the momentum carrying the back through the block. His eyes are up, his elbow is high, he should have a tight squeeze between his neck and the blocking surface, his chest is on his thighs, his butt is over his heels, and, finally, he should have the bag between his legs. After the first blocker goes, the second blocker, who was holding the bag, comes over and takes his turn to block. The coach is standing back, watching all of his blockers, and can see if anybody is out of place. He makes his corrections and then is ready to move on to the next drill.

Once the players are to the point where they can take their first step, replacing their toes with their heel, they are ready to execute the drill without stopping on the first step. Do not make robots out of your players. Get past this part of the progression as quickly as they are ready.

Run and Hit

The final drill in the progression is called run and hit, where backs will simulate blocking linebackers. The blocker will run at the bag and block it as if he were blocking a linebacker. When a halfback has to run at and block a defensive end and is in a diveback position, he will start from four yards away. If the fullback has to run through a hole to block a linebacker or block a linebacker stepping up into the hole, he will be starting from four yards away. The run and hit drill puts the back in these types of situations. You also bring the bag right up on the blocker. The drill is now called hit and run, which means backs hit first and drive the bag four yards. This drill is an alternative to run and hit.

The same blocking fundamentals apply in run and hit. If the backs block with their right shoulder, then they must step with their left foot first. It should work out so contact will occur with the right shoulder contacting the bag on the fourth step, when he is four yards away. As the blocker drives the bag, he will drive the bag straight back with his right shoulder.

The final blocking fundamental is the finish. You teach the backs, as well as all of your players, to finish their blocks by swinging their tail. When coaches say swing the tail, the blockers will turn their butts into the hole in order to turn the defender. This case is where blockers will use their hands to help finish the block. As they make contact, they drive the bag, using their off arm like a piston, and punch up through the bag. They bench press with that arm and turn the bag at the same time. The bag should remain between their legs. One of the cardinal sins occurs when the blocker approaches the bag, makes contact, and begins to swing his tail, with his feet outside the bag. He will cross over as he turns the bag. At this point, he will lose the defender. Instead, the blocker should keep the bag between his legs and keep his feet apart. He should accelerate his feet on contact, but keep his feet apart through the whole block, finishing as he swings his tail.

The command to use is, "Run and hit, right shoulder, on sound." On "Set," the blocker will take off, run four yards, drive the bag backwards for two steps, swing his tail with his feet wide apart, and drive the bag to the side for five yards. He can drive the bag farther, if he wants, further emphasizing the finish of his block.

Next, the drill is reversed so it is, "Run and hit, left shoulder, on sound." The same fundamentals are used here as in the previous phase. As the back drives his forearm through the bag, his chest will be on his thighs, he will have a good, tight neck squeeze, his off arm will bench press, and his elbow will lock out. This method is how he can turn a defender. He keeps the defender between his legs, drives his free hand into the bag, and bench presses. (This technique is one of the major reasons to do the bench press in the weight program.) As the back swings his tail, his butt should turn into the hole and the man should stay between his legs. Next, his partner switches over and takes his turn. The man who held the bag is the blocker. The man who blocked holds the bag.

When your coaches do these drills, they are coaching a line of blockers. They can watch them all block, watch them all turn the bag, and check them when they finish. You blow the whistle to have them stop and hold their block, so you can check all of them. Have they finished in the correct blocking position? Do they have a tight neck squeeze between the side of their neck and the blocking surface? Is their chest on their thighs, butt over their heels? And, is the man between their legs?

Types of Blocks

In addition to the shoulder skill progression, the backs are taught different types of blocks. Two wingback blocks exist and are called gap and down, along with one diveback block, called log. Regardless of what position the backs play, they all learn the wingback blocks, just as all linemen learn how to do waggle and sweep drills and all running backs learn to execute all three types of motion. Coaches cross-train all of the players so they learn all of the skills.

Wingback Blocks

All of the backs work on wingback blocks. The blocking bag simulates the defensive end whom the wing will block on the sweep. The blockers are in a wingback position about a yard back and a yard outside. The two wingback blocks are the gap block and the down block. Differences exist between the two blocks, and different times exist to use them. Anytime the defender is a player who likes to penetrate, the wingbacks use gap technique. They must cut penetration off. If he is not a penetrator, but is a reader who is playing on the line of scrimmage, the wingbacks use down technique. If any doubt is in their minds, they begin with gap technique and react from there. Since the tight end has the assignment of gap, read down on sweep, he will block inside, leaving the wing on the defensive end. How the wing attacks him depends on his style of play. You use gap technique versus a penetrator and down technique versus a reader. If the end is a penetrator who runs upfield when the tight end blocks inside, then the coach's job is to call the companion play and not try to run outside. If the end is not a penetrator and tries to jam the tight end and then seal into the hole, he has set himself up for down blocks. The wingbacks must be ready for either reaction. They must be ready for him to penetrate or to read and not penetrate. Coaches attempt to know by film analysis, stance, or alignment which technique the end uses, so the wingbacks can anticipate the type of block to use.

Gap Block

When you have called the sweep, the wingback has to live with it. He may have expected the end to seal, but, instead, he is a penetrator. The wing must block him anyway. He will use gap technique. His first step should be flat, for the inside foot of the tight end. It is like a pull step. The wingback's head will be across the front of the belt buckle of the penetrator. The key is to get the head across the front of the belt buckle in order to stop penetration. Even though you put the head across the front, the blocker must keep the defender between his legs. The bag (or the defensive man) is always kept between the wingback's legs when he makes this block. A common error is for the wingback to try so hard to get his head across the front of the defender that his feet wind up across the front as well. In that case, the defensive end can spin out of the block and beat the wing. You coach the wing to step flat enough so he can cut off penetration, but still be able to adjust the angle enough to keep the man between his legs when he makes the block.

You first drill the right wingback's block with the right shoulder. The command will be, "Gap left, on sound." Coaches should look for head up; good, tight neck squeeze between the blocking surface and the neck; chest on the thighs; back flat; butt over the heels; and the defender between the legs. You check the first step, the gap step, the flat pull step for the inside foot of the tight end. The second step should occur on the contact phase. The step and hit techniques learned in shoulder skill period will finish the block. You then practice gap block to the right, which is executed with the left shoulder. The first blocker will block once with each shoulder. Then, the second blocker will block once with each shoulder. They then switch back and go to the next drill. The players get a lot of drills done in a short period of time, provided they are blocking correctly. On the first day of training camp, as well as the first day of spring practice, you allow 15 minutes for this period. This long period will enable you to teach the shoulder skills thoroughly.

The reason to coach chest on thighs is that, when the blockers make contact, they will make contact at the hip. No one lifts weights with his hips. Players do not do presses with the hips. They are not doing squats with their hips, the way they do with their thighs. No strength exists in a man's hip. If backs block at the hip, they will push the defender all over the field. No matter how much he resists, they can still push him. They can do it with one hand. Take the biggest player on the team and have the smallest player push on his hip with just one hand. He will move him all around the field, as long as that hand is at the hip. One of the hardest things coaches will ever have to do is get players to block at the hip. Once the blockers understand that principle, they will bury people. They will not just block them; they will bury them. The man who blocks at the shoulders has the toughest time. The defender has much of his strength in his shoulders, and all that resistance will defeat the block or, at least, get it stalemated. This method enables the defender's bench workout in the off-season to help him defeat the block. If the blockers strike at the hip, the defender has no strength there, and the blocker will rarely be beaten. Painting a white line on the bag at about the hip area emphasizes the chest on the thighs and the importance of striking at the hip.

Down Block

The second wingback block is called a down block. On a down block, the defender is no longer a penetrator, so the blocker can put his head behind. Since the man is not a threat to penetrate, he will probably play parallel to the line of scrimmage and laterally up and down the line of scrimmage. The wingback's job is to cut off this lateral/parallel movement. His head is placed on the upfield side of the defender, as opposed to in front. Backs only do this when they are absolutely sure the end is not going to penetrate. The wingback is one yard outside and one yard back from the tight end. He will then execute the block down left. He will step with his right foot and block with his left shoulder. As the blocker steps with his right foot, the toes of his left foot pivot as he moves his right foot. His second step will be with his left foot. The opposite arm and leg action still applies. Next, you drill the same block to the right. This drill will be down right for left wingbacks and is done with the right shoulder, with the head on the upfield side of the defender. He steps with his left foot, blocks with his right shoulder, and keeps his head behind.

Diveback Block

Log Block

After the backs have executed both wingback blocks, one more block is executed from the diveback position. This block is called a log block. The defender is aligned in a 9 technique on the outside shoulder of the tight end. The diveback is lined up behind the tackle's outside leg and is four yards deep in the backfield.

On this block, the first step should take off for a point 1.5 yards outside the tightest man on the line of scrimmage. This man could be a tackle, if the diveback is on the split end side, or it could be the tight end, if the diveback is on the tight end side. The first step only establishes the initial angle of takeoff. From there, the back must adjust on the basis of the defender's reaction. If the defender is sliding out, the halfback will let him go and wall off on the next inside defender. At this point, the guard will kick out the defensive end, and the ballcarrier will make his cut inside the guard. If the defender seals inside, then the halfback will adjust his path to pin the defender inside. The guard will then kick out the next man. The divebacks will execute this block with their inside shoulder. As they finish the block, they will finish by swinging their tail and taking the defender inside on a 45-degree angle, away from the line of scrimmage. The blocker must adjust to the defender on the basis of his reaction. The coach will put the blocker in a two-point stance and execute log block with the left shoulder. If he blocks with the left shoulder, he steps with the right foot. He will make contact with the head to the outside, swing his tail, and drive the bag in the opposite direction. His chest is on his thighs, his butt is over his heels, and the man is between his legs. You then will log block with the right shoulder. Do the two blocks and have the players switch. The man who was holding the bag gets to be the blocker, and the man who was doing the blocking gets to hold the bag.

That drill completes the blocking skill period, which covers the shoulder skills. In review, surface, strike a blow, step and hit, and run and hit are the four main steps in the progression. Then, wingback blocks and diveback blocks exist. Once the backs learn gap, down, and log, they have learned the blocks they need to use.

Routine Period

The next part of practice for backs is called the daily routine period (Diagram 3.2). This time is when the coach will teach the proper stance and how the players should take off. The players work on the first step for as long as it takes them to explode correctly. The four parts of this drill begin with the stance. The second part of this drill is bird-dog. The bird-dog drill is a one-step drill. The players explode out of their stance as fast as they can for one step and then hold it to see if that first step is a good one. The next part of the period is takeoff. When they practice bird-dog, they can go straight ahead at a 45-degree angle, pull step to go lateral, or crossover step to go lateral. When they practice takeoff, they use those same first steps, but also take off and run. They can take off straight, take off at a 45-degree angle, take off with a pull step to go lateral, or take off with a crossover step to go lateral. The final drill during routine period is the timing of all of the motions, which can be mixed into the takeoff phase.

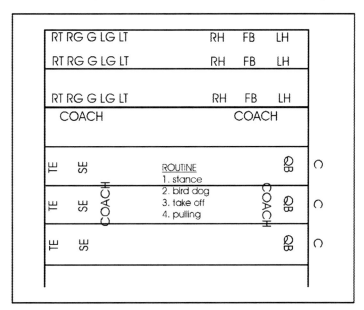

Diagram 3.2

Stance

The first phase begins with the stance. The backs learn the wingback stance, the diveback stance for the halfback, and the stance for the fullback, which are all the same. When coaches line this up on the field, they have all of their people in squares and on yard lines. Coaches want five yards between players and five yards from the players behind them. The first thing you teach in the stance is the feet. You use a stance where the feet are underneath the armpits. The feet should not be any wider, so the back can explode on the first step. The wider the feet, the tougher it is to explode, because the first step will be shorter and less powerful. Backs need to be able to explode out of that stance. You coach a slight bend in the knees and ankles. You tell the backs to get their heels up to the top of the grass.

The backs are in a two-point stance at all positions. The fullback is standing up; he does not get down in a three-point stance. The divebacks and the wingbacks stand up. They keep their shoulders parallel to the line of scrimmage and their hands rest comfortably on their thighs. They do not want to push weight down into their thighs with their hands because that weight makes for a slower takeoff. The backs rest their hands comfortably on their thighs and even pat their thighs so they are not grinding too much weight into their thighs. Some coaches instruct their players to put their hands down on their knees. That technique lowers the shoulders too much. Preferring to be more upright allows you to see. Sometimes, backs feel comfortable turning their toes out slightly, so they can push off the ball of their foot. That stance does not pose a problem. If the backs feel comfortable, they can use that stance. For the most part, however, the toes are pointing north and south, the feet are parallel and underneath the armpits, the knees are slightly bent, and the heels are to the top of the grass.

The running backs should be fairly upright, with their backs slightly arched and their eyes looking straight ahead, so they don't give away their keys. The diveback and the fullback are in the exact same stance, feet parallel. The fullback is straddling the midline, so he is behind the center and the quarterback. The halfback is straddling the outside leg of the tackle. If the halfback is required to line up as a wingback, his alignment will change. The halfbacks will take their alignments from the tackle, because ends will always be changing. The ends could be tight, split, or flexed to two yards; they could be unbalanced or not. A slot could exist, or a split end could be closed down. When the halfbacks align in a wingback position, they line up from the tackle in order to always start from the same spot. They align from the outside foot of the tackle. The wing's outside foot should be 3 to 3.5 yards from the outside foot of the offensive tackle. The football is in front of the center, reached out as far as possible. The wingbacks align with their toes two yards from the back tip of the football.

Wingbacks line up according to the football and the offensive tackle. You want the wingbacks in the same position all the time, because they will be going in three-step motion. When they go in three-step motion, you want the back to be in the diveback position after the third step. On his third step, the wing in motion will be at the outside leg of the tackle. Timing of plays requires the wingbacks to line up from the tackle, who does not change his alignment, as opposed to the ends, who do change their alignment. Consistency requires the handoff to be in the same place all the time.

The wingback stance is the same as the diveback stance, with the exception of the inside foot. Wingbacks drop the inside foot back so the toes are even with the heel of the outside foot. This method facilitates the pull step and three-step motion. The wingback uses the pull step when he has to block a penetrating defensive end. This slight difference in the wing's stance enables him to keep his first step flat. This stance also allows the three-step motion to be quicker. This stance does not hinder the wing from going straight ahead, nor does it hinder him from releasing outside, if he has to flare to block the fourth defender on the flank. The only change is the inside foot is back, with the toes back as far as the heel of the outside foot. Everything else is the same. Shoulders are still north and south, square to the line of scrimmage. A slight bend is in his knees, which happens when he gets his heels to the top of the grass, and he is upright, so he can see the defense to read it correctly.

The backs are never down in a three-point stance. Sometimes, you take the halfbacks and flank them out wide. They can use a wide receiver stance when flanked. You do not widen halfbacks very often. You want a four-back attack, with the backs in the core, so you can execute the wing-T offense. The passing game is executed this way, and so is the running game. No tips should exist for the defense.

Bird-Dog

The next drill is called bird-dog. In this drill, the backs explode out of their stances as fast and as hard as they can for one step. Coaches can check the first step by calling, "Bird-dog," plus a type of step with it. If the coach says to step straight ahead with the right foot, then the backs take their right foot and step straight ahead so their toes are replaced by their heels. As they take that step with their right foot, their right arm should be thrown hard behind them. Their chest should also go down to their thighs. When they check the first step, coaches check for these points. The drill is called bird-dog because a bird-dog in the woods, pointing to a bird out in the field, would look just like this. He would have his nose pointing toward the target, his tail straight back, and his whole body pointing at the bird.

The first step you bird-dog on is a straight-ahead step. The command given to the players is, "Bird-dog, right foot straight ahead, on sound." To set up the drill, the coaches place all players five yards apart, with the backups five yards behind each other. The coach can stand out in front of the drill and see the entire drill. He can see who has not thrown the correct arm behind him and who does not have his chest on his thigh. The coach checks all the backs in the group, then tells them to relax and get ready for the next step. Everyone does the drill at the same time; that way, you are mass teaching. You are getting a lot of players reps at the same time. They are learning by doing, rather than by watching, and do a lot in a short period of time.

In the first practice of the year, routine takes 10 minutes. By the second or third practice, it takes five minutes, and, by the end of the year, you can do this in two minutes.

The next step in bird-dog is a fire step. Their toes are still pointing north and south, but the step is on a 45-degree angle instead of straight ahead. The call is, "Bird-dog, fire right, on sound." Then, they fire left, on sound. Next, the backs step with their left foot so their left arm throws hard behind them. This step will simulate the first step in the log block, or any time you have to run for a point 1.5 yards outside the tight man. It will be used on runs and on pass patterns. You coach the same takeoff angle, so both plays look the same.

The next step will be a pull step to the right. Coaches will work the backs on the pull step, just as the linemen do. When backs take the pull step, the first step points the toes toward the sideline. That foot comes up and goes back down again. Since the backs are stepping with their right foot, they will take their left arm and throw it hard behind them. As with the quarterback in the 20 series, the most important part of this technique is to have the back foot pivot as the front foot steps. A common error is for the back to try taking a pull step without first pivoting his back foot. That action will force the body momentum to go on a 45-degree angle, as opposed to straight down the line of scrimmage. It is very important to pivot the back foot on the pull step. Backs should step with their right foot, throw their right arm hard behind them, and pivot their back foot. This action will turn their shoulders and give them the necessary speed and momentum as they get into their block.

Coaches should continue to check the basic fundamentals: chest on the thighs, back foot pivoted, right arm thrown hard behind, and proper bird-dog position. When the backs learn to master these fundamentals, the coaches know they will be able to explode out of their stance at full speed.

On the sweep, you teach the halfbacks to cross over on their first step, because it is faster. When a baseball player steals second, he also crosses over from first base. To add momentum to the crossover, the backs take their backside arm and throw it across the front of their chest as they take off and run. You do not overcoach this, because it is not opposite arm-leg action like you normally emphasize. To enable the backs to get their shoulders turned as they cross over is important. When they take the crossover step, they throw that arm out in front of them, and then the opposite arm and leg action will take over naturally. You also practice the crossover step in bird-dog drill. Backs will cross over and hold it for one step. When crossing over, they rip their backside arm across the front of their chest so their shoulders will turn and enable them to get momentum into the crossover.

Takeoff

In routine period, the first phase is checking stance, the second phase is bird-dog, and the third phase is takeoff. Players begin five yards apart and five yards behind one another. They all sprint off the line at the same time with the proper foot. They will explode out of their stance and sprint five yards at full speed. Coaches tell them which foot to take off with and which type of step to use. They explode out of their stance. They run five yards as fast as they can and take about five more yards to slow themselves down. (You need 10 yards to do this drill.) Next, all the backs turn around and face the other direction. At this point, they explode with their other foot. If they exploded with their right foot the first time, then, the second time, they explode with their left foot. After doing the drill once in each direction, they will end up in their original starting position.

If coaches want to work on pulling in the same drill, they have the backs face the sidelines. The coaches will then call, "Take off, pull right, on sound." The backs will pull right, sprint five yards, slow down for five yards, then reset, and pull left. The players explode out of their stance with a pull step. The first step is a pull step, and then they sprint down the line of scrimmage.

During routine period, your backfield coach will also work on three-step motion, one-step motion, and extended motion as part of this routine period. All backs learn all three types of motion.

Handoff Drills

The next part of the running back practice is called handoff drill. Diagram 3.3 illustrates the handoff period. All of the backs and quarterbacks are involved in this drill. Your coaches teach extra players on the football team (e.g., the kickers or the players sitting out with an injury) to execute snap technique so each quarterback will have a snapper in the drill.

You set up four stations. In one, a center, a quarterback, a fullback, and his backup behind him take part. In another station, a center, a quarterback, and another fullback are participating. One station will run fullback plays to the left; the other station will run fullback plays to the right. Two other stations will be about 15 yards down the field and

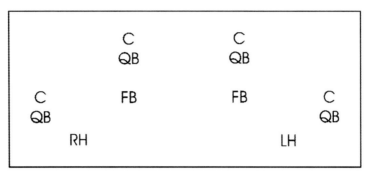

Diagram 3.3

include a center, a quarterback, and a halfback. The left halfbacks will be on one side, and the right halfbacks will be on the other side. The quarterbacks and the fullbacks could be working on the belly play. The fullbacks on the left work on belly to the left. The quarterback and the fullback execute their footwork for the belly play, and then the quarterback finishes by doing a good job of faking. It is important for the quarterbacks to fake well. The fullback rotates from the left side over to the right side. Halfbacks continue working in their two stations on halfback plays.

If two fullback stations cannot be filled with players, then it's okay to use only one. All stations are independent of each other. They use spacing boards during handoff drills. Spacing boards are 16 feet long, one inch thick, and four inches wide, with paint on the spaces for the holes and the players. The backs work with these boards so they can line up according to where the linemen will be. This setup enables you to get lined up correctly on the practice field and not mistime the plays. The spacing boards consist of two separate boards, so they can be picked up and moved if coaches want more space between the fullback stations.

The quarterback will rotate to each station as the period progresses. About one-fourth of the way through the period, the quarterbacks coach will be yelling, "Quarterbacks, rotate." They then rotate with the clock and go to the next station to work on a different technique. Every time they rotate, they work on a different technique.

The backs stay at the same station and work on the same play over and over again. Backs get many reps during this period. Coaches should allow five minutes for this period. They can reduce the period to two or three minutes, but, if they use five minutes, it will guarantee a lot of reps on just a few plays.

The backfield coach and the quarterbacks coach will rotate around and make sure they can observe all the stations. They might miss something one time, but will not miss it over the course of a few practices, and whatever needs to be corrected will get corrected.

Pitch Drills

The next drill the backs do is pitch drill. In pitch drills, two different stations are used. A group consists of a center, a quarterback, a fullback, and a left halfback. This group will work options to the right. The quarterback is working on pitch technique during this drill. The halfbacks are working on catching the pitch. Diagram 3.4 illustrates trap option.

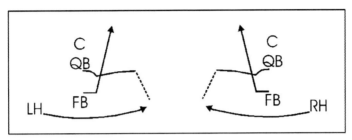

Diagram 3.4

Halfbacks do not block in this drill. A fullback fakes, and the halfback is receiving the pitch. Another fullback holds a bag, so the fullback participating in the drill, after faking, can make a good block. An extra quarterback is the pitch key. The quarterbacks will challenge each other during this drill. You want them to make it hard on each other.

The halfback establishes pitch relationship with the quarterback, which is five yards in front of him and three yards deep. As he catches the pitch, he bounces to the outside. He will bounce in order to stay away from the free safety in the middle of the formation. As the back catches the pitch, he will bounce from hash to alley to numbers to sideline. He keeps working his way outside. As he bounces, he starts up the field, sets up his block, and then bounces to the outside. One station of backs is working on options to the right, while the other station of backs is working on options to the left. Both groups work independently on their own cadences and get as many reps as possible in the allotted time.

Full Backfield Technique

The next drill is called full backfield technique. Diagram 3.5 shows an entire backfield—center, quarterback, fullback, left halfback, and right halfback—working on sweep to the right. During this period, they will work on any play, which the coaches feel they need to perfect. This time is great for working on techniques needing to be corrected. Also, this time is great to work on most of the flank passing, keep pass, counter bootleg, waggle, and trap-option pass.

When working on sweep, for example, the quarterback takes the snap, hands the ball to the left halfback, and then fakes waggle. The left halfback runs the sweep; the

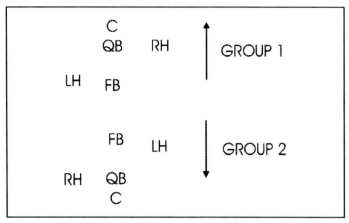

Diagram 3.5

fullback and the right half are assigned to block on this play. An extra fullback and right halfback will be holding big bags. The players block the bags, so no one is just going through the motions. Everyone is executing their assignment and technique for the sweep. While one group works in one place, the second group is in another. Both groups work on the same play at the same time. Each cadence is independent of the other, so, as soon as they are ready, they can go on the next play.

Passing with Ends

The final phase of individual practice is called passing with ends. Diagram 3.6 shows the backs working on the waggle play, where they fake the sweep to the right and the quarterback keeps the ball in the opposite direction. The spread end runs an out route. The fullback will block, if the linebacker either threatens him or blitzes. If not, he is in the flat. The left halfback fakes the sweep and becomes a blocker. The tight end either runs a crossing route or splits a two-deep coverage. The backside halfback fakes a sweep block for one step and then runs a fly on the backside. In this drill, you are working on pass patterns, throwing the ball, and catching the ball.

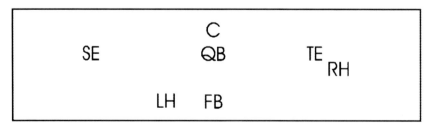

Diagram 3.6

Another way to do this drill is have each quarterback and a line of receivers work on individual routes. The drill can be done with a full backfield and the ends, or with just the quarterback and the receiver throwing routes versus air. Those drills are what the backs do in the practice plan: shoulder skills, routine period, handoff drills, pitch drills, full backfield technique, and passing with ends.

Technique and Footwork

While discussing the exact techniques the backs use, along with their footwork for each play, the first play will be the sweep play. Many coaches think the sweep is the wing-T. Even though this play is one of the primary plays in the wing-T, the wing formation, and the sweep to the wing, does not, by itself, represent the wing-T. The wing-T is much more. It is important to develop formation integrity and run-pass balance so the defense will not overload to stop the sweep series.

The 20 Series

28-29 Sweep

The fullback lines up directly behind the quarterback, with his heels four yards from the back tip of the football. He should be straddling the midline with the quarterback and the center. The halfback will line up in a diveback position. His heels are also four yards from the back tip of the football. If he were to run the sweep from the wingback position, he would start in three-step motion and then execute the play from there.

When running sweep to the right side, the fullback will take a crossover step. His first step will go for the left foot of the center. As the quarterback reverse pivots on his first step, their shoulders are tight to each other. On the second step, the fullback passes the quarterback and makes a proximity fake. He will close down over an imaginary ball, grab his jersey, and sprint through the line of scrimmage to his blocking assignment. He will have his arms in, and the defense will think he has the ball. The quarterback does not fake to the fullback. As the quarterback reverse pivots, the proximity of his shoulders to the fullback and the action of the quarterback provide the picture of trap to the defense. As the fullback takes his second step and passes the quarterback, he will be faking into the line of scrimmage. The quarterback's back is to the line, and the play has good deception, with the fullback faking over an imaginary ball. The fullback blocks the area on the backside of the center. Sometimes, the center will block that backside area and the fullback will adjust to his right and pick up a linebacker at the second level.

As the fullback crosses over for the backside foot of the center, the halfback will take his first crossover step, throwing his left arm hard across his chest to gain momentum. On the halfback's second step, the quarterback is ready to give him the ball. As he takes his third step, he will receive the ball.

The halfback's technique, after he has the ball secure, is to get his eyes on the down block by the wing. The halfback's eyes should be looking upfield as he runs across the backfield. Some coaches tell their halfbacks to catch the frontside guard before they cut. You should coach your halfbacks to get outside the down block by the wingback on the defensive end and then make a north-south cut. The halfback should turn up quickly.

The wider he runs, the more delayed he will be, and the more time he will give the pursuit to catch up. As the halfback crosses the backfield, he will stretch the sweep, get to the outside of the down block, and cut on a north-south path. As the halfback pops the line of scrimmage, running lanes will open up for him. He can break all the way back across the grain. Sometimes, the whole pursuit will overrun the play and he can get the big touchdown run by cutting back. Sometimes, the flank may be blocked very well and the cut will be north-south or possibly to the outside. The major coaching point is to get the shoulders square and cut north and south.

A halfback drill for this play really helps them to learn how to cut north and south. It is the cone, or four corner, drill. In this drill, the backs run and cut off of their right foot all the way around four cones as they make four cuts. They run across the cones to the right and plant their right foot as their eyes look to the inside. As the halfback plants his right foot, he steps upfield. In order to get his shoulders turned upfield, he will pivot his right foot. As his right foot pivots, his shoulders will turn north-south. He runs five yards and cuts, always keeping his eyes upfield. He repeats this technique until he makes four sweep cuts. He will go around all four cones and then go to the left. The backs get four sweep cuts in both directions. It is a pre-practice drill. They can work on planting their foot and pivoting so their shoulders turn north and south.

In review, the quarterback takes his first step on the midline. The fullback takes his first step for the left foot of the center. The halfback takes his fist step by crossing over. On the second step, the fullback will fake over an imaginary ball, and the quarterback will continue with his second step on the midline. The halfback will take his second step to the handoff position. On the third step, the fullback continues through the hole. The quarterback will cross over on a 45-degree angle and will hand the ball off to the halfback.

The halfback will take the ball with his inside thumb down and the fingers of his outside hand spread straight from his belly button. As the quarterback lays the ball in, he will put the ball on his hip and the halfback will let the quarterback bring the ball to him. The halfback should not reach for the ball. His bottom hand is the table, and his top hand is the stopper. The quarterback will put the ball on the table so the nose of the football goes into the stopper hand, and the ballcarrier can tuck the ball away with either arm.

On the third step, the quarterback will make the handoff and continue to the flank, faking the bootleg. This play will have great deception because, as the quarterback reverse pivots away from the center, he pulls the ball into his belt buckle, keeps his elbows in tight, and, as he reverse pivots, places his back to the line of scrimmage so the defense will not be able to see the ball. With the proximity fake to the fullback, the play will have effective deception.

The mirror to this play, 28 sweep, is 29 sweep. The right halfback will now be the ballcarrier, when the play goes in the other direction. The wingback is executing a gap block or a down block on the defensive end.

24-26 Fullback up the Middle

The next play in the same package is 24 and 26 to the fullback. Many different blocking schemes can be used for the fullback up the middle, including some schemes from the trap option package. The blocking schemes include on, gut, and guard trap. Five or six different ways to block this play exist and will be discussed at a later time.

The fullback footwork adjusts slightly against odd or even defenses. The quarterback's footwork is also based on odd or even defenses. In an even defense, when the center is uncovered, the center will probably be blocking back to his left. Therefore, the fullback can take his first step for the left foot of the center. When running 24, the 4 hole is at the right guard. The fullback will run for the backside foot of the center, then break to the 4 hole. As the fullback makes the cut, his eyes are on the center's block. If the man the center is blocking fights across the front of the center's block, then the fullback will run the ball off the backside of the center's block. If the center gets movement, the fullback cuts playside.

If it is an odd defense, with the center covered, the fullback should run straight on the midline, through the quarterback and the center. The quarterback, as he reverse pivots, will pivot beyond the midline, allowing the fullback to run on the midline. The fullback will option run the defender on the center. Regardless of the blocking scheme, the fullback will find the hole, once he sees how the center is blocking the noseguard.

On this play, the quarterback executes the same technique as he does on the sweep, except here he gives the ball to the fullback. He will fake to the halfback. The wingback will fake his sweep block and then block at the cutoff point. The quarterback makes a one-handed handoff to the fullback. The quarterback will deal the cards. All handoffs will be made from forearm's length. The quarterback should never reach to make a handoff. If he has to reach the ball to the fullback, he will have poor deception on the play. The footwork of the quarterback will probably be poorly executed as well. The 26 is the opposite. On 26, the fullback starts for the right foot of the center and breaks to the 6 hole, which is the left guard's area.

If the play is 24 with on blocking, then everybody on the line of scrimmage blocks the man on him. The block on the noseguard versus a 50 defense will determine the cut by the fullback. He needs the midline. The quarterback will reverse pivot slightly beyond the midline, allowing the fullback to have the midline. The fullback will option run the center's block. The center will take his man in any direction he wants to go, and the fullback will cut off of his block.

21-29 Waggle

The next play in this series is 21 waggle. The backs will fake the sweep, and the quarterback will keep the ball to attack the flank. They all execute the same technique as sweep, at least for the first few steps. The quarterback will have the midline as he reverse pivots. The fullback will step for the left foot of the center, and the halfback will cross over. The next steps on waggle begin to change. On the fullback's second step, as he closes over an imaginary ball, his path will widen to the outside foot of the guard, and he attacks through the line of scrimmage, reading the linebacker. As he runs through, he reads the linebacker. If the linebacker blitzes the A or B gap, the fullback will block him with his inside shoulder and with his head outside. The point of attack is to the outside. The fullback's head is between the point of attack and the defender. If the linebacker does not blitz, the fullback is free to continue into the flat as a receiver.

The halfback, after he passes the quarterback on the fake, will gear down and block anyone who shows outside the right tackle's block. This waggle coaching point is very important. Many coaches will have the halfback who fakes the sweep run around the end. He can be a very valuable blocker on the backside of the quarterback. If the quarterback is forced to pull up, he has to get his shoulders upfield and is more of a stationary target. You need the halfback to be a backside blocker in case anyone is blitzing off the edge on the weakside of the play. The quarterback is attacking the flank and has the option to run or throw. The mirror play is 29 waggle, in which the quarterback bootlegs to the left. His read progression is deep, flat, or run. He will throw backside only when the free safety rotates with the quarterback's action. The wingback is a pass receiver. He will fake the sweep block and then run his route.

22-28 Off-Tackle

The next play is called 22 and 28. This play is a great companion play to the sweep. If the wingback on sweep has to block a defensive end who is a penetrator running into the backfield, then he should not run outside, because that block is so tough for the wingback. Against a defensive end who is not allowing the sweep, you should change the play to the off-tackle play, which is 22 and 28. This play hits off-tackle, inside the defensive end who is penetrating, and takes advantage of his upfield charge. The coach calling the plays must know what the third defender, the defensive end, is doing. If he penetrates, run inside of him. If he seals, run outside of him.

The techniques for 22 are pretty much the same as the techniques for all the 20 plays, with one notable exception. The fullback uses 21 technique and will step with the right foot for the left foot of the center. On his second step, he will fake over an imaginary ball and then adjust his path for his blocking assignment.

This play can be blocked with power blocking, where the backside guards pulls to kick out the end. It is then a double-team and kick-out. It can be blocked with gut blocking, where both guards pull the way they do on the sweep, but the first guard guts and the backside guard kicks out the defensive end. It can be blocked with tag blocking, when both the backside tackle and the guard pull. The guard kicks out the defensive end, and the tackle pulls through the hole and walls off inside. The fullback's blocking assignment is based on which blocking scheme is used. After the second step, the fullback will adjust his path according to the blocking scheme.

22 tag is a favorite scheme for this play and requires both the backside tackle and guard to pull like counter trey. In that case, the fullback's first step is for the left foot of the center. On his second step, he fakes over an imaginary ball, and, on the third step, he adjusts tight off the pulling tackle's tail and fills the area behind the left tackle.

The halfback's technique is to take the same crossover step he takes on the sweep, take one more step, and then bend for the 2 hole. He will bend for the inside foot of the tight end against an odd defense or the inside foot of the tackle against an even defense. He receives the handoff on the inside from the quarterback. The quarterback will take his sweep footwork, but, instead of handing the ball off outside, he hands it off inside. The quarterback does not have to reach to make the handoff because, if the handoff can be made at forearm's distance, the backs can run their course, and the play looks just like a sweep, except that it hits off-tackle. Some coaches teach this play with an outside handoff, but the halfback has a tougher cut into the hole. If the play is executed correctly, the defense will not notice a difference in the play.

Waggle Solid

The next play in the 20 series is waggle solid, which requires the quarterback to keep the ball, but also to pull up instead of attacking the flank. The fullback takes his first step. On the second step, the fullback fakes over an imaginary ball and begins to attack his area. On the third step, the quarterback will step toward the flank to show the picture of waggle, but then drop back. The play turns into a dropback pass. With waggle solid, both backs are blockers. This play will also keep one of the guards in to provide as much protection as possible. It is a three-man route. As the fullback takes his footwork and fakes over an imaginary ball, he will break down in the hole and block that area. The halfback takes his footwork, gears down, and prepares to block the backside of the quarterback. This play gives coaches a dropback game with waggle action and misdirection.

The 60 Series

It is important to be able call plays on the line of scrimmage and not have the players get confused. Many coaches call the trap option series with 20s, but you should call them 60s to avoid confusion when calling them at the line of scrimmage.

63-67 Guard Trap

One of the first plays setting up this series is a guard trap at the 3 and 7 holes. It could be 23 guard trap or 63 guard trap, depending on the action chosen. The fullback will run a guard trap like 24 guard trap, but 63 guard trap is one hole wider. With all the even defenses and 4-3 defenses that teams have employed lately, this play has become an increasingly major factor in game plans. If this play is called and the defense is odd, the play goes back to being 24 guard trap.

Against an even defense, when running 23 guard trap, the backs will fake 20 action and the quarterback will fake waggle. On 63 guard trap, the backs run that same 20 action, but the difference is the quarterback turns and fakes trap option. This play is the first in the 60 series, because it sets up the series. On this play, the quarterback will take the snap and reverse pivot beyond the midline, because the fullback steps for the frontside leg of the center, since he has a wider point of attack. The fullback will still step with his right foot, as he does in all 20 series plays to the right, but the difference is he will step for the frontside foot of the center. On the 3-hole or 7-hole guard trap, the fullback must step for the right foot of the center because the point of attack is wider. The quarterback, regardless of his fake, must get beyond the midline. On the second step, the quarterback will make the exchange, and the fullback will make his cut. On the second step, the fullback will stay on course and begin to adjust as he receives the ball. After he has the ball, he cuts off the right tackle's block, which establishes the hole as he blocks down on the man over the guard. The guard will trap the first man outside the offensive tackle. The fullback will stay tight to the down block. A trap one hole wider affects the quarterback's technique and the fullback's technique, but does not affect the halfback's technique.

If the call is 23 guard trap, then after the exchange, the quarterback will cross over, make a great fake to the halfback, and sprint to the flat. To run the same play, but call it 63 guard trap, the quarterback will fake trap option and the fullback's footwork will be exactly the same. The quarterback's footwork is the same for two steps. The only difference is the quarterback will turn and fake trap option. As the halfback comes across the backfield, he will be the pitchback. The quarterback now must snap his hands back inside and his chin to his left shoulder. He will begin to pivot his right toe so he can come downhill on his third step to fake trap-option action. The quarterback fakes to the playside instead of faking waggle.

61-69 Trap Option

When running 61 trap option, the point of attack is the flank to the right. The 61 trap option is 20 technique for the backs. The fullback steps for the left foot of the center and will be a blocker. He will block either an area or a linebacker off the backside. If the center blocks back, the fullback will cut off his tail, get to the second level, and block the linebacker upfield. The halfback is the pitchback. He will sprint across the backfield the way he does on 20s, beginning with crossover footwork, and then will establish pitch relationship with the quarterback. The quarterback takes two steps on the midline, turns downhill on the third step, and executes the option by reading the third defender. The right halfback is given his blocking assignment. He will flare and block the fifth defender, because the end will crack the fourth defender.

The quarterback will attack downhill, to the inside shoulder of the third defender. The backside guard will pull to log and protect the quarterback from pinches or slants inside. The quarterback will get in the face of #3 and pitch the ball. If #3 comes right at the quarterback, then he will break down and step to the back he is pitching to. The pitch is taught two ways. The quarterback can use the basketball pitch or can snap his elbow and turn his thumb down. If the quarterback pitches and the ball is spinning too much, it makes the pitch hard to handle. If he cannot slow the spin with his thumb down, then the quarterback will use the basketball pitch. The ball will not spin as much with the basketball pitch. Normally, you teach the quarterback to turn the thumb down and snap the elbow, and the ball will rotate slowly. If the defense sends the third defender in his face, the quarterback will give with the hit the way a boxer gives with a punch. He wants a nice soft pitch. The halfback will be five yards in front and three yards deep as he catches the pitch. Against defensive players who slow play, or play cat-and-mouse, you want to attack them with the quarterback until they make a decision. If the defender is trying to slow the quarterback down on the way to his pitch, his momentum will be carrying him outside. The quarterback will give him a pitch fake, tuck the ball, and get to the option alley.

61 Trap-Option Pass

The companion play is 61 trap-option pass. If the fourth defender is coming hard up the field to beat the crack block, you throw a slant route by the wide receiver, in behind the strong safety (#4), to the void area he created by attacking the line of scrimmage.

The backfield technique is exactly the same. The quarterback is on the midline for two steps. The fullback steps with his right foot for the left foot of the center. The halfback crosses over and establishes pitch relationship. The quarterback begins to attack downhill on his third step. On steps four, five, and six, the ball should be thrown. Those steps should be choppy. The backside guard will pull to protect the quarterback as he throws the slant route behind the strong safety. If the corner chases the slant route, the quarterback can throw to the right halfback, who flared as if he were blocking the corner on the option play. If the strong safety stays back and the corner stays back, you could also pitch the ball to the trailing halfback.

61 Trap-Option Reverse at 9

A great play off the trap-option series is where the ball is pitched to the split end coming back through the backfield. The play is called 61 trap-option reverse at 9. The opposite would be 69 trap-option reverse at 1. The backfield technique on this play is the same as on the other 60s. The fullback will run to the backside flat, exactly as he does on waggle. He gets himself set up to block any defender who is chasing the play from inside out. The halfback uses the same action he does on 61 trap option, except he needs to get more depth as he crosses through the backfield, especially as the quarterback gets ready to pitch the ball to the split end. The halfback will reach his hands as though he's catching a pitch. Between steps four and five, the ball should be pitched to the split end. The quarterback should pitch the ball straight back, not in front, as if to pitch to the halfback. The spread end will appear as if he is intercepting the pitch. He then carries the ball around the opposite end.

67 Counter

Other good plays are included in the 60 package. The 67 counter will show the trap-option action. The quarterback will start downhill, as if he is running the trap option, then hand the ball to the right halfback from the wingback position, and run a counter play. On this play, the quarterback, the fullback, and the left halfback look exactly as they do on 61 trap-option crack, but only for the first two steps. The fullback then runs through the hole, bends, and blocks the frontside linebacker. The halfback continues to fake 61 trap-option crack. The wingback is not in motion. He leaves on the snap and takes the same footwork, as if he is going in three-step motion. After the third step, he runs for the outside leg of the left guard, where a double-team will occur. The quarterback will hand the halfback the ball on the inside. The quarterback continues to fake the trap option, and the right halfback is the ballcarrier.

69 Counter Sweep

A companion play is 69 counter sweep. This play is interesting. Everyone executes 67 counter, but, when the wingback receives the ball, he gets extra depth and runs a sweep around the left side. The fullback, the quarterback, and the left halfback will run 61 trap-option crack. On the fourth step, the quarterback will hand the ball to the right halfback. The quarterback then continues to fake trap option.

67 Counter Bootleg

Another companion play to 67 counter is called 67 counter bootleg. On this play, everybody uses the same action as on 67 counter, except the quarterback will keep the ball at the flank and have a run-pass option. His first step is the same as it is on all 20s and 60s. The quarterback's second and third steps are the same as on 61 trap option. On the fourth step, the quarterback will fake the ball to the wingback—who is running the counter—with his hand and not with the ball. The quarterback keeps the ball in the crease of his pants and will attack the flank with the football. The receivers are the fullback, the tight end, and the backside spread end crossing. The left halfback passes the quarterback and will work downfield to block the first free man at the flank from the outside in. He uses log block technique with his left shoulder.

The 30 Series

31 Sweep

The last two packages of plays to review are the 30s and the 80s. The 30s are similar to the 20s, since they both feature a sweep play. The first play to review is 31 sweep, which is very similar to 21 sweep. The difference is the line blocking is fire-on-backer. The halfback will cross over, receive the handoff, and make a good sweep cut, when he gets outside the block at the flank. The line could make a six call, to pull the backside guard to wall off. Do not do this when playing against a penetrating eight-man front, because the defenders will be stunting and blitzing. Against those types of defenses, the line will block with fire-on-backer technique across the front.

Instead of the guards pulling to kick out the force, the fullback will kick out the force. On the 31 sweep, the fullback will take a lead step, with his toes pointing north and south (like the belly cross block play), and then drive tight off the wingback's block to kick out the first defender outside that block. The difference on this sweep is no buck or misdirection action happens. This sweep includes full-flow action with solid zone blocking up front. It is an effective alternative, because you can pick up the stunts with solid fire-on-backer blocking. If the defense is stunting, they are not keying the tailback or the guards; therefore, no concern is necessary about the full-flow action in the backfield being too fast or bringing the defense to the play too quickly. The right halfback will use that same down technique on his block. The tight end will post the defensive end, thus setting up the right halfback's block.

The quarterback technique is exactly the same as it is on the 20s. He will hand the ball off to the halfback, as in 21 sweep, and fake the waggle. The big difference on this play is the fullback's action.

32 Off-Tackle

If #3, the end, is a penetrator, the companion play in this package is 32, an off-tackle play. A double-team will be on the man over the offensive tackle in an odd defense. If it is an even defense, the line will double-team the man over the offensive guard. The fullback will kick out the defensive end. The halfback will run directly for the off-tackle hole.

The quarterback opens directly to the halfback and hands him the ball. The halfback must have a chance to get quickly to the hole, so you make this handoff quickly, enabling the halfback to run directly off-tackle. The wingback has a blocking assignment. The fullback will cross over with his left foot in order to get a good inside-out path on the defensive end. He will run to the tail of the double-team, as does the ballcarrier. The ballcarrier should run right over the tail of the double-team as tight as possible and as far as possible from the kick-out. It is an off-tackle power and a good short-yardage call, as well.

34 Blast

You can also run 34 blast over the guards. On this play, the center and guard will double-team the noseguard and the fullback will block the playside linebacker, with his head to the inside. The fullback will take off with his left foot, staying tight to the double-team, and isolate on the linebacker over the guard.

The halfback will use the same footwork and same technique as on 32, except he must get turned up into the 4 hole quicker. The halfback gets his shoulders turned up fast and should be square in the hole, which invites the defense to overrun the play. The cutback to the backside often results in good yardage. The halfback must stay tight to the double-team and follow his fullback through the hole.

31 Roll Pass

The 31 roll pass means the quarterback will fake the sweep and then roll in the direction of the play-action. On this play, the left halfback will block the defensive end. This play has the tight end running a corner route behind the corner. The fullback will run at the corner, as if to kick him out, and then slip into the flat. The left halfback will fake 31, come across the backfield, and log block the defensive end.

The first two steps are like 20s for the quarterback, like 31 for the fullback, and like 21 for the left halfback. On the third step, the quarterback will fake the sweep to the halfback and then roll in that same direction. The quarterback's pass progression is to look deep, then to the flat, and then to run. He can throw the ball to the tight end deep or the fullback in the flat, or else he can run the ball, if the flank is pinned down.

34-36 Counter

The rest of the 30 series are counters. They are blocked several different ways. In fact, 34 and 36 counter to the halfbacks has been blocked with eight different blocking schemes over the years. The tackle-trap counter has been one of the best of the schemes. Another blocking scheme is counter draw blocking, which has been exceptional, leading to many big plays and many touchdowns.

Another misdirection is the counter crisscross play. The counter crisscross is a play where the quarterback hands the ball off to one halfback and the halfback hands it off to another. This play can be run either to a tight end or away from a tight end. It also can be run with two different kinds of blocking schemes. You teach the quarterback to open to the left halfback, as if it is a 32. He will take the ball and reach it to him. He wants the defense to see him give the ball, so they will begin to flow. The halfback will take a crossover step, as if he is going to run 31 sweep, and the quarterback will give the ball to him as soon as possible.

The fullback will block the way he did on 32. He will cross over to run a tight, kick-out path inside out. He will run for the outside foot of the tackle and, as soon as the tight end passes in front of him, will kick-out whoever is chasing off the backside of the tight end. When running counter crisscross, the blocking can pull the guard and the tight end, pull the guard and the tackle, or pull the tackle and the tight end. Three different ways exist to block the play, depending on what kind of defensive spacing you see.

This play is one of the main reasons you teach the halfbacks to take the ball with their inside thumb down. When the quarterback hands the halfback the ball, the halfback can push it back to the other halfback without taking the ball and turning it over. The ball is placed on his table, and, as he crosses the backfield, he will simply push the ball out. After the quarterback gives the ball to the halfback, he will fake waggle and bring defensive players with him. The wingback will not go in motion, but, on the snap, he will use the same footwork he would use on three-step motion. He will get depth, as if he is coming back to his diveback position. On the third step, he should be back to where his diveback position is, receive the handoff, and run to the hole. As he clears the off-tackle hole, he will run north and south. The ballcarrier does have one option left. The quarterback, who handed the ball off and then faked waggle, is running down the sideline. As the right halfback clears the line of scrimmage, he can pitch the ball to the quarterback. This option is fun for the players to practice, but be careful allowing the halfbacks to pitch the ball in a game. The ball can be pitched right to a defensive corner, who can run it 60 yards the other way. Be sure the defense has collapsed before trying to execute this part of the play.

To complete the 30 package, you use 34 and 36 tackle trap counter and the bootleg off the play. A lot of technique is involved, and it is very important this play is coached with detail. When running 34 counter, you will fake action to the left and the left halfback will receive the ball, countering back to the right at the 4 hole. The 34 counter tells all the backs, except the ballcarrier, they are running in the direction opposite the football play. If they are running 34 counter, the play will hit over the right guard. All of the other backs will be running to the left. The wingback will go in three-step motion behind the fullback. As he clears the mesh between the quarterback and the left halfback, he will start downhill and log block the first free man on the flank from the outside in. The fullback will show belly and fake over an imaginary ball. Although the quarterback will not fake to him, the action will still indicate belly package to the defense. The fullback must run for the outside leg of the guard at full speed. As he takes off, he will cross over to get there faster. The fullback steps for the outside leg of the guard, fakes over an imaginary ball, and then blocks his area.

In the tackle trap counter, the fullback must stay on course for his landmark. He should be in perfect position to block off the tackle's tail, as the tackle pulls to trap block. As the tackle pulls to execute the trap, the fullback fills tight off his tail and blocks the first defender who shows. If the defensive end is closing down, he blocks the defensive end. If the defensive end is up the field, he will not make the play, and the fullback will continue on to the next level. The fullback is a blocker on the play, but will also fake to show the picture of the belly play.

The halfback carrying the football from a diveback position will rock his weight to the outside. He will throw his hips to the outside. He will not rock the weight and step with his outside foot, because that action causes the halfback to run on a flat angle. As he rocks the weight, he will throw the weight to the outside. The first step will be with the inside foot. When he steps inside, he will use a lead step; his toes will be pointing north and south. The halfback will gain six inches of ground towards the line of scrimmage, keeping his toes north and south and his shoulders square. On the second step, the halfback's feet cross over. The third step squares his shoulders, his toes are still pointing north and south, and he will be square to the line of scrimmage, putting him in perfect position to accept the handoff.

The quarterback's technique is to reverse pivot, depending on whether he is facing an odd defense or an even defense. The ballcarrier's path will bend, also depending on whether it is an odd or an even defense. If it is an odd defense, the ballcarrier should run for the near foot of the center, which would be the left foot of the center when running 34 counter. The center and the right guard will double-team the noseguard. The center will step with his left foot and post with his right shoulder to elevate his pads. The right guard will use down technique to block the nose with his left shoulder at the hip and with his head behind. Both linemen will swing their tails driving the nose flat down the line of scrimmage. The ballcarrier will stay tight to the tail of the double-team and explode through the line of scrimmage. You coach the backs to stay away from where the trapper is, because the ballcarrier will trip over the trapper's feet. When that happens, the ballcarrier is too wide.

If the noseguard is in a 0 technique, as in an odd defense, the aiming point for the halfback is the near foot of the center. If it is an even defense, the aiming point is a shorter hole, because the double-team will move over one man. The double-team will occur with the left guard as the post blocker and the center as the lead blocker. The double-team now will take place over the left guard. Therefore, the halfback bends his path for what is called a short hole. A short hole means the back will run for the inside foot of the guard on his side of the line. In that case, the quarterback has to reverse pivot beyond the midline. If it is an odd defense, the quarterback will reverse pivot directly on the midline. If it is an even defense, he will reverse pivot six inches across the midline, because the halfback will run to a shorter hole.

One of the worst things that can happen on this play is when the quarterback reaches the ball out to the halfback. Instead, you want a close, tight handoff from forearm's length. When looking at this play on film, the line of bodies is straight; the fullback, the ballcarrier, the quarterback, and the right halfback are all in a direct line, which gives deception to the play. It makes it hard for the defense to read. If coaches stop the film after the third step and the bodies are in line, then the players are executing the play correctly. The guard and the pulling tackle may also be in the line of bodies.

The quarterback will drag his right hand, keep his left hand in, and pump his arm as he attacks the flank. The ballcarrier runs tight to the double-team. He can bend the play to any daylight. If the man being double-teamed fights across the face of the double-team, the ballcarrier can break behind the double-team. Against an even defense, the double-team is moved a man over; therefore, it is a shorter hole for the halfback and more of a reverse pivot for the quarterback.

On 34 counter, the ball is usually given to the diveback, but it is possible to run the same football play and give the ball to the wingback, who will start in three-step motion. In that case, the right halfback would be in a diveback position. He can cross over and run to the flank, in order to be a log blocker. You can also use a technique with the halfback called right half dive. The halfback will dive to the outside to block the outside linebacker, as if he is running a load option. The fullback will go in one direction, the halfback will go in another direction, and the ballcarrier will be in motion, which divides the defense. If the linebackers key the backs in the backfield, they have a tendency to divide and open up a hole for the ballcarrier.

Another form of 34 counter is run with both halfbacks in a wing position. The ballcarrier will go in motion, but the other halfback will flare. He will flare as if he is blocking on trap option. The left halfback will go in three-step motion, and the quarterback will give him the ball. Be careful not to overcoach the wingback on this play. Allow him to go in three-step motion and aim for a point deeper than his normal diveback alignment. Tell him to square his shoulders to the line of scrimmage and let the wing and the quarterback work out the mesh. The quarterback makes the handoff from forearm's distance away and should not be reaching for the handoff. The quarterback takes the exact same footwork, reverse pivots, and wraps his second step tight around the fullback. Then, the wingback will adjust to the quarterback from there. The players work the mesh out between themselves.

34 Counter Bootleg

The last play in the 30 series is 34 counter bootleg. It is almost the same play as 34 counter, except the quarterback will have the ball and the halfback will fake 34 counter. The quarterback will take the ball to the flank and execute a run-pass option. When you are pulling the tackle to run 34 counter bootleg, the fullback will widen his aiming point, because he is a blocker. He will cross over, but, instead of aiming for the outside leg of the guard, he aims for the outside leg of the tackle. If any 5-technique penetration exists, he must block it with his head to the outside, with a right shoulder block. You are calling this play because, as you are pulling the tackle on the tackle-trap counter, the defensive 5 technique has been chasing the tackle inside. If the 5 technique does not chase, but you still need to call the counter bootleg, you call counter bootleg solid, which tells the left tackle to block on, instead of pulling.

If the fullback checks his area and no 5-technique penetration exists, the fullback can release into the flat. If you call counter bootleg solid, the fullback attacks the outside leg of the guard for his aiming point and, at this point, his block is on the linebacker. If the linebacker does not come, he will release to the flat and become a receiver. If the linebacker does come, he blocks him. The tackle and the fullback assignments are interchangeable, depending on how the tackle will block the play. The halfback will fake 34 counter and always fakes over a short hole. He will use the inside leg of the guard for his aiming point. This way, if the tackle pulls, they will not collide with each other. If the left halfback aims over the center when the tackle pulls, then they will collide. If he is on a short-hole course, then, as the tackle pulls, he will come right off the tackle's tail behind him. The tackle's technique is to sprint to the opposite guard and then gear down. Even if the play is counter bootleg solid and the tackle is not pulling, the left halfback will use short-hole technique.

The quarterback will step across the midline to get to the flank quicker. The quarterback is beyond the midline and wraps tight around the fullback's tail. The fullback fakes over an imaginary ball. The quarterback will hand fake to the left halfback, dragging that hand as he goes by. The ball is tucked in the left side of his body, in the crease of his pants. As the quarterback attacks the flank, he has a deep receiver, a flat receiver, and a crossing receiver. He also has the option to run.

The 80 Series

83-87 Belly

The primary play in the 80 series is 83 and 87 belly. It involves a good deal of important detail for both the fullback and the quarterback. This play is one of the most productive plays in the offense. If executed properly, it can gain a thousand yards a season by itself.

The first variation is called 83 cross block (87 cross block to the left). This play is 83, which means the fullback will carry the ball on a belly play. The right halfback will lead him through the hole. A favorite blocking scheme when running this play is cross block. The tackle's rule is gap down-on, and the guard pulls to trap outside. The halfback is responsible for the inside linebacker. At the college level, you can cut the linebacker.

This play will show the same full-flow action as the 30 package. The halfback will take a short jab step out and up (a very important coaching point). From there, he must attack through the hole, and his landmark is the outside leg of the guard, not the tackle. As he takes his second step, he will continue for the outside leg of the guard, reading the first defender from the nose of the guard out. This read is his key for whether he will block inside or outside. This read is also the key for the ballcarrier to make his cut. If it is an even defense and a man is over the guard, then that defender will be the key, because he is the first man from the nose of the guard to the outside. If nobody is on the guard, but a man is over the tackle, then he is the read for the ballcarrier and the blocker, because he is the first man on the line of scrimmage, from the nose of the guard outside. This defender's defensive reaction will tell the back whether to go inside or outside of him. The backs should run off their short jab step, out and up. As he takes his second step, he will continue for the outside leg of the guard and read the first defender from the nose of the guard out. If the tackle blocks down on the man over the guard and the guard pulls to cross block the defensive end, the backs should run off the tackle's block. As they come through the hole, they will adjust their course. If the tackle blocks down and the defender fights outside the down block, the backs should run inside.

You use the same keys if the guard is uncovered and the tackle is covered. The defensive man over the tackle is the key. If the blocker turns him out, the ballcarrier and the lead halfback go to the inside. If the defender slants inside and the tackle blocks him down to the inside, the ballcarrier and the lead halfback adjust and slide to the outside.

The left halfback will be in a wingback position. He will go in three-step motion. When he passes the quarterback-fullback mesh, he will attack downhill and block the first free man on the flank, from outside in. When working on this play in practice, you use an extra fullback to hold a big bag and move the bag, so the backs will have to cut. An extra halfback will also be holding another bag, so the log blocker can execute his blocking technique.

The fullback has specific footwork he should use. The worst thing he can do is get into the hole before the blocking has had a chance to develop. This play is like the sprint draw of the wing-T. The footwork is vital. The first step by the fullback will be a lead step, with his toes pointing north and south. He will gain about six inches of ground toward the line of scrimmage and will keep his shoulders square. On his second step, he crosses over, keeping his shoulders square and his toes pointing north and south. On his third step, he also gains six inches of ground, with toes north and south and shoulders square. This step is the fullback's square-up step and is when he will receive the ball. Since he has gained only six inches with each step, he will receive the ball deep enough in the backfield to read and make a cut. The halfback's body is about a yard to a yard and a half directly in front of the fullback. The quarterback reverse pivots beyond the midline to give the ball to the fullback and wraps tight around the fullback before faking keep pass. The cross block makes six bodies in a straight line as the handoff occurs, which adds deception to the play, even though it is a full-flow play. It will be tough for the defense to read what might happen here. Again, stop the film when it gets to the handoff point to see if the team executes the play with correct timing and deception.

The quarterback will reverse pivot to a 60-degree angle, beyond the midline. On his second step, he will reach the ball to the fullback's far hip. The quarterback hands the ball off on his third step, snaps his hands back in, and goes behind the fullback to fake keep pass. On this third step, you will see the line of bodies starting to form and the correct relationship forming between the halfback and the fullback. A common mistake on this play is when backs execute poor footwork and are running through the hole, side by side. If coaches see this error happening, then one or more of the backs did not use the proper footwork and the fullback will have no protection. It could be a fumble play. The fullback can be protected by keeping him a yard behind the lead halfback.

The belly is the same as an iso or blast from the traditional I formation. The lead blocker will be about one yard in front of the ballcarrier as they go through the hole. The right halfback takes a jab step out and up on cross block, because he wants to give the cross block time to happen. The tackle will block gap down-on, and the guard will pull to trap. They need time to execute the cross block, so the halfback will jab step. The linemen can block the play with blast blocking, double the nose, pull the backside guard around, and lead the halfback through. They can also block this play with on blocking, where everybody blocks straight ahead.

As you can see, four or five different ways exist to block this play. The only time the halfback needs to take a jab step is if you call cross block. On any other blocking scheme, the halfback can run immediately for the outside leg of the guard with no jab step.

The belly is the top play in the offense. It will make many yards every year, but it has to be executed correctly. You do not want poor timing on this play, and it takes work to get the fullbacks to take correct footwork. The fullback must not be in too much of a hurry or be impatient. He can be quick, but not in a hurry. One of the biggest mistakes is when a fullback takes a lead step, crosses over, and, on his third step, runs immediately into the hole. When the fullback does that, the halfback will not be able to lead him through the hole and protect him from the linebacker, who is free to run through and cause a fumbled handoff.

81-89 Keep Pass

The companion play to the belly is 81 and 89 keep pass. Here, the quarterback will keep the ball in the direction of the flow. He will reverse pivot the way he did on the belly, will poke the ball into the fullback's pocket, and snap it out quickly. He will fake to the fullback for an arm-length ride, snap the ball back quickly, and get the ball up to a passing grip.

The halfback will be a legitimate receiver at the flank. From a diveback position, the outside halfback will run for a point 1.5 yards outside the tight man. If the tackle is the tight man in the formation, the halfback will aim his first step for a point 1.5 yards outside of him. Keep pass blocking will block down with the tackle and log with the guard. They may also block straight ahead. Regardless of the scheme, the halfback can help the block on the 5-technique defensive end. He will dive for a point 1.5 yards outside the tight man and, on his way through to the flat, will punch his left hand into the shoulder of the defensive end. He will then work his way up the field for two steps and bend to the flat. Halfbacks sometimes make the mistake of getting to the flat too quickly by running straight into the flat, thus forcing the quarterback into a longer throw than necessary. When this happens, the halfback catches the ball too close to the sideline, with no room to maneuver. The quarterback should be in a good relationship with the halfback and should be able to complete an easy pass to him, because he is the primary receiver. You should run the play to a tight end or a spread end with a reduced split. The halfback can out-leverage the defense in the flat quickly.

A variation is to keep the spread end out wide and call keep pass out, so you can throw an out cut to him. When trying to get the ball to the spread end, it's a good idea to keep the spread end wide. When trying to get the ball to the halfback, bring the spread end in and out-leverage the defense in the flat. Against a team running two deep and really jamming the spread end, his out route will convert to a fly and a high/low read will be on the corner. The quarterback can throw the ball in the hole behind the corner. He can also throw the ball in front of the corner, to the halfback, depending on the corner's reaction.

The fullback, in keep pass, will use belly footwork. His steps will be lead, crossover, and square-up, and he will widen his aiming point to the outside leg of the tackle. The fullback will block the 5-technique area, which is the outside shoulder of the tackle. Against a 50 defense, the tackle could block all the way down to the nose. Then, the pulling guard will have to log the defensive end, giving the fullback the defensive tackle. Keep pass fire will require the tackle to block on. The guard will pull to log the defensive end, and the fullback will then have the linebacker. You could also have the entire line block on, which will give the linebacker to the fullback and the defensive end to the motion halfback. The fullback will make a good belly fake and then block an area.

The left halfback will be sprinting in three-step motion. When he passes the mesh between the quarterback and the fullback, he will start downhill and execute a log block technique on the first free man at the flank from the outside in.

The quarterback will give a quick arm-length ride to the fullback, snap the ball back in, and get the ball ready to throw in a passing grip. He will get the ball quickly to the halfback in the flat. If he gets the ball to the halfback, the halfback can catch the ball and quickly get turned up the field. If the halfback breaks one tackle, he will run down the sideline for a big play. Sometimes, your quarterbacks are a little gun-shy on pulling the trigger and wait too long, allowing the defense to react and catch up to the play. If the quarterback will throw the ball quickly off the mesh, the halfback will have the ball quickly and will have a better opportunity to make a big play.

The halfback does not have to be in a diveback position. The coach can also put him in a wingback position. The blocking halfback could also be in a wing or diveback position. From the wingback position, the halfback can get to the flat quicker.

83 Pass

Another play in this series is the fake to the fullback and dropback. Instead of the quarterback attacking the flank with a run-pass option, he can drop back. This play is called 83 pass, with a suffix to attach the route. The right halfback will be in a wing position, because he is one of the primary receivers on the play. The left halfback and the fullback are primarily blockers on this play. The quarterback takes the snap and reverse pivots, as in 83. The fullback takes the exact same footwork as before. As the quarterback meshes with the fullback, instead of attacking the flank, he drops back for three steps to throw. The left halfback will go in motion. If he is in a wingback spot, he goes in three-step motion, and, if he is in a diveback spot, he goes in one-step motion. As he goes in motion, he will pass the fullback-quarterback mesh and then gear down to pass protect from inside out. This motion will result in the same blocking scheme an I-formation team would use on the sprint-draw pass. The fullback will have the inside linebacker, and the motion halfback will have the outside linebacker in pass protection. If the fullback does not have to block, he will hook inside over the ball. If the halfback has nobody to block, he will flare. This play-action, dropback type of play allows for five receivers in the route. As the quarterback reverse pivots, he fakes deep in the backfield. Not only does this move freeze the defense, but it also gains the quarterback depth away from the center. As he drops, the defenders are late in reacting, because they have been held by the depth of the fake to the fullback.

As the fullback fakes over the ball, he attacks the line of scrimmage under control. After the mesh, he will make a decision on whether he has to block the linebacker. If he does, he will break down, get into the proper football position, and be ready to pass block. If not, he can continue through the line and hook either outside or inside, depending on what kind of pass pattern he is running. As soon as the halfback passes the mesh, he gears down and works up into the line of scrimmage from inside out. If the outside linebacker or defensive end is blitzing, he must pass block him. If not, then he will flare with depth, get width, and become a fifth receiver for the quarterback to throw the ball to.

83-87 Counter

Another 80 series play is 83 and 87 counter. It calls for the same blocking schemes used on 37 counter crisscross. On 87 counter, the quarterback will hand the ball to the wingback. He will fake the belly with the fullback, while the backside halfback goes in motion to be a log blocker at the flank. The word counter means all of the other backs go away from the hole. The fullback will fake the belly as if he is running 83. He takes lead, crossover, square-up footwork. The quarterback will use the same footwork as on the belly, faking the ball to the fullback. He will hand the ball to the wing, who leaves on the snap and will not be going in motion. The wing's footwork is the same footwork he would use if he were using three-step motion. He takes three steps and then starts downhill to the hole, which is at the outside leg of the backside guard. The quarterback will reverse pivot, fake to the fullback, and hand the ball off on the inside. The backside halfback goes in on step motion. He runs across the backfield through the heels of the fullback and, as he passes the fullback, will attack downhill and block the first free man at the flank from outside in. He will block with his inside shoulder and use log-block technique. The fullback's footwork is lead, crossover, and square up, and, as on all other counter plays, he has a blocking assignment. He will fill off the tail of the last man to pull. If you pull both the guard and the tackle, it will be off the tackle's tail. If you pull the guard and the tight end, it will be off the tight end's tail. He puts his head inside and blocks with his outside shoulder. The quarterback will hand the ball to the wing and attack the flank the same way as on keep pass.

The Down Series

Although the 82 and 88 down is a belly play, it is a direct-hitting, quick, off-tackle play to the fullback. Since no deliberate footwork exists for the fullback, he will cross over and run as fast as he can. The quarterback, instead of reverse pivoting with depth into the backfield, will reverse pivot flat down the line of scrimmage. The quarterback gives the ball to the fullback with a quick ride into the line of scrimmage and then fakes option with the halfback. The playside halfback will be a blocker. He will block an inside linebacker or the strong safety at the cutoff. The backside halfback will go in motion to get in pitch relationship. If he is in a wingback position, he will go in three-step motion. If he is in the diveback position, he will go in one-step motion. He will be the pitchback on the option, so, when the play is 82 down to the fullback, he will fake the option with the quarterback. The fullback will cross over and run through the outside foot of the tackle. You tell the fullback to square his shoulders as soon as he feels the mesh and to get north and south. The quarterback will give the ball to the fullback off-tackle.

The next play is down option. When the fullback gets the ball (82 down), the play is blocked like a trap: down, down, pull the guard, and kick-out. The down option play is blocked down, down, pull the guard, and log. The frontside halfback is a blocker either on the safety, on the inside backer, or on the corner. The backs use the same techniques they used on 82 down. The quarterback will ride the fullback into the line, snap the ball back, and attack downhill to option the fourth defender. The guard will log block the third defender. The fullback has two options: one, he can keep his shoulders square and run vertically through the line of scrimmage as he goes through the hole to block the free safety, or, two, he can bounce to the outside to block the free safety. This option makes for less of a fake, but is probably more effective in getting the fullback downfield to be an extra blocker. Often, the free safety is very active and will support, so the fullback's block becomes critical. The quarterback can either keep the ball or pitch it to the halfback in motion. You will also use keep pass to a tight end-wingback, 83-87 pass, and 83-87 counter as companion plays to the down series.

The Quick Belly Series

The last part of the 80 package is the quick belly package, used to gain belly option when not running the 40 series. This package is an alternative to the triple option. The series features the quick belly option and the quick belly to the fullback. In the package, the quick belly is 84 and 86, which is a handoff to the fullback, followed by a fake option. The companion plays are 81 and 89 option, which call for a fake to the fullback and an attack down the line of scrimmage to run the option. You also have 84 scissors at six, which is a handoff to the wingback, countering flow. The last play in the series is 81-89 waggle, which has been used with higher frequency in the last few years.

In the quick belly series, the fullback's footwork changes slightly. He will take a quick lead step, but his second step is a dive for the butt of the guard. It is a quick path. The quarterback will reverse pivot, give the ball, run the option, or give the ball on the scissors. The frontside halfback has a blocking assignment unless the play is scissors. The backside halfback will go in motion and be the pitchback.

84-86

The first play to start with is 84, to the right, or 86, to the left. This play is a quick belly, and the fullback will take a lead step and then drive for the butt of the guard. The quarterback technique is to jab step forward, reverse pivot flat, handoff to the fullback, and then fake option. The backside halfback will be coming in motion, three-step motion from a wing alignment, or one-step motion from the diveback position. The quarterback should be up on the balls of his feet, so he can reverse pivot off his near foot. He reverse pivots flat down the line of scrimmage, reaches the ball to the fullback, rides him, snaps his hands back in, and then fakes the option. The play can be blocked with different schemes up front, but works best with fire-on-backer rules, or zone blocking. The fullback can cut to either side.

81-89 Option

The next play in the series is 81 option. The fullback will use quick belly technique. The backs do the same thing, but the quarterback now pulls the ball and reads pitch or keeps off the third defender. The backside halfback is the pitchback.

84 Scissors at Six

On 84 scissors at six, the backside halfback will do the same thing he did on 81 option and 84. He will go in motion across the backfield and become the pitchback. On 84 scissors at six, the quarterback is going to reverse pivot, fake the ball to the fullback, step back, and hand off to the right halfback. The fullback's technique is exactly the same as on 84. The ballcarrier leaves on the snap, but does not go in motion. His first step is back for depth, and his shoulders are square and facing the quarterback. From here, he should run right for the tail of the center and adjust to the quarterback. As he receives the handoff, his shoulders should be north and south as he goes through the hole. It is very important that he does not take a second step for depth. Rather, he should take his first step for depth and his second step for the tail of the center, and then he should be running downhill with his shoulders square.

This play is blocked a bit differently from the way Sally is blocked. It has the right tackle pulling and leading through the hole. The tackle is assigned to block the backside linebacker as he comes through the hole. He will read the center's block. If the center is blocking in the left direction, the tackle pulls through the hole behind the center. If the center is blocking in the right direction, the tackle pulls around the center's tail. If he pulls up through where the center is in presnap alignment, he should be in good shape. The ballcarrier should make the same read as he attacks through the hole. If he goes right over the tail of the center, he will be able to run vertically and also be able to cut in either direction. The quarterback will ride the ball to the fullback, pull it back out, step back, give the ball to the halfback, and attack the flank. The opposite play is 86 scissors at four.

81 Waggle

The last play in this package is 81 waggle. This play has been popular of late, because many coaches have begun to instruct their inside linebackers to key the fullback. Rather than run 21 waggle and have the fullback run to the playside of the center, thus bringing the linebackers to the play, the fullback will use 84 footwork until he passes the quarterback. He can bend back to the left, as on 21 waggle, and still become a receiver in the pass pattern. The pivotal problem occurs when the linebacker becomes a blitzer. As a preventive maneuver, you do not run this play if the defense has shown that tendency. It is very difficult for the fullback to start to the right of the center and then come back to block a linebacker lined up to the left of the center, if he is blitzing quickly. This play comes out of the game plan if the defense has shown a tendency to blitz inside backers.

The right halfback will be in a wingback spot and run the crossing route. His technique on this play is to start down through the middle of the two hash marks. As he does so, he reads the deep middle of the field. If a safety rotates to the middle, between the two hash marks, then at 10 yards, the halfback will break it off flat and stay between the hashes. He will not cross to the outside of the hash marks. He must now find an opening and sit down. As the right halfback runs down through the middle of the hash marks—and if he sees no one in the middle—he will split the middle of the field for a touchdown shot. If the two safeties stay outside the hash marks, the right halfback will divide the field down the middle. At the same time, the quarterback should be reading the safety correctly and then get the ball to the right halfback.

The fullback's footwork is the same as on 84—a quick lead step to the right, diving right for the butt of the guard. As he clears the quarterback, the fullback will bend his path to the left and run in the flat. The left halfback will go in motion. As he passes the quarterback, he will gear down, work inside out, and be a blocker on the backside of the waggle. If nobody shows for him to block, he will flare. Rather than teach the quarterback to come all the way around and fake a belly play to the fullback, you simplify the action and have the quarterback reverse pivot on the midline, as on 21 waggle. He will execute the same footwork, so he does not have to learn another set of footwork. The play does not look any different to the defense than the belly play or a 30 sweep with all backs flowing. The fullback will fake over an imaginary ball, with the halfback faking sweep, just as he does on all waggle plays. The quarterback will attack the flank, with the outside receiver going deep, the backside inside receiver running the crossing route, and the backside outside receiver also going deep.

Summary

This chapter has presented a detailed description of everything the backs must execute in the wing-T offense. Included are many of the details important to the execution of the wing-T. Without those details, the wing-T is just a group of plays. Although they are nicely packaged plays, the details make them successful. Anyone who wants to coach wing-T running backs needs to coach details very thoroughly. He will find, when executed properly and with precision, these plays will gain a great deal of yardage.

The Wing-T Receiver

In this chapter, the wing-T receiver—or, as some commonly call them, the ends—techniques will be discussed. This program has tight ends and also spread ends, or wide receivers, or split ends—whatever you want to call them. All receivers are going to learn the same techniques. Again, you are going to cross-train your people. With very few exceptions, most of the ends will learn how to do every skill required of all the end positions.

Qualities of Receivers

The single most important quality for the tight end, as well as for all the other positions, is being an unselfish football player. You must have a tight end who is just as willing to block as he is to run down the field and catch the waggle play. In terms of their physical attributes, the tight ends should average about 6'3" and 233 pounds. Those attributes do not mean a tight end has to be that big, or that he cannot be smaller or bigger to play the position and perform well. But, most successful teams have tight ends who are in the neighborhood of 245 to 255 pounds. That size means they are great big offensive blockers. These tight ends must be dominating players at the line of scrimmage. An athletic tight end is also preferable, because you like to throw to the tight end. He is the number one receiver on many of the patterns, and you expect him to be able to get across the field or down the field and get open. Therefore, athleticism is imperative. When you are looking for a tight end, you want someone who is big and strong enough to block down on defensive tackles or defensive ends. It is extremely important that the tight end be able to gap block. He must be able to stop any penetration from a man playing 7 technique, inside him, or in the gap, or even all the way down on the tackle. He must be able to come down and execute a block on that defender. The flip side to blocking is he also must be athletic enough to run down the field and get open against a defensive back. Usually, the tight end has to play against the safety, whether it is a strong safety or a free safety. Coaches recruit corners and put them at those positions, anyway, so the tight end needs to be athletic enough to get to the assigned spot on the field with the correct timing and, hopefully, also get open. The tight ends are worked on what is called 2-corner drill, or 1-on-1, versus defensive backs. They have to be able to win those match ups.

The wide receivers, or what are called spread ends, are sometimes going to be off the line of scrimmage and, therefore, flankers for you. Sometimes, they will be on the line of scrimmage and, therefore, split ends for you. You can call them wide receivers or whatever you want to call them; it makes no difference. Again, the first quality to look for is unselfishness. You know the spread end is going to be the number one receiver on the majority of the routes, so, obviously, he must to have receiver skills. But, you want a spread end who is also willing to block. That attribute does not mean he has to be a great big, giant, physical specimen. He simply has to be willing to block, meaning he must be willing to go down in there and throw his body at a defender, if you call option crack or a split sweep, where he has to come down on a defensive end. Whatever the case may be, you need a split end who is willing to come down inside and really strike someone. You try to teach all of your players to block with their head across the front and above the waist. Times exist when you can cut. The majority of the time, when the receivers block, they are going to have to block with their shoulders and block hard. Whether they are asked to execute a crack block or whatever you would like them to do, their willingness to block is probably the most important thing they can have going for them. Will that split end run and hit somebody? Many wing-T coaches find their best wide receivers, or split ends, are kids who played running back in an offense similar to the wishbone—players who have some pretty good speed, but also have been trained to block. If you have a wide receiver coming from a program where they throw the ball 45 to 50 times a game, he is probably not the wide receiver you are going to get into your program. You are probably not going to throw the ball 50 times a game, unless you are just so good at waggling you can do throw that often. You can throw that often in this offense, but, normally, it is a ball-control type of offense based on running and play-action passing. Therefore, you will need to recruit a spread end who is unselfish.

Another key quality for receivers, of course, is good hands. Receivers can get open all they want and can run great routes, but, if they can't catch the ball, all that running talent is not doing much good. Can good hands be developed? Situations have happened where a guy would come in as a freshman and really not have a very good set of hands. The receivers coach would then work with him all through the season and the off-season, give the player a lot of drills, and have the quarterbacks throw to him a lot. Many players can go from not having a good set of hands at all to being top-quality receivers. Now, if receivers initially come to you with not-so-great hands, then, obviously, you want a player who is either really fast or who has great shake-n-bake moves, great quickness, or simply a knack for getting open. Hopefully, then you can help him to develop his hands as time goes on. Also, all coaches have experienced players who have come in as freshmen and graduated five years later, and their hands never got any better.

Finally, the ability for a receiver to run pass routes is essential. The receiver must have either great speed or great quickness. Some guys can get open underneath, can run great routes, and can shake loose from the defender covering them, because they have really fine quickness and good moves. Some can burst off the line of scrimmage, give a head fake, give a jab step with a head fake, and find themselves wide open. Some receivers have the ability to really get a guy leaning. They can work one side of the defender or the other and then break off in the opposite direction. Receivers who have great moves can make it. They can be good receivers, especially in this offense, which contains so many intermediate routes. The flip side to great moves is a receiver who has tremendous speed. Obviously, at the college level, you can try to recruit those people. But, they are hard to get, because every coach wants them. If you can get a guy with great speed, then a lot of things will open up for you in any offense, especially if that great speed player can also catch the football. With tremendous speed, you can get a guy down the field, can throw him a fly route, can throw him a post route, or can throw him a corner route. You can get him down the field, make some big plays with him, and back the secondary off. This attribute allows you to run the ball without the safeties and the corners, who are always sticking their nose up in the line of scrimmage, trying to be a factor in your running game.

It is most important to have players on your football team who are unselfish. You cannot have people who want statistics for themselves only. Athletes have to be happy with winning the football game and also with accumulating statistics as a team. When you have those kinds of guys, you are going to win. The worst thing to mess those guys up is usually the attention given to them by the people in your town—patting them on the back, grumbling about the coach, telling the kid he should be a 1,000-yard rusher, or telling him is not getting the ball enough. A kid buys into that attention. It causes problems. Your players have to buy into what you are teaching. They have to buy into a team philosophy. They have to be hungry and have to be unselfish. Those attributes are the principal qualities to look for in your receivers.

While going through the different drills the receivers do in every single practice, many of them are going to sound like some of the other descriptions in this book, because everyone is taught to block. You teach the same blocking fundamentals to all receivers, backs, and linemen. You teach the same fundamentals to the backs, the linemen, and the receivers, when working on their first step and their stance during the routine periods. While discussing this, some of the practice periods, such as shoulder skills and routine, will sound similar to drills already discussed regarding the other positions. But, once through shoulder skills and routine in practice, then the descriptions of the duties of the spread ends and the tight ends become noticeably different from the descriptions for the other positions.

Shoulder Skills Period

The first thing the receivers start with, as you go to the individual part of the practice, is the shoulder skills period. Diagram 4.1 illustrates what this part of practice is like for the receivers. You may have one coach or may have two coaches. If someone is available to help your receivers coach, that situation is great. Then, you can have two sets of eyes watching these drills.

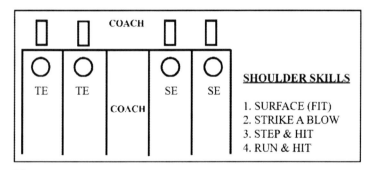

Diagram 4.1

Shoulder skills period includes surface, where you are going to fit into the bag and make sure you have the proper blocking surface. The second drill in the progression is strike a blow. You position the players in a six-point stance for both drills. You will have the bag between the legs, will be working on a good blocking surface, and then taking that blocking surface and actually driving it through the bag and rolling the hips. A receiver blocks just like a lineman, a back, or anyone else in your program. The third part of this progression is step and hit, where receivers work on taking the first step and then striking the bag. The final phase of the blocking progression is called run and hit, which can be turned around to hit and run. In run and hit, receivers are going to block a defender off about four yards, or linebacker distance, away, and then finish the block after that. The opposite of the hit and run occurs when the receivers have to block a man who is directly on top of them and then have to drive and run him, finishing the block that way.

You use the sideline for organizing shoulder skills drill. If you had four tight ends in your program, two tight ends would block two bags, which would be held by the other two tight ends. The wide receivers or spread ends would also be blocking the bags, with partners holding them. If you had four of each, that number would be optimal for the purposes of practice. If you do not have those kinds of numbers, then you should combine the groups and let one tight end and one split end work together and match them up that way.

The bags are intersected by the sideline. The bottom of the bags should be placed right on the sideline and should be placed between the five-yard stripes on your field. You can put them right on the corners of the five-yard stripes on the sideline. The coach stays on the inside of the action, so he can see the blockers from behind. Once in a while, the coaches move to the other side to look into the blockers' eyes.

Surface

The first drill in the blocking progression is called surface. When you do surface, your players are going to be down in a six-point stance. The players know, when they get in those six-point stances, their hands and their knees should be spread enough so the bag stays right between their knees. The six-point stance means, basically, the cage of the face mask is right up on the bag. If you do this without requiring a helmet, you can tell your players to put their nose right on the bag. Their knees should be straight down from their hips. They should not have their butt cocked way back so the blocker is sitting on his heels. You coach your players to position their feet so their toes are not curled into the ground. You want their feet flat, and, that way, when they do the drills, their knees will not lift up off the ground. This positioning will enable their hips to roll through the block.

The first part of this block is nothing more than a matter of fitting the blocker's surface into the bag. This part is called surface. It is a fit drill. No hitting is done. All you are doing is fitting into the bag. The blocking surface will include the thighs; the front of the shoulder, all the way down to the elbow; the forearm; and the fist, which is placed right next to the pec. At the contact point, the receiver is going to strike and drive that shoulder and forearm hard through the bag. The receiver is doing nothing more than fitting himself into the bag. Not a lot to striking is done. Not a lot of contact occurs (you will be doing that in the next drill). The key coaching points are that the hips should be rolled down and through, the eyes should be up, and a squeeze exists between the side of the neck and the entire blocking surface. If blockers squeeze the neck and the blocking surface, then they will squeeze the defender, which will give them a better chance to control him. Another point is that the receivers' toes should not be curled underneath their feet.

Your commands to your receivers are going to be, "Surface, right shoulder, on sound." Each fits in with his right shoulder. Next, you want to see them fit in with their left shoulder, as well, so the next command should be, "Surface, left shoulder, on sound."

Strike a Blow

One of the reasons why the bag is placed on the line, on the sideline on the field, is so the line can intersect the bottom of the bag. You want to see the player knock that bag off of that line. You want to really strike a blow. The name of the drill is strike a blow. You want these guys to really strike the bag. You want to see if they can knock a 100-pound bag off the line scrimmage with one hit and not even use their feet. The strike has to be nasty. You want to see how hard your players will hit when they get a chance to block someone.

Strike a blow is done from a six-point stance. The blocker places his nose on the bag, both hands on the ground, knees straight down from the hips, and toes uncurled behind him. The player who is making this block is going to rock back just slightly and then explode through the bag, using that same blocking surface just mentioned and knocking the bag off the line. You will have him go with his right shoulder, then with his left shoulder, and then will switch your guys around.

At the beginning of both training camp and spring ball, you ask players to hold their block so the coach can check it. If the coach is instructing six to eight different ends, they will all be on the line. Still, he's got to be able to coach them all, look at them all quickly, make the necessary corrections, and have them come on back. Everybody gets off on the "s" in set.

Step and Hit

The third step in the progression is called step and hit. In this drill, you teach from a two-point stance. You want the receivers to be about an arm's length away from the bag. You tell the players to reach out and touch the bag. You want a good base. You are going to emphasize having the bag, or the defender, between your legs as a blocker. You are going to work on the proper footwork first of all, and then you are going to strike a good blow and block the bag off the line. This drill is first done in a two-step progression—step and hold—and then, after a while, you do the whole thing.

One of the key fundamentals in blocking is, if a blocker is going to block with his right shoulder, his first step should be with his left foot. He should be vertically back off the ball as far as he is allowed to be. You want your players to take a short power step on the first step and then make contact on the second step, where they will actually drive the defender. On the first step, the blocker replaces his toes with his heels, which constitutes the length of the step. The second step is an up step, which is done with his right foot. His right shoulder will make contact. On his third step, he will drive through naturally. Another important coaching point is for the blockers, when they step with that first step, to place their chest down on their thighs, because you block at the hip. The reason, as noted before, is no strength exists in the hips. Players who work on the hip sled, doing squats and legs lifts, have all that strength get transferred down into the quad area and the glutes area, but not at the hips.

After you have worked step and hold for a few days and are satisfied that your players are keeping their chest on their thighs, keeping their feet apart, and stepping with a power up step so their heels replace their toes and are not overextending, then the next thing you want them to do is the whole drill on one command—and watch the whole thing take place. Next, the players will do the same thing with their left shoulder and are also going to do the entire drill without stopping.

Run and Hit

The final part of this progression is called run and hit. You are going to have the receivers practice blocking linebackers, who are lined up four yards away. You are going to have the receivers run at a linebacker as if they are going to be blocking a linebacker (or it could be a corner in the case of the wide receiver). The receivers are going to run at the bag at full speed. When they get to the contact point, then the other fundamentals are going to fall into place. One of the things you tell your players to do is drive the bag back a couple of yards, swing their tail, and take it down the line a couple of yards, just so they get a feel for what it is like to finish the block, as well as do all the other fundamentals.

One of the cardinal sins of blocking is when the blocker decides to start swinging his tail and finishing his block to the right and then throws both feet outside the bag. If the blocker's feet slide over and are all the way outside the bag, the defender will be able to penetrate at him. The blocker will not have the necessary control on the defender he needs to block. The defender can also spin out of this block. The steps and the footwork are short, choppy steps, and, as he turns, the blocker takes his outside arm, throws it up into the numbers, and bench presses.

In one drill, you are going to have the blocker run for four yards, as if he's going to block a linebacker. When he does, he makes contact, drives the bag, and finishes the block. The opposite is hit and run. You also teach the receivers to block a man who is right on their nose—to drive him and then swing their tail and finish him. That action emphasizes leg drive. This drill is a good substitute for sled drill.

If your players execute the proper fundamentals, they will block at the hip, keep the man between their legs, and have good control of him as they throw their shoulder and forearm through the block. You finish by having the receivers squeeze their neck and their shoulder and keep the defender controlled on that blocking surface.

Routine Period

The next part of practice that the receivers go through is called routine period. Routine period is really a footwork period. This period is where they concentrate on a proper stance and a correct first step. With the wide receivers, you teach two different stances. The tight ends can learn the wide receiver stance, which makes a total of three for them. The inside hand is always down for the receivers. That stance facilitates the release technique, the blocking, and the way you teach blocking. Diagram 4.2 illustrates how to organize the routine period.

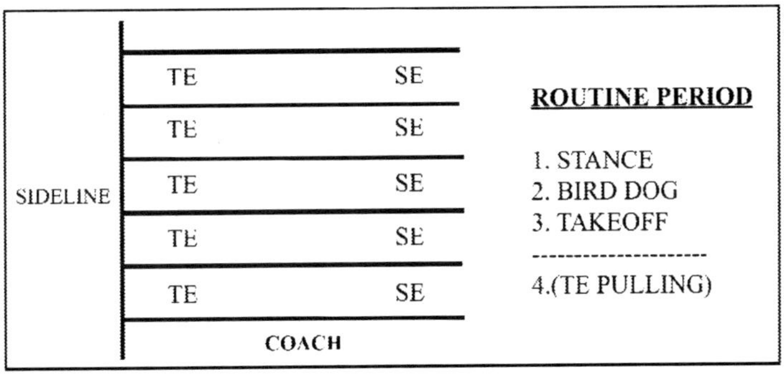

SIDELINE	TE	SE	**ROUTINE PERIOD**
	TE	SE	
	TE	SE	1. STANCE
	TE	SE	2. BIRD DOG
	TE	SE	3. TAKEOFF

			4.(TE PULLING)
	COACH		

Diagram 4.2

Routine period includes, first, work on the stance, and, second, the bird-dog drill, which is simply a step and hold (i.e., take the first step and hold it). And, when you do this, you really throw the arms hard, having one arm pointing straight ahead and one arm kind of pointing behind you. You will actually look like a bird-dog going out pheasant hunting when you do this. The third part of the progression is takeoff, where you are going to work on exploding off the line of scrimmage for five yards with the correct foot. The last part is just for the tight ends and only if you ask your tight end to pull on any of your blocking schemes. If you never ask your tight end to pull at all, you would not do this drill. It is a linemen's drill, but the tight ends have to pull through the hole and wall off on counter plays; therefore, you teach the tight end pulling drills.

During routine, you want the receivers coach to be in a centralized location, as mentioned earlier. He needs to be in a centralized location, where he can see all of the receivers. What you do is put all the receivers in a line, right behind each other, five yards apart and five yards in width. With this spacing, the receiver coach can look out over his people, see all of them doing the drill at the same time, and make quick corrections. By following this procedure, you get in a lot of reps in a short period of time.

This drill starts out as a 10-minute drill on the first day of practice. By the time you finish your season, the drill will be down to about two minutes. You go fast in this drill. Once you're convinced your people are comfortable with the proper stance, then you do not necessarily have to work on the stance anymore. You can eliminate that from the progression. On bird-dog, you step and hold at the beginning of the year, just to check the footwork, but you rapid-fire bird-dog later in the year, meaning you can go three steps very fast and then on to the next footwork.

Stance

Since the receivers are always going to have their inside hand down, you must tell them which side the ball is on. The tight end stance is just like the offensive linemen's stance. First of all, they should use a narrow base. You do not want a big, wide, giant base, because you want their first step to have power to it. You want their feet right underneath their armpits. That width is as wide as they need to be. Their feet should be parallel. You do not want them to stagger either foot back. You want them to have a perfectly balanced stance, so they can go in all four directions equally well. You want their toes to point in just slightly, because, when they get down in their stance and bend their knees, their power-producing angles will still be going forward. If their toes are way out and they get down in their stance, then their knees will point in the opposite direction. That position is counterproductive to what you want them to do (if you have a football player who is a slightly pigeon-toed, then, by turning his toes in, it is actually going to help him, because it will lock in the power-producing angles). You want the receivers' inside hand down and their off arm wrapped tight around their knee in order to lock those power-producing angles in even further. You also want to emphasize the heels up to the top of the grass. If the receiver brings his heels to the top of the grass, he is automatically going to bend at his ankles. As he gets into his stance, he should have bend at his knees and at his hips. You want him to have a nice, flat back in his stance. You want his hand to be extended as far in front as possible, yet not have any weight on it. You want him to be able to pick his hand up and down without having any weight on it. You want his hand as far out as possible, because you want the defense looking at that stance to think it is a run stance, even though it might be a pass play. Another point is, if he has too much weight forward or backward, the receiver won't have proper balance in his stance. By having proper balance, the receiver can go in all four directions equally well with power. The four directions are straight ahead, left, right, or even backward, if the receiver needs to be a pass protector. You want his inside hand down, because the number one block the receiver has to execute is a gap block, where he blocks a defender in the gap between him and the tackle, or a defender on the tackle who might penetrate. If he keeps his inside hand down, then it will be easier for him to take the pull step and get his head across the front.

The first stance to teach a spread receiver is a three-point stance. Eventually, you are going to have him stand up in a two-point stance. The fundamentals should be almost the same as when he takes a three-point stance. The advantage of being up, obviously, is he can see a little bit better. He will have a better awareness of what is going on around him. Clearly, he can make moves on people who are right in his face. He can still get off the line of scrimmage quickly, as long as his feet are disciplined. Anytime you see the receivers start to false step, you put them back down in a three-point stance for a while and make sure they understand the fundamentals of stances. Then, you go back to standing them up again. The one thing to make your receivers understand this message faster than anything is, if they have been in a two-point stance for a while and, as a coach, you are seeing a bunch of false steps, you make them go back into a three. They do not like the three-point stance nearly as much as the two-point stance. It is of the utmost importance to eliminate false steps from the receivers.

When having them take a three-point stance, you teach the receivers to maintain a narrow stance. Their feet should be about as wide apart as a yard stripe on the practice field. You want the receivers' feet in a narrow stance, like a sprinter's. You want their back foot back. You are going to have them put their inside arm down and their inside foot back. You have them bend their knees and get their heels up to the top of the grass. You can look inside to the ball, if you have to. A wide receiver has no excuse to be offside or jump the gun, because he can always turn his head to the inside, see the football, and move on the snap. He does not even have to hear the quarterback's cadence. He puts his back arm up a little bit, so he can throw his arm forward and really get his momentum generated to go straight ahead.

The spread ends are told to go down into a three-point stance and keep their feet the same and stand up. That two-point stance is best to use. You like their arms in a position where they can explode off the ball. What you would like is for the spread end to come off the ball just as he would in a three-point stance. You do not want him to false step. A false step occurs when the first step goes backwards. That error means the step has to come back to the line of scrimmage. What has happened to the receiver is he has taken two steps and gone absolutely nowhere. When a man releases correctly off the line of scrimmage, he takes two steps and is a good two yards up the field. That mistake is what you are trying to eliminate. Those two yards can be the difference between scoring a big touchdown or being covered. You want to make sure the receiver does not false step, and that stance is what you are looking for by the receivers.

Bird-Dog

The next part of routine period is called bird-dog. Bird-dog is a step and hold. The receiver is going to work on one step at a time, and that step is all he is going to do in this drill. At the beginning of training camp, you have the receivers take one step and hold it and then check to see if that step is where you want it. Three different steps are done using bird-dog with the receivers. The first one is straight ahead. The second one is called a fire step, where they step with their inside foot at about a 45-degree angle. The third step is a pull step. You have them pull step both ways, inside and outside.

You have the receivers work on firing out straight ahead. The tight end can work on firing out with his left foot and his right foot. For the spread end, normally, when he steps straight ahead, he is going to step with the back foot.

A fire step means the receiver is going to step at a 45-degree angle with his feet, but his tail will still be pointed north and south and his shoulders will still be square with the line of scrimmage. You do not want them to get overextended, because it is very easy for the receiver to be pulled out of his stance or fall down. He has no power or balance when he does that; therefore, he is not going to be as effective either as a blocker or as a receiver releasing off the line of scrimmage.

On a pull step to the left, the receiver should take his left foot and step toward the sideline. It should not be a big, overextended, giant step. All he basically needs to do is pick his foot up and put it back down again. But, the most important coaching point is, if he picks up his left foot, his right foot needs to pivot so his toes are also pointing to that sideline. Another important point is, if he steps with his left foot, he should throw his left arm hard behind him. In this case, that movement will help him turn his shoulders.

Takeoff

On takeoff, what you are going to do is have the receivers sprint five yards. You want them to get off the ball. It is not a long sprint. You are not interested in conditioning the receivers at this point. Instead, you want to see them explode out of their stance, but you are going to give them the foot you want them to step with initially. On the practice field, what you are going to do is have the receivers sprint five, jog five, and then turn around. Then, you can do the same thing, coming back with the other foot.

Pulling Drill

The tight ends are taught what is called an 11-step pull drill, so they can pull through the hole and wall off on certain counter plays. Therefore, they have to know pulling techniques. You are going to teach the pulling techniques at the end of the routine period and have only the tight ends do this. If you have only one receivers coach, send your tight ends to the offensive linemen for routine period. That way, they can work on pulling while you are working with the wide receivers on other things.

In the 11-step pull drill, if you are going to go to the right, the receiver will post up with his right foot first. His second and third steps both have him going down the line of scrimmage. On his fourth step, you want him to reach down with his left arm and grab grass, because this movement simulates where the contact is going to occur. If he were pulling to the right and going to log a defender, contact would occur on this step right here. If he is going to gut or pull through the hole, then his fifth step is going to go straight up the field to finish the block. You want him to be nice and low. From there, steps six, seven, eight, nine, and 10 all go back to where he came from, and 11 is nothing more than getting back down in his stance. He should have completed a pull and returned to where he started. When you teach this drill to your players, you want to walk them through it once or twice, but no more than twice. They have to learn to do it. You can walk them through it once, have them walk really fast, and then count the numbers for them the second time. After that, just say, "Set," and have them sprint all 11 steps. You do not want to make robots out of your players. You do not want kids out on the field doing things one step at a time. You want this drill to be smooth, fluid, and fast.

The linemen grab grass on their fourth step. They dip their shoulders so they can rip through on the next step, because steps four and five are where they make contact on log blocks. Sometimes, the tight end might have to do that, but most of the time— 99 percent of the time—he is going to pull through the hole and wall off on a linebacker.

Blocking Technique Period

The next phase of the receiver practice plan focuses on what the receivers have to do in terms of individual techniques. You begin with blocking technique period. The tight ends have quite a few blocks. They have individual blocks, but, sometimes, they are involved in combination blocks. They have to be able to execute the same blocks as the offensive linemen on a defensive down player. They also have to be able to execute the same blocks as the wide receivers on defensive backs.

Tight End Blocks

On Block

The first block to teach the tight end is the on block (Diagram 4.3). Just like everyone else, his head goes to the side of the hole, and he finishes the block by swinging his tail. You like to have the tight end take the man down the line of scrimmage parallel to the line of scrimmage. In on right, he is going to block with his right shoulder; therefore, his first step is with his left foot. Contact occurs on the second step with the right shoulder. And, he drives the defensive man to the right.

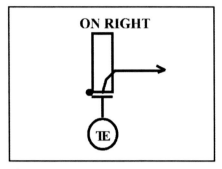

Diagram 4.3

Gap Block

Gap right means a defensive man has either lined up in a 7-technique inside shoulder, in the inside gap, or possibly over the next player inside (Diagram 4.4). He is a threat to penetrate the neutral zone inside you. In this case, you put the bag inside and even with the tight end, so as to simulate someone who has just penetrated the neutral zone. On gap block, when the receiver executes a gap technique, his head goes in front. You tell him to drive his head right across the front of the belt buckle and block with his left shoulder. Even though you are gapping in the direction to the right, the block is made with the left shoulder. This technique would be gap right. You have the blocker step with his right foot, and that first step is a pull step. The gap block technique consists of a pull step, and the blocker also puts his head across the front, blocks with his left shoulder, and finishes the man directly down the line of scrimmage. This block is done versus any defender who is a penetrator or a threat to penetrate.

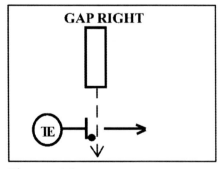

Diagram 4.4

Down Block

The next block is down right (Diagram 4.5). This same technique is the technique for lead or double-team whenever you double-team a player. On this block, you are simulating blocking a man who is over the tackle. You place the bag where the tackle would line up, his ghost alignment. You are going to put your head behind on a down block, because you have determined, at this point, this man is not a penetrator. He is a line-of-scrimmage, reading type of player. Therefore, you don't have to worry about putting your head across the front because he is not going to penetrate. Down right is executed with the right shoulder. Because the head is behind, you would step with the left foot. What happens in this block is the right foot merely pivots and the left foot steps, in order to get your shoulder square to your target. Contact occurs with the right shoulder. You finish the block down the line of scrimmage.

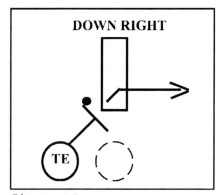

Diagram 4.5

Fire Block

The next block is called the fire block (Diagram 4.6). The fire block means you are going to take the fire step worked on in bird-dog period, the 45-degree step, with your shoulders still square to the line of scrimmage. Your toes are still pointing north and south. You are simulating blocking a man who is lined up on the outside half of your body. You put the bag on the outside half of your body. When you say, "Fire right," you have to block the man who is to the right, but you also have to get your head to the outside. Therefore, even though you are saying, "Fire right," it is a left-shoulder block. The blocker will take a 45-degree step, toes north and south, shoulders square, and make contact with the left shoulder. The second step drives right through the crotch of the defensive man, and you are going to drive him and knock him off the ball. If you can, knocking him off the ball is great. If you feel you can do that, try to swing your tail and finish the man on a 45-degree angle back away from the direction the play is going. You do not want your blockers to try to round off the block. What you want to do is block and drive the man back at a 45-degree angle and just knock him off the line of scrimmage. Once you have good control of him, then you will swing your tail and finish the block.

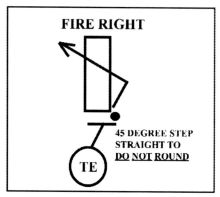

Diagram 4.6

Reach Block

The next block is called a reach block (Diagram 4.7). Reach and fire are very closely related. A reach block is used versus the defender who would be over the man adjacent to the tight end on the inside. When you take a reach step, you are either going to block this defensive lineman, if he slants to you, or are going to climb up the field, right through his inside hip and try to cut off a linebacker. As a tight end, you are also often assigned to block a loose 9 technique and reach him. This man would be lined up outside of you by a whole man. When you take the reach step, you are taking a flat 90-degree-angle step, with the toes pointed north and south and shoulders square to the line of scrimmage. Then, if that defensive man comes on an angle toward him, the blocker will go ahead and execute a fire technique after the reach step. The second step is right through the middle of the man. You will drive this defender straight off the line of scrimmage and later swing your tail and finish him off inside on a 45-degree angle.

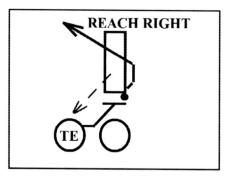

Diagram 4.7

Bump Lead Block

The next block to work on is called a bump lead (Diagram 4.8). Lead means you are going to double-team. It is the terminology for double-teaming. The blocking bag is placed on the offensive tackle. The tight end is going to come down, as if he is going to double-team on the man lined up over the tackle. You get a good strike on this man and then climb vertically to the linebacker who is scraping. From there, the tackle takes over the block by himself, using wheel technique (which is explained in the offensive line section).

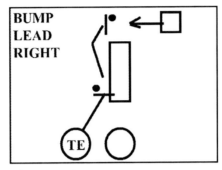

Diagram 4.8

Post Block

The post block is done by the tight end when he knows the wingback is going to come down and double-team with him from the outside (Diagram 4.9). If you are going to post lead and take the defender to the right, then the tight end is going to use his left shoulder. The tight end steps with his right foot, places his head to the inside, and posts with his left shoulder. What you do with the post block is try to raise, or elevate, the aiming point for the block. Normally, you block at the hips. But, this time is one when you can block up in the numbers. You want to raise the defender up and elevate him so the lead blocker can come down at an exposed hip. Once the post is made, the eyes should be to the inside. If a chance exists the linebacker might run through the C gap, the tight end must come off and gap block him. If not, then you can finish the double-team block, and the two, the post and the lead, will get their tail ends together, swing their tails, and take the defensive player flat down the line of scrimmage, parallel to the line.

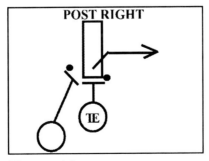

Diagram 4.9

Cutoff Block

The last two tight end blocks are done with the tight ends and the spacing boards (Diagram 4.10). Those spacing boards are 16 feet long, an inch thick, and four inches wide. You need a set of spacing boards for the receivers to work on blocks. You want the tight end to be able to block at the cutoff. You will put a defender with a hand shield in a defensive back position above the play. You will then have him mix up the kinds of looks he gives to the tight end. As the tight end comes across to the cutoff point, if that safety penetrates really hard, the tight end will gap block him by putting his head across the front. If the defensive player has backpedaled to the middle third and then is coming, by the time you get to the cutoff point, you should be able to square up on him—and, actually, at that point, use stalk block technique.

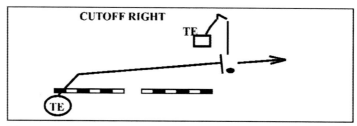

Diagram 4.10

You might also encounter a defender who is on the far side of the line of scrimmage and, thus, simulates the tight end blocking all the way across at the cutoff. This block will usually consist of the head across the front and gap blocking technique. That drill would simulate a sweep play to the opposite side from the tight end, common blocks that the tight ends have to make.

Walloff Block

The last one is the walloff block, which is the reason you taught the tight end how to do pulling technique (Diagram 4.11). The tight end will post up and pull down the line of scrimmage and turn up somewhere over the outside leg of the center or the outside leg of the guard on the far side. The tight end will wall off on a linebacker, who should be misdirected. Because most of these walloff blocks are on the counter type of plays, where you start flow one way and bring a wingback through in the other direction, the

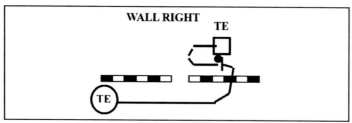

Diagram 4.11

tight end has to wall block through the hole and block the linebacker, who should, by that time, be scraping back to the hole. You tell the linebackers in the drill to take a shuffle step or two toward the middle and then come back on the tight end, so he has a fair chance to execute his blocking assignment.

Spread End Blocks

Stalk Block

The first block is the one the spread end has to use more commonly than anything else in the offense and is called the stalk block (Diagram 4.12). Four or five parts to teaching this block are very important. The first phase is similar to the shoulder skills, in that you simply focus on the fit. You get the receivers and a defensive back, who could be another receiver simulating that position, locked up with each other. You start the spread end with his knees bent and his hands inside. Normally, you use a blocking shield to begin with during the early days of camp, but, eventually, you throw the shield away and just have the spread end get his hands on the actual defensive player. You want him to bend his knees, put his hands on the inside of the man, and basically fit into the block to see how it feels.

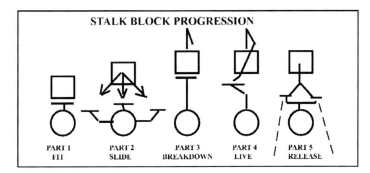

Diagram 4.12

In the second stage, you teach the spread end to slide his feet right and left. What you do in this part of the drill is take the defensive player and back him up to where he is about three yards away. You tell the spread end to get down, as if he is ready to make contact. At this point, the defensive guy has a three-way go. He can blitz fast to the inside, blitz straight ahead, or blitz to the outside. In this particular drill, you do not want him to head fake and try to go to one side or another. All you want from the spread ends is to get down in a good hitting position. If the defender goes inside, you slide left. You get squared up on him and make the block. If the man goes outside, you slide to the right, get squared up on him, and make the block. If he goes straight ahead, you take him on as he comes. You are still fitting into the defensive man, but here you are doing it with him coming forward, so a little bit of contact is involved as well.

In the third part of the stalk block progression, you have to learn when to break down. You just call this the breakdown phase. The defensive back takes the hand shield and backpedals. When he breaks down and stops or begins to drive forward, the spread end is going to break down at the same time. On the command, the spread end starts sprinting off the line of scrimmage. As soon as he sees the defensive man stop or break forward, he comes under control and gets into a good hitting position. No contact happens in this part of the drill. All you are really doing is teaching receivers when to break down. If the defender does not break down, you want the receiver to run him to the goal line every single time. If the defensive back is in man coverage and has his back to the quarterback, turned inside out, facing the receiver, then you should run him to the goal line. He is not looking at anything else. Run him all the way to the goal line. That situation leaves two less bodies to step over when you pitch the ball.

The fourth phase of this progression, which is the live part, is the total combination of the other three and is called go live. Actually, you are combining drills one, two, and three. The defensive back will backpedal as the spread end comes off the line. When he starts to drive forward, the spread end breaks down. When he gets to a place where he can attack you, as he comes forward, you can let him go to his left, to his right, or up the middle. The spread end, as he pushes off the ball, breaks down when the defensive back starts forward. If the man breaks inside, you slide inside and make the block. If the man goes straight ahead, you are in good position. If he slides to the outside, you slide to the outside to make the block.

The last thing you can do is have two spread ends facing each other. You have the spread end, who is simulating the defensive player, go ahead and use his release technique. You tell the spread end, who is simulating the blocker, to use his stalk block technique. At this point, both of them can work techniques they use all the time—and get better at doing them. One man is working on release techniques. He is going to drive forward and try to release inside or outside. The blocker is coming straight ahead. He is going to slide left, slide right, and then try to stop block the man who is trying to release around him. You should be able to turn this into a competition and have an especially successful drill.

Crack Block

Four other blocks are taught to the spread ends (Diagram 4.13). These blocks are all different from the tight end's blocks. The first one is called crack. It is a change-up way to block the flank on option. Normally, the spread end is going to release and stalk #5 on the option. If you call option crack, then the receiver will post up inside, come flat down the line, and crack the fourth defender. The halfback, who usually blocks the fourth defender, will flare and stalk #5. It is just a switch in assignments between the spread end and the halfback.

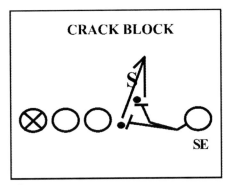

Diagram 4.13

When you crack block, you want to take a good pull step to the inside. You want to come flat down the line of scrimmage as far as you can go until you have to start turning up. It depends on how aggressive the strong safety is. If he sees option and comes flying, you might have to go flat all the way down the line of scrimmage to crack him. If he backs off a little first and then starts coming, read steps, freezes, or pauses, by the time you get to a position to block him, you can usually start working up the field on that man. The receiver should always start with a pull step down the line of scrimmage and then adjust to the strong safety from there. When you crack block, you want the head above the waist and the head in front so it is legal.

Cutoff Block

Cutoff blocks can be simulated many ways (Diagram 4.14). A spread end, who has to cut off a corner, will simulate a play going away from the receiver in the opposite direction. Usually, in this case, no quarterback faking is coming back to him. If the quarterback was faking waggle to your side, then you could fake a pass route and set up a waggle or a counter bootleg. But, on a full-flood play away from the spread end, he must get inside out and cut off the corner on the backside.

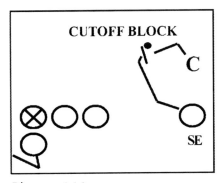

Diagram 4.14

Down Block

The last two blocks are related to each other (Diagram 4.15). A down block is done from what is called split alignment. The spread end is four to six yards from the offensive tackle. He is going to come flat down the line of scrimmage and put his head across the front of the end man on the line of scrimmage. It is similar to a crack block or a tight end's gap block. It is a down block, because you are coming from four to six yards outside and are blocking down on the defensive end. If the end manages to penetrate and beat you before you get there, you will climb to the next level. You usually do this in those instances where you know the end is a line-of-scrimmage player and not a penetrator. You are going to come flat down the line of scrimmage, put your head across the front, and block him. You would like to finish the block parallel to the line of scrimmage.

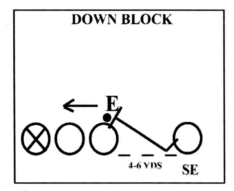

Diagram 4.15

Wall Rock Block

The final block is called a wall rock block (Diagram 4.16). You are going to come down and fake the crack on the defensive end. You hope the end will penetrate or widen out to beat the spread end's block. When you use wall rock block, you are going inside to influence the end and make him either step outside or penetrate across the line of scrimmage. Then, you go to the linebacker level and wall the linebacker off. In the

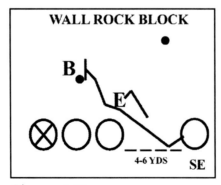

Diagram 4.16

meantime, you are going to run some kind of a play coming up inside that defensive end. You are going to influence him to work out and then run the play inside of him.

Release Period

The next part of the receiver practice plan is the release period, where you emphasize to the receivers the importance of getting off the line of scrimmage. You remind them that they cannot get jammed or held up at the line and back up your verbal instruction by working on their release techniques every day. You teach the receivers five release techniques, four of which are for both the spread end and the tight end and one of which is for the tight end only.

Pull Release

The first release to work on is a pull release (Diagram 4.17). If the receiver needs to release to the outside, then he is going to take a pull step with his outside foot. On a pull release, he pull steps with his outside foot, then dips his inside shoulder, rips his inside arm through, and starts working vertically up the field as fast as he possibly can. This release can be used by a tight end on the line of scrimmage with the defensive end directly over the top of him, trying to jam him, or by a spread end with a corner in a press position, right up in his face. In either case, you need to be able to pull release around the defender. The spread end needs to pull release when he is running a fly route. You try to release outside on the fly routes to really stretch the secondary. Against a cover two-deep corner who is right his face and pressed, the receiver is going to release to his outside and run the fly. A tight end might have to do the same thing—take a pull outside release and then run his keep pass pattern, a seam route.

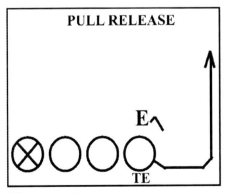

Diagram 4.17

Down Release

A down release is the second release (Diagram 4.18). It can be used by a tight end releasing off an outside backer or a spread end releasing off a corner—any situation where you want the inside release and also want to get vertical. If you are using a down release, you take a down step on a 45-degree angle to your inside. The shoulder nearest to the defender must dip, and your arm nearest the defender must rip. You want the outside half of your body to dip and rip and then get vertical up the field. One of the things coaches should teach their players is how far up the field they should sprint at full speed. It is good to put a cone at least 10 yards up the field so they do not just release off the line and gear down. That move is not realistic to a game. They need to release off the line and then burst up the field.

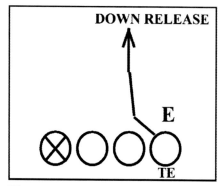

Diagram 4.18

Fake Release

On a fake release, you are going to fake to one side and release to the other (Diagram 4.19). You use several types of fakes, but a mere head fake can suffice. You can just throw your head to one side and then step with the opposite foot. You can step with left foot and then go to the right. Or, you can combine both of those. You can head fake, step to the left, and then break to the right. Whatever works best for each receiver. A lot of players like to do them in different ways. Most players choose to combine the head fake and the outside step and then try to release to the inside, or vice versa. They

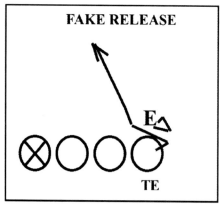

Diagram 4.19

go head fake and step inside and then release to the outside. Times exist when the tight end has the release technique dictated to him (e.g., on a waggle route, a counter bootleg route, or a keep pass route). You do not let tight ends experiment with different types of releases on certain plays because of the way the base play is getting blocked. But, plenty of times also exist when the tight end can fake release and run a drag route or crossing route to the other side. On pure dropback, where you are protecting from inside out, the receivers can basically take the release they want.

Swim Release

On the swim release, obviously, you are going to try to swim right over the top of the defender or right over top of the defender's hands and arms (Diagram 4.20). It is good to pin the arm in the direction you are releasing to. If the defensive man has his left arm sticking out at you as a receiver and you are trying to release to your right (his left), then you want to take your hands and get his left arm off of you. You can pin his elbow or can swat his hands down. Whatever technique your coach is partial to will work. On the swim, you want to get the defender's hands off of you and want to punch right over the top of his arms with your near arm as you burst vertically up the field.

All of these releases—the pull release, the down release, and the swim release—can be combined. If you want to, you can head fake and swim, head fake and down release, or head fake and pull release. You can combine the fake release with any of those.

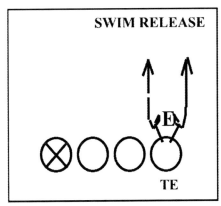

Diagram 4.20

Block Release

The last release to discuss is strictly a tight end release (Diagram 4.21). This situation is where the tight end has a 7 technique, or an inside shade, lined up on the inside half of him. This defender has shown a tendency to penetrate into the line of scrimmage and cause problems for your blocking scheme. The block release simply means you are going to try to log this guy from outside in, but, since he is penetrating, you cannot get it done without some help from the tight end. The tight end comes off on a block release. He is going to make contact with his head to the outside. If the ball is on the right, the tight end is going to make contact with the right shoulder; therefore, he steps with the left foot, hits the defender with the right shoulder, and, in one continuous motion, bursts up the field. You do not want the tight end to hit, stop, hold, and then be late getting to his pass pattern. You want him to strike and take his second step in one continuous motion. It is done at full speed. No slowdown aspect exists. As he strikes, he runs his second step right to his route. The tight end does not slow down, but, if he makes some decent contact, plenty of slowing down happens for that defensive player. The guard, who has to log him, can pull, and, since the defensive player has been slowed down, you can get that man log blocked.

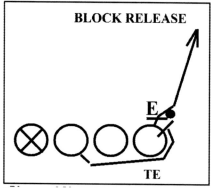

Diagram 4.21

Pattern Drill

The next phase of the practice for the receivers is pattern drill. You have patterns specific to the tight end and specific to the spread end and will work on those in this particular drill. You are trying to teach precise route running and are not necessarily working on releases. You are also not necessarily working on catching the ball. What you want to do is teach the receivers the proper depth, the proper footwork, the proper cut, and not have them mix and match other drills at the same time. You could work the release, the pattern, and catching the ball, all three at the same time. That drill is done often and is called passing with backs, or four-corner drill, or any type of team setting such as skeleton. The receivers get all that work in those periods, but, in this drill, you are going to work on just the pass pattern and precise route running.

Tight End Routes

Waggle Route

You teach the tight ends nine basic routes (Diagram 4.22). The first one is called the waggle route. On the waggle route, you want the tight end to take an inside or down release. You teach no faking in this release, because you do not want the defensive man leaning outside. You want the defensive player to seal down with you so you can log him. You want the tight end to take his down release inside and burst vertically, getting as deep as he can, running right down the numbers on the field. If the ball is snapped from the left hash and the tight end was into the short side of the field, he will inside release, burst vertically to the numbers, and stretch the defense. It is amazing how many times over the course of a season a tight end will run that route, and the corner, who is supposed to be in deep thirds, will come flying up and let the tight end go, leaving him wide open for a possible touchdown shot. You put a cone deep down the field and on the numbers. The tight end has to sprint to the cone. Normally, you put a cone at the depth you want any kind of cut to be made.

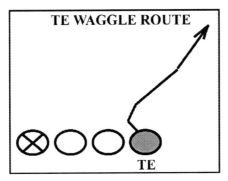

Diagram 4.22

Step and Cup-Drag Route

The second route is called step and cup-drag (Diagram 4.23). This pattern is the backside route of the keep pass play for the tight end. If you need to worry about four rush players coming off the backside, blitzing the backside of the quarterback, you can run keep pass to the spread end side away from the tight end. Then, you can use the tight end as a fourth blocker. The techniques on step and cup-drag call for the tight end to quickly check if either one of the two linebackers drops. He will step with his inside foot, cup back, and check the inside backer to the outside backer. If they both rush, he must stay in. If either one drops, he can go ahead and run his drag route over the center.

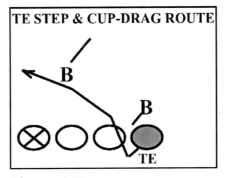

Diagram 4.23

Seam Route

The next route for the tight end is the seam route (Diagram 4.24). This route is run when he has keep pass coming to his side. The tight end takes an outside release, usually a pull step outside release, and climbs to a point seven yards deep and three yards outside his alignment. As the tight end pull releases and gets up the field to that point, he is merely going to bend to the sideline and look over his outside shoulder for the football. The quarterback gets him the ball if the corner reacts to the flat route.

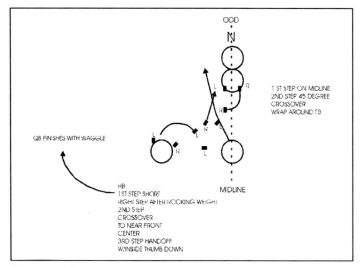

Diagram 4.24

Drag Route

A lot of drags routes are run as crossing routes for the tight ends (Diagram 4.25). When you call tight end drag or any route with the tight end dragging, you usually show play-action to the tight end side and have him drag back across to the other side. In that particular case, you want the tight end to drag on a shallow route and work for a point six yards deep all the way at the opposite sideline. If the defenders are reacting to play-

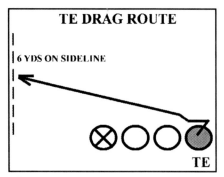

Diagram 4.25

action, they usually overrun the tight end, and, by the time they realize it, he is wide open in the opposite flat. You can use any kind of release and encourage the tight ends to use their fake releasing and so forth.

Hook Route

The hook route is similar to a spread end's curl route, which you also teach to the tight ends; therefore, you need to differentiate between the hook and the curl (Diagram 4.26). On the hook route, the tight end is on the backside of a play-action pass. You feel comfortable with releasing the tight end and do not need him to block. On a hook route, you are going to release outside. You will take a pull-step release and get vertical. You burst vertically to a point 14 yards down the field and then hook up. If the ball was snapped from the hash mark, and the tight end was into the short side of the field, you want him to get as wide as the numbers and then hook up and slide to an open area. If you show play-action away from him, he is on the backside for the quarterback and is almost always open.

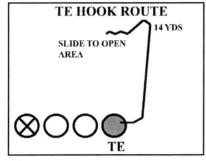

Diagram 4.26

Crossing Route

You use the crossing route for a tight end when he is on the backside of waggle or for the counter bootleg play (Diagram 4.27). On this particular play, You want him to take an inside release and do not care how he sets it up, because you are not trying to log the backside of the waggle. The tight end takes any kind of release he wants, but he has to release inside. He can combine pull release with fake, down release with fake, swim, or whatever. But, he needs to release inside and get vertically down the field as fast as he can. You would like him to be between the two hash marks. He works to the area somewhere between 10 and 15 yards deep, where he is behind the linebackers. If a free safety is in the middle of those two hash marks, or any safety, or any rotated defensive back in the middle, he breaks it off and stays in the middle of the two hash marks. You do not want him to cross the hash mark and work to the outside of the field. If no safety is in the middle, you tell him to run right down through the middle of the field and be the deep threat. If you throw the ball back, this pass should be a touchdown shot.

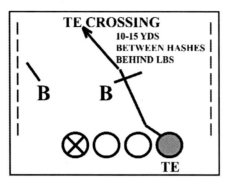

Diagram 4.27

Hitch Route

You teach the tight end a hitch route (Diagram 4.28). He has a lot of hitch routes in the offense, especially if you are running a smash combination. The tight end will basically burst off the line of scrimmage. When he gets to six yards of depth, he just turns and faces his numbers to the quarterback. Other ways exist to coach the hitch, but this way is very simple and direct.

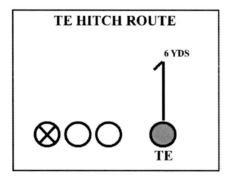

Diagram 4.28

Out Route

For the tight end, the out route can be run at 12 yards back to 10, if you have a quick tight end (Diagram 4.29). On a later-developing pass play, you can run it at 16 back to 14, or 14 back to 12, whatever times out best with your quarterback and receivers. Normally, when you do the out, you have the tight end in a flexed position. He is either flexed from the tackle or spread from the tackle, using spread end rules in a wide receiver stance. You are going to burst up the field, try to get the corner to turn his shoulders one way or another, and then break back to a point 12 yards deep. As you make this break, you want to lean forward into the cut, accelerate your arms as if you are going to go deep, and then plant and break. He also could run speed outs, where he does not come back to the ball, but simply rounds it off and tries to go full speed through the route. At this point, a lot of out routes are coming back, in the traditional sense.

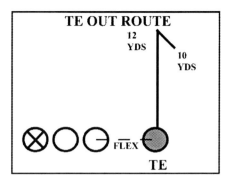

Diagram 4.29

In Route

Last, but not least, you teach the tight end an in route (Diagram 4.30). Basically, it is a route anywhere from 14 to 18 yards deep, depending on how it times up with both the speed of your tight end and whatever passing action you're using. In this case, the receiver can go straight down the field and break to the inside. When he gets to his landmark, anywhere from 12 to 18 yards, he breaks flat across the line and is basically running away from any man coverage. As he breaks across, he settles in any hole in the zone he can find. Something similar is called a dig route. At 10 yards, you have the receiver fake to the post, and, then at 18 yards, he breaks back across the field. You get the corner to back up, work to the middle, and then break away from him, creating separation to the inside.

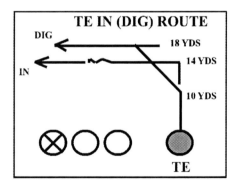

Diagram 4.30

Spread End Patterns

Post Route

The spread end has nine basic patterns, as well (Diagram 4.31). They're obviously different and usually done from the wide receiver position. The first one is the post route. The spread end will take his split, and, as he pushes vertically about 12 yards, breaks to the post. Most of the post routes are skinny. You want them to be a vertical cut, not really flat, where you come across to the middle of the field. In fact, what you would really like to do is split the area between the corner and the free safety as they backpedal into thirds. You want to stay away from the free safety. The spread end post route is going to split those two defenders. You want him to stay outside the hash mark when he runs a post.

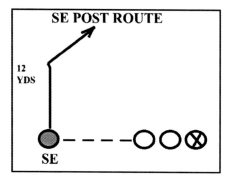

Diagram 4.31

Out Route

The out route can be 12 back to 10, 14 back to 12 (Diagram 4.32), 16 back to 14, or 18 back to 16, whatever you want to teach, based on the timing of your play and the speed of your end. You want to capture one of the shoulders of the defensive back and get him to open his shoulders one way or another. You usually push vertically to a point about 14 yards and then break back to 12. In the last few years, a lot of mileage has been gotten from out routes. The quarterbacks get adept at throwing that particular pattern, the receivers run the pattern very well, and you get a very high completion percentage with out routes. One of the favorite combinations is off waggles, keep passes, and counter bootlegs.

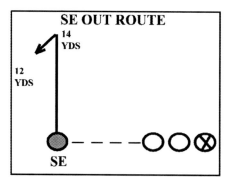

Diagram 4.32

Fly Route

One of the things to always insist on is, if you run a fly route, you want to release outside the corner at all times (Diagram 4.33). No excuse exists for releasing inside the corner. If the corner is pressed right up in your face and you are assigned to run a fly, then you must take a pull step outside release to get outside him. You want to get to a point six yards down the field, get the corner to lean one way or the other, and then burst outside of him. Obviously, getting him to lean to the inside is best. Somehow or another, you want to get his shoulders turned or get him to squat his feet (fake hitch) and then release to the outside of him, bursting north and south up the field.

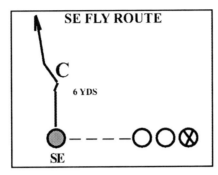

Diagram 4.33

Dig Route

The dig route for the spread ends is the same as the tight ends, in terms of the route depth (Diagram 4.34). You want the receiver to sprint to 12 yards down the field, break to the post, and, at 18 yards, once he has the corner really running with him, break flat across the line of scrimmage. If it is man coverage, he will run away from the man. If it is zone, he will sit in the open areas of the zones.

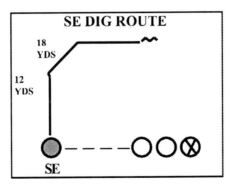

Diagram 4.34

In Route

You also teach the spread end to run an in route (Diagram 4.35). The depth can be anything you want it to be—14, 16, or 18. You are going to push north and south, then break flat, parallel to the line of scrimmage, and burst away from man coverage. Or, if it is zone, as you break across the field, you will find the open zone and sit in it.

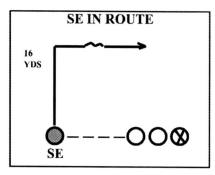

Diagram 4.35

Angle Flag or Q Route

On the frontside of the counter bootleg play, the spread end has been running what is called an angle flag route (Diagram 4.36). The angle flag is a push vertical, about four steps on a 60-degree angle, and then a burst deep to the numbers. Recently, a route called Q route has been introduced, which is similar to the angle flag. You want the spread end to burst vertically for about 12 yards. Somewhere around 12 yards, you want him to stick and step inside. He can head fake at the same time. But, it is just one step to the inside, which is all you want. You want him to basically push off his left foot, stick step inside, plant his right foot, then roll over, and just bend the pattern to the area somewhere around 20 to 22 yards at the sideline. As he looks over his outside shoulder, that action bends his shoulders enough so the quarterback can get the ball in there. Normally, in order to hold the corner, someone will be in the flat when you run the Q. Some people also run the post corner, where they come down, break to the post, and then break to the corner. The Q route pretty much does that for you, but faster, much faster, using the slightly different technique of a stick step inside, roll over back outside, and burst.

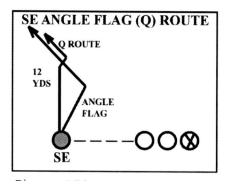

Diagram 4.36

Slant Route

The slant route can be run off a three-step drop and also off the trap-option pass action (Diagram 4.37). You are going to come off the line of scrimmage and attack the outside shoulder of the corner, trying to create width. When you get to six yards, you are going to make a skinny break. You want to break on an angle about halfway between 45 degrees and 90 degrees. So you can call it a 22-degree angle if you want, but it is halfway between a 45 and a flat break. You will gear down in the open seam and run away from man coverage.

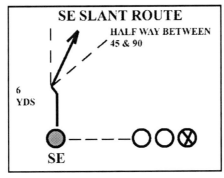

Diagram 4.37

Curl Route

The curl route is very specific (Diagram 4.38). You are going to split about 12 yards between the spread end and the tackle. You do not want to be oversplit on the curl route, because you are going to threaten the flat with another one of the receivers. On the curl route, for the first two to three steps, you stem slightly inside. Then, you break vertically up the field. You want to really burst and to run like you are going to run a fly route. At 12 yards, you are going to plant your outside foot and come right back down the stem of the route. Once you start down the stem, you can slide to an open area, if you need to do that, in order to be in a good passing lane back to the quarterback. Normally, you simply come right down the stem of the route. If the corner is going to really sit on this, then, in combination with the curl, you can run a route called stutter, where at 12 yards you stutter your feet, or basically gear down, and then burst on the fly. The stutter and the curl route work hand in hand.

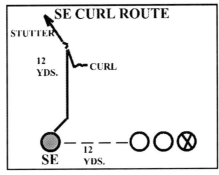

Diagram 4.38

At 5 Route

The last route is called an at 5 route (Diagram 4.39). If you are going to put your spread end in a split alignment four to six to eight yards from your tackle, this route becomes a valuable alternative on the backside of waggle. The spread end will step down as if he is going to sweep block for just one step. Next, he climbs vertically to a point about five yards up the field and then becomes the crossing receiver, just as the tight end was on the backside of waggle. He will start down the middle of the field, and you want to keep him right between the middle of the two hash marks. If no safety is between the hash marks, he is going to split the hashes and go right down the middle and deep. If a safety is between the hashes, somewhere between 10 and 15 yards he breaks it off and stays between the hash marks, not crossing the hash marks to the outside of the field.

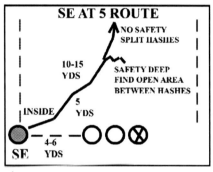

Diagram 4.39

Ball Drills

As you notice when you go through this practice plan, the receivers work on releasing off the line of scrimmage in a separate drill. They work on patterns in another drill. And, then they work on ball drills, which is another type of drill. Those drills are really what comprise the three parts to running a route: the release, the pattern, and the actual catching of the football.

The ball drills discussed in the following sections are nothing revolutionary. All of you who have been coaching for quite a while probably have lots of different ball drills that you do, and they are probably the same as these. Or, maybe you have some different ones that you prefer. But, in any case, these drills cover the fundamentals you need.

Tuck and Cover Drill

The coach pairs his receivers up, with one football for every two guys he is working with (Diagram 4.40). You tell the receivers to throw the ball at all different strike points.

You want them to throw the ball right at their partner's face, over their partner's right shoulder, over their partner's left shoulder, and at their partner's numbers. They should throw it low, throw it low to the right, and throw it low to the left. You work on catching the football in all those different ways. They just play catch. It is that simple. But, you want them to concentrate on the fundamentals of catching the football. You tell your guys that the only catch made with their thumbs together is the ball coming at their upper body, straight down the middle. For all the other catches, you tell them to put their pinkies together and turn their thumbs out, so they are not fighting the ball or pressuring the ball away from them. You also emphasize the fact that as soon as they catch the ball, they have to tuck it away. Then, if contact is going to occur, they can cover it up. Those points are the three most important you try to accomplish in this drill: catch, tuck and cover, and catch the ball at different strike points. You do not want the receivers to always catch the ball in one place in this drill, because this repetition makes it really too easy on them. You want them to practice making those catches away from their body and down low. A lot of times in games, the ball will come and is not going to hit you right in the exact strike point that you expect.

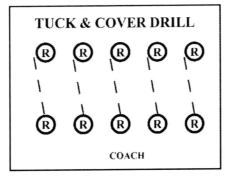

Diagram 4.40

Bad-Ball Drill

The next drill done with the receivers is called a bad-ball drill (Diagram 4.41). Many ways exist to set this up, but what you do is have a line of receivers standing one behind the other. The coach will be back five, 10, or 15 yards away, whatever he deems necessary in terms of the length of the throw. Each receiver takes off across the field. The coach is going to throw them a bad ball. You want the ball to be thrown low. You want the ball to be thrown high. You want the ball to knuckle by taking the ball, holding it at the back tip, and throwing it with a locked elbow. The receivers really have to concentrate on catching it. The first guy runs across the field and catches a ball from the coach. Next, he runs over to the other side of the drill. Then, the next receiver will go. You can get a lot of reps on a lot of bad balls in a short period of time by doing this drill. A five-minute period is provided for bad-ball drills every day, and you can get at least two bad-ball drills per five minutes.

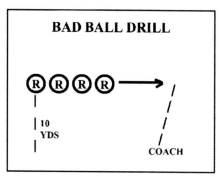

Diagram 4.41

Break-Point Drill

Two things to mention about this drill are, first, you do not work on the release, and, second, you do not work on the pattern. All you are doing is putting receivers in the place where they would have finished their pattern and then having them accelerate to the football from what is called the break point. You are going to throw them the ball and work on the fundamentals of catching the football. If the ball is in the upper body, right down the middle, you will catch the ball with the thumbs together. If the ball is away from the body, up high, you try to catch that ball with the pinkies together and the thumbs spread out. What happens is, if the ball is away from your body and you put your thumbs together, when the ball hits your hands, it tends to bounce off your hands and away from your body. Whereas, if you turn the thumbs out, then the ball hits your palms and tends to bounce back toward your body.

One-Handed Catch Drill

The next drill focuses on the players concentrating so intensely that they can catch any football with just one hand (Diagram 4.42). You will throw the football over their shoulder, about where you want the fade ball to go. You can throw the ball up and over and try to hit the outside shoulder. You can also throw a ball on more of a straight trajectory and have the receiver work on bringing that ball in with one hand. But, the important thing here is, as many times as you do it with your right hand, you probably should do it twice as many times with your left hand, if you are a right-handed receiver—and vice versa, if you are left-handed. The line of receivers will go straight down the field, the coach will throw the ball in that direction, and they can work on catching the ball with just one hand. Then, the next guy goes, and the next guy goes, until you are finished. As the receivers wait, the coach will run down quickly and throw the ball from that end down their way. At this point, the receivers are working with their left hand. The coach moves around, but the receivers do not have to move around. You save time in your drills and are not wasting time. This method goes back to the racehorse practice philosophy.

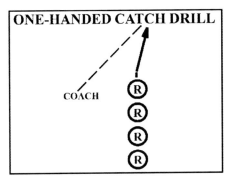
Diagram 4.42

Turnaround Drill

In the turnaround drill, you simulate a man running a route (Diagram 4.43). He turns around quickly, and the ball is already on him. He has to focus, catch the ball, and get it tucked away, all within a relatively short period of time. You hear many coaches talk about throwing on the break. If the quarterback goes back, sees the receiver break, and lets go of the ball, if he has some strength to his arm, that ball is going to be traveling before the receiver can get his eyes focused back to the quarterback. In that situation, the receiver must have fast focus, good concentration, and the ability to get the ball tucked away when it is right on top of him. Sometimes, the quarterback will see a receiver is going to be open. He will be getting pressured in the pocket and will need to get the ball off a little bit early. Because of this, you must have your players trained to get their head snapped back around, to get their eyes trained on the football, to focus, to concentrate, and to get the ball locked away. The receivers are facing away from the coach. The receivers have their backs to the coach. You will tell them whether you want them to turn over their right or left shoulder. You want the receiver to snap his head around and get his shoulders around as quickly as possible in whichever direction you are working on. You work equally on both directions. The coach is going to give the command as he lets go of the ball. The ball is in the air by the time the receiver gets his head and shoulders snapped around. You usually do this drill from about 10 yards apart.

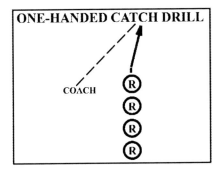
Diagram 4.43

Comeback Drill

In this drill, the receiver is going to come back to the coach, or the quarterback, and catch the ball on the way back to him (Diagram 4.44). You take the release and the route out of this drill. All you work on is the actual coming back to the quarterback. You have heard a lot about receivers running a route with coverage on them, having to turn around, and coming back to the quarterback, so their numbers face the quarterback (so the defender is behind them) and their body seals the defender from the throw. You can be open with guys close to you, as long as a man isn't in the throwing lane between you and the quarterback—assuming the quarterback has pretty good zip on the ball and can get the ball there with confidence. When the receiver gets his shoulders snapped around, what you want him to do is be able to come back to the quarterback. If he just turns around and stands there, the defensive back can then react through him to the football and swat the ball down. If you have pushed the coverage enough to make a good cut, you make the break, and, as you see the quarterback, you come back to him, you then have a chance to keep the separation between you and the defender, or, at least, keep your body between the ball and the defender. The receivers are about 10 yards away from the coach. The receiver who is going to catch the ball takes a step forward to simulate the last step in his pass pattern, then plants his foot, and comes driving back to the coach. You want him to come right back down his stem toward the coach and are going to throw him the football. You can have him plant his left foot and turn back over his right shoulder, or plant his right foot and turn back over his left shoulder. Once the ball is tucked away, you want him to burst up the field. You do not want to get into the habit of catching the football and stopping. You want to teach your players to avoid that bad habit. It is really important that, as each kid catches the ball, he tucks it away, covers it up, turns, and bursts up the field. You put a line of cones about 10 yards up the field, so he has to break all the way past the cones. The cones help the receiver get used to catching the ball, turning upfield, and running. You do not want your players catching the ball and falling to the ground, or catching the ball and slowing down. Once they have the ball in their hands is when the action should begin.

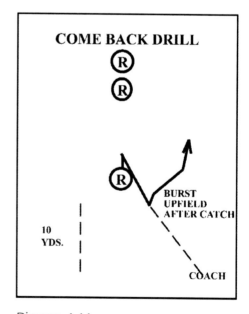

Diagram 4.44

Sideline Drill

In high school and college, you only need to have one foot in bounds when you catch the football (Diagram 4.45). You teach the receivers the same drill the pro coaches teach. You learn to do a little tap dance on the sideline. For a number of reasons, you are going to teach them to keep both feet in. If they are concentrating on it, one foot for sure will probably stay in, maybe even two. You will have a lot of receivers make catches, right at the sideline, with both feet in bounds. Another reason is, if the receivers ever do make it to the pros, they will have already been trained in those techniques. You know sometimes a receiver is going to catch the ball on the dead run, get one foot down, and step out of bounds. But, if this technique is coached into them thoroughly enough, they will tap dance on the sideline and try to keep both feet in. Sometimes, keeping both feet in is not possible. It is not always possible at the pro level, either. But, you are going to work on it right from the very beginning of their freshman year, all the way on through their career. You set a receiver who is going to catch the ball about five yards away from the sideline and have the extra receivers lined up right behind him. You take the final step of the route, one step forward, and then break back toward the line of scrimmage toward the sideline. The coach is going to throw the ball, simulating a quarterback throwing the ball on a comeback or an out. The receiver will catch the football and try to tap dance right on the sideline, keeping both feet in and catching the ball. Sometimes, they even drag their feet and fall down as they are catching the ball and trying to keep both feet in bounds. You like to get each receiver four or five throws on two different drills every time you do a ball drill period.

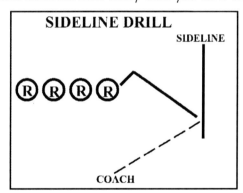

Diagram 4.45

Distraction Drill

This drill is good because it forces the receivers to concentrate, which is a big help, especially if they are going to be trying to catch the ball in a crowd (Diagram 4.46). The distraction drill can be set up many different ways. One of the easiest ways is to have two receivers serve as the distracters. The line of receivers is going to run straight across the field. The coach, from about 10 yards away, throws the football right between the two distracters. The distracters, only two to three yards apart, wave their arms, jump up and down, and put their hands between the ball and the receiver's eyes to disrupt his concentration. As the receiver runs across the field, he has to focus on the football, keep his concentration on the football, and not allow those players to be any kind of a distraction to him at all. As he catches the football, he goes across to the other side. Once the receivers are done running in one direction, then they start from the other side and run in that direction, and you throw the football. Here, they are looking over their left shoulder instead of their right shoulder, as they run horizontally across the field. One variation is to have two lines of receivers on the opposite sides of the field and have both run across in opposite directions. You throw the ball to the back receiver, and the front receiver acts as a distracter. You try to simulate those game day situations as much as you can.

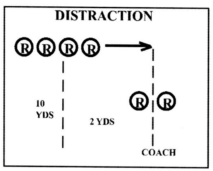

Diagram 4.46

Gauntlet Drill

The final ball drill is called gauntlet (Diagram 4.47). Here, you really try to make the receivers concentrate on catching the football. You do that by trying to strip the ball, trying to knock those receivers down, anything to cause problems for the receiver. In this phase of the drills, you are working on making sure each receiver has caught the ball and tucked it away. As he turns up through the gauntlet, you try to do everything you can to get that ball out of his hands. You have two lines of receivers forming a gauntlet, or a tunnel, with the receiver turning up into that gauntlet. The players in the gauntlet are going to strip him, bang him with hand shields, and bump him. They are going to do anything they can to try to make him lose the football. You put the receivers really close to the gauntlet. As they start to run, the coach, from about 10 yards away,

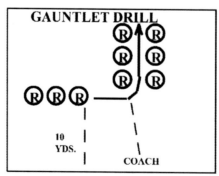

Diagram 4.47

will throw the ball at the first line of gauntlet defenders. As the receivers come across, they catch the ball and have to turn up immediately into the gauntlet. This drill gives them good practice at turning up the field and getting the ball tucked away quickly, so it does not get stripped.

Those drills are the basic ball drills. They are not revolutionary, and you as a coach have come up with even better ball drills than these. But, these techniques are what you want the receivers to concentrate on when they catch the football: catch, tuck and cover, get upfield, come back to the quarterback, keep their feet in bounds, concentrate on the football when they are getting distracted, and keep the ball tucked away when they are getting swatted, stripped, bumped, and everything else. You do the drill five minutes almost every day of the whole year. When you first start doing it in training camp and then again the first day of spring practice, you allow 10 minutes for the period, so your coaches will have plenty of time to introduce all these ball drills to the players and get reps on it. Shortly thereafter, it becomes a five-minute drill.

Passing with Backs

The last part of the individual portion of the receiver practice plan is called passing with backs (Diagram 4.48). Passing with the backs concerns the receivers and the running backs getting together with the quarterbacks and running pass routes. This drill can be an individual or a group drill. You do it at least once a week each way. You can have more than one drill going on at the same time. Sometimes, you can have as many as four different drills going on at the same time, where the quarterbacks are just dropping back and throwing a certain route to a certain type of receiver. If you want to get a lot of work on throwing the out route to the wide receivers, you will have one quarterback do that. Possibly, another quarterback will be working on throwing to his tight end the corner route, the angle flag, or the crossing route. You just give them one route at a time in that particular setting.

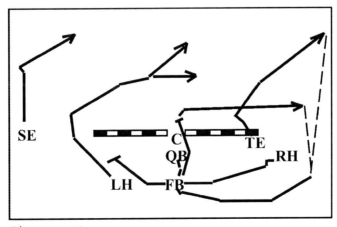

Diagram 4.48

You should also try to do a lot of group work as well, where the entire backfield and the ends run through what they would do on a certain passing play. Take, for instance, the 129 waggle, where you fake the sweep to the left and the quarterback keeps the ball and bootlegs out to the right. In this case, the tight end is going to take a down release, go vertically, and get deep on the numbers. The split end is going to run a skinny post and stay outside the hash mark on his side. The left halfback is going to run the crossing route, where he can split two deep or break across the middle. The right halfback is going in motion, faking the sweep, and then blocking the backside of the quarterback. The fullback is going to block the linebacker, if he is a blitzer, and, if not, he is going to slip out into the flat. The quarterbacks come up and call the cadence. All the backs and the tight ends run the pattern. One thing you can do to spice up the drill a little bit is put a free safety in for the quarterback to read, or else put some corners in and have them just back up or come forward. As a coach, you can direct what you want the defensive backs to do, so you can also control what the quarterback is going to see in terms of a read and who he should be throwing to. You tell the quarterbacks when they do this drill that, if you repeat the same pattern, they should not throw the ball to the same guy twice. You want the quarterbacks to keep mixing up their throws so they get practice at throwing all parts of a particular play.

5

The Wing-T Offensive Linemen

This chapter will deal with every technique an offensive lineman has to use in the offense. You will begin with the qualities to look for in the linemen, position by position, beginning with the offensive center. The offensive center is first because, in this offense, you put the best people down the middle. You need a strong, athletic center, just like your quarterback and fullback. A football team is similar to a baseball team. In a baseball situation, you want to build strength up the middle—your pitchers, catchers, middle infielders, and center fielders. Those people are vital to the operation of your baseball team. It is exactly the same with the wing-T. You want to have a strong center, a very good quarterback, and an outstanding fullback in this offense to make it work as effectively as possible.

As you look for the desired qualities in the offensive linemen, you go through several testing procedures. You test the players on any skills to get useful information. You use the same combine workout the NFL scouts use. You will test all players in their height and their weight, their bench press, their 40-yard dash speed, their vertical jump, their broad jump, their 20-yard shuttle times, and the list goes on and on. You test them in about as many areas as you can come up with, areas you think will give you useful information on the athletic abilities of your players.

Once they have finished the tests, you take all the big men and look at their test scores. You find out which ones are the best overall athletes. Those players are candidates to play center. Often, you have two or three different players who can play center. The second opening for a big man is at tackle. Next come the offensive guards, who don't have to be big, but do have to be among your best athletes. As a clarification, saying the best big man plays center means he should be one of your finest athletes, in terms of his test results, who is also a big man. He is the guy you are going to put at center. The guards should be very good athletes, without respect to size, although, clearly, the bigger they are the better it will be for the offensive line.

Centers and the Snap Technique

You must first teach the center the proper hand-up technique. You can take anybody and teach him the snap technique used in the wing-T offense, so the center doesn't have to be someone who has played the position before. Regardless of his experience, in time, he will learn to execute the snap technique properly. The best way to illustrate this point is through the following example: if I were at a clinic lecture someplace, in front of a large audience, I might pick out somebody who has played football, yet has never snapped the ball before in his life. In front of all those people, I could teach that person how to snap the ball in a little over five minutes. In short, the techniques to teach your players are both easily learned and easily taught at every level.

You want the quarterbacks and the centers to work every single day on the hand-up technique, which is what most people refer to as the quarterback-center exchange, or, just simply, the snap. The snap technique is the most important skill in football; after all, nothing else will happen if you do not snap the ball correctly. You teach the quarterbacks to put their hands straight up in the air, with their fingers pointing vertically north and south. They then turn their hand a quarter turn to the right, if they are a right-handed quarterback, or a quarter turn to the left, if they are a left-handed quarterback. The V between the thumb and the forefinger should point straight up to the sky. You want to take the hand and bring it down so the hand is parallel to the ground when you stick your hand under the center. If you do that, you should be able to take the snap with one hand and not use the left hand, if you're a right-handed quarterback. The quarterback is going to be only wrist deep under the center.

When you teach snap progression, you teach a three-part progression to the center snap. The first thing you do is get the quarterbacks to hold the ball exactly the way they want it to come from the center. When the ball comes up the quarterback, you would like him to receive the laces in his hand, in order to get the ball into a passing grip as quickly as possible. You want the fat of the ball between the V of the thumb and the forefinger and want the quarterback to have his hand on the back half of the football. This positioning is exactly how it should come up from the center.

No turn happens during the center snap. The center does not snap the ball and turn it as he snaps it. He brings the ball straight up. You describe this motion with the center's hand as the same motion he would use if he were down in the basement and had to turn on a light bulb with one of those cords hanging down that turns the light bulb on. The center is going to grab the cord and pull it. That movement is what the center's arm and hand should take as he delivers the ball. As he brings the ball from the ground, he brings it straight up. The first few times centers do this their forearm will snag right across their thigh and their thigh will bruise a little bit. But, the bruising subsides quickly, and they learn how to handle it.

The three-part progression works like this: you have the center down in a good offensive lineman stance. The first part of the progression is called the fit. You want the quarterback in a fairly narrow stance. You want him to be only wrist deep under the center. You do not want him any further than wrist deep under the center. You want him as upright as he can get. A slight bend will be at the knee. The quarterback will take the ball and get in his good stance. He will hand it to the center, who then takes the ball from the quarterback and brings it down to the ground in the opposite motion he would use to snap. He gets the feel of the ball, of where it should be, as he hands it to the quarterback. He reverses the trajectory of his arm motion back down to the ground. After he has done that, he passes the ball back around to the side. The quarterback will take the ball again, put it in the good grip in which he wants to receive it, and pass it back to the center, who will again take the ball and bring it back down to the ground. The important point here is that the center must get a feel for where that ball has to come when he brings it up to the quarterback. You will repeat this hand-up as many times as you have to, until you feel the center has that motion down.

The next part of the progression is called the six-inch snap. In this part of the progression, the center will take the ball and snap it to the quarterback. He is going to snap the ball from somewhere around his knees, at least six inches off the ground. At this point, the quarterback just directs the center in terms of where that ball came back. The quarterback will tell him the ball did not come back far enough or came back too far. It is too far to the left, too far to the right, turn to the left, turn to the right, or whatever that direction might be. The quarterbacks really need to know how they want the ball, and your best center coach, a lot of times, after a few years in the program, will be your quarterbacks.

The third part of this progression is the full snap. At this stage, the center will use all his fundamentals. You would like the ball stretched out as far in front of the center's face as possible, because that stance gives the offensive line room, where the defense has had to back off. The center knows how the ball needs to come in, because you did fit. He knows how the ball should snap when he snaps the ball and how it should feel as he brings it up to the quarterback. You should be able to execute this snap in a short period of time, as long as you have coachable people. When fumbles occur, the quarterback and the center need to communicate. If a fumble ever happens in a game, you give both players minuses, regardless of whose fault it was, because those two need to communicate with each other.

Offensive Guards

Your offensive guards will actually have a lot of fun playing in this offense, because they get to pull, trap, block down, kick out, and lead the backs on the sweep. The wing-T is not the kind of offense where your linemen either go straight ahead or straight back all day long. In this offense, your linemen have a lot of fun because they get to do everything. They really get to showcase their talents and their abilities.

The offensive guards must have good coordination. They must be able to pull and also to maintain their body control and balance as they pull. Many athletic movements are involved in the offense, and the offensive guards must have good body control and must be fine athletes. They have to be big enough to block down on a defensive lineman. Sometimes, people think you can put the 5'9", 160-pound kid at offensive guard. Maybe that choice will work in high school, but it certainly will not work in college. Many times exist when guards have to block on or block down against some big football players in college football. Consequently, guards have to be at least big enough to block down on a large-size defensive lineman.

The guards also have to be fast enough to pull out on the flank and lead a swift running back on the sweep or on an option play or the quarterback on the waggle. The guards must have good athleticism to be able to pull and lead those backs on the sweep. The average center in a league weighs about 250 to 260 pounds. He is usually at least 6'2". The offensive guards in a league are actually big people. They are usually in the 6'3" range and about 270 pounds. In high school, you are not going to have those kinds of kids. You cannot recruit players to play with. Therefore, you are going to have a mixture of different body types on your offensive line. Putting your best big man at center, your quickest big man at left tackle, and then your best line athletes at offensive guard is suggested.

Offensive Tackles

The offensive tackles are the big linemen in your offense. They are the players who are going to be asked to block down on defensive tackles or block straight ahead with on technique on defensive tackles. They must have considerable size to play this position. You put your best line athletes at guard and then take your big men and find out who is going to be your center. The rest are tackles. Your quickest tackle needs to be on the left side, assuming you have a right-handed quarterback; on the right side, if you have a left-handed quarterback. You want to be able to protect the quarterback's blind side. If he is your best athlete, you do not want him to be taking a lot of blind-side shots.

You want that guy to play 11 games. The tackles are your largest people. They do the least amount of pulling, yet they do some pulling. You do cross-train all of your players to play all positions. Therefore, they must be athletic enough and must have quick feet to be able to execute those pulling assignments. Also, more important, they must be able to execute a gap or a down block, where they have to step down inside and cut off penetration, or block down on a defensive tackle who is lined up inside of them. The offensive tackles are great angle blockers. They must be able to block down on angles. You will always try to scheme so the tackles will be able to block on angles as often as you possibly can in the offense.

Offensive Line Practice Plan

The next topic to discuss is all the techniques taught during the offensive line practice plan. Many of these skills will be repeated by other position groups, because blocking and shoulder skills are taught to all position players.

Shoulder Skills

The first thing you do during practice with the offensive linemen is shoulder skills period (Diagram 5.1). Using sleds or coming out from chutes and boards and doing those kinds of skills instead of shoulder skills is fine. Wanting to combine them is fine, too. Some coaches do use the sled at times and then will use chutes and boards next year, at times. But, the first thing you do on the first day of every practice and training camp, spring ball, whatever, is teach shoulder skills.

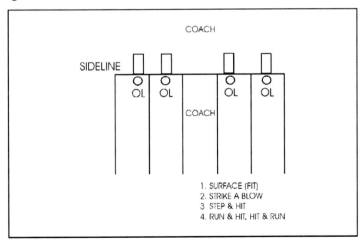

Diagram 5.1

Four parts make up this blocking progression. The first one is called surface, which is nothing more than a fit drill. You do the surface drill from a six-point stance. Some fundamentals in blocking are emphasized all the time, namely, keeping the defender between your legs, having your chest on your thighs, keeping your butt over your heels so you do not overextend, and finishing your block by swinging the tail. The six-point stance means your hands, knees, and feet are touching the ground. An important coaching point is the toes should be flat and not curled underneath the feet. You do not want to curl the toes underneath the feet because, if you do that, as the blocker strikes, his knees will lift up off the ground and you will not be emphasizing rolling the hips.

Surface merely means you are going to fit these men into the bag. This drill involves no contact and no strike. You are going to have them form a good blocking surface and fit themselves into the bag. When you block, you drive your forearm and shoulder through a bag. You do not want to block at the man; you want to block through the man. As you make contact, the blocking surface includes the side of the neck; the front of the shoulder, all the way down to the elbow; the front of the forearm; the fist right next to the pec; and the pec. As you make contact on a block, you explode and drive that surface through the bag. During surface, you are going to fit these young men into the bag and make sure their surface is correct. You cross-train all of the players on all the techniques, and you mass teach, meaning you structure as many drills as possible so all the players are working at the same time. Therefore, many players get a chance to do a lot of reps. The players learn more by doing than they do by watching. You are going to try to get as many of them in a drill as you can at the same time.

Using all of the offensive linemen, you have one bag for every two players. You line all the bags up on the sideline, going right down the line, and the blockers are lined up on the inside of the field. The bottom of the bag should be intersected by the white yard line. All the blockers are facing into the bag. The coach can stand back and look at his linemen from behind. From behind them, he can see what kind of strike angle they have. He can make a lot of corrections from this angle. The coach can then come around to the front and can watch their eyes to make sure they are looking where they are supposed to be looking. You do all of these drills on the first sound. You do not waste time with a whole bunch of cadence during practice; you get more reps without doing it that way. You do the drill with one shoulder, and then you repeat the same drill with the other shoulder. After that, the blocker gets up and holds the bag, and the person who just held the bag will come down and take his turn to execute the blocking assignment. You emphasize some key fundamentals in this drill. You want to make sure the blockers' eyes are up. You want to see them looking up to the sky. The coach can stand in front and can see that the eyes are up, or he can stand from behind and see the other fundamentals. When you are behind, you are looking to see that the blockers have a good surface and that the bag, or the defender, is squeezed between the side of the neck and that blocking surface. You want to get a tight neck squeeze. If you are going to control this defender, the best way to control him is for you to have him between your legs and to squeeze him with the blocking surface and your neck.

You want to see the off arm posted into the ground. It is also very important that you see the hips down and make sure the toes are flat and not curled.

You need to check just a couple of things at the outset of this drill. You want to see that the players are in their six-point stance and also ask the linemen to put their face mask right on the bag. If you are doing this in preseason and are not using helmets, you can tell them to put their nose right on the bag, if you want. You want a direct angle up and down in their knees. You do not want them cocked way back or hunched back on their heels. You would like them to be upright. You would like their knees right under their hips. You do not want their toes curled into the ground.

The second part of the progression is also done from the six-point stance. The second phase is called strike a blow. In strike a blow, you want to do exactly that. You want to really strike the bag and roll the hips through; you want to make contact hard enough so the bag is knocked off the white yard line. You want to have hardness here. This move is explosion. This drill is full speed live, in terms of the hit. At this point, all you are going to do is see if the hips roll through the block. You will do the same drill again, only with the left shoulder. The command to the players would be, "Strike a blow, left shoulder, on sound."

Part three of this progression is called step and hit. This phase is very important to the entire drill because you are true to a fundamental principle in all of the blocks. The linemen get down in their stance. The center has the ball and reaches the ball out in front of him as far as he can. The guards will put their hand down on the center's toes. That position puts the guards back off the ball as far as legally allowed. The helmets must break the plane of the center's belt as he gets down in his stance. That position is legal for an offensive linemen to be in. Because of that distance, contact really is going to occur on your second step.

The one thing you want to avoid is an overelongated first step. You want the first step to be a good six-inch power step, with the second step driving through the defender, or the bag in this case. What you want, and what was mentioned as a very important fundamental in the blocking, is anytime you are going to block with the right shoulder, you are going to take a short, six-inch power step with that left foot. When using the right shoulder, the left foot will step first. When using the left shoulder, the right foot will step first. This fact holds true in all blocks. You begin to teach that principle in this part of the blocking skills or shoulder skills progression. This drill is called step and hit for that reason.

What you do in this drill is take the first step and then drive through the bag. At the beginning of training camp or spring ball, when you take the first step, you ask the players to step and hold it so you can check that their first step is exactly the way you want it. If you are going to block with the right shoulder, you want the blocker to take a short step with the left foot, with his heels replacing his toes. The step should go no farther than this. You do not want the blocker to be overelongated. If the first step is too big, the blocker does not have the proper balance he needs to block. If he gets any contact from the side, he is going to lose his balance. You are going to do the step and hit, and, the first few times you do it, you are going to say, "Set," and they are going to take the first step and hold it. Then, you will say finish or count to two, and, on the second command, the players will block through the bag on their second step. Their third step will actually follow naturally right with them. Another important fundamental in this phase should also be emphasized. You would like the blockers to be as close as they possibly can, every time they make contact, so their chest is on their thighs. When you take the first step, you are not only going to look at the step, but you are also going to make sure the chest is down on the thighs. The reason you want the chest on the thighs is to block at the defender's hip. Defensive players have all their strength in their upper body, but, right at the hip, a man has no strength. He cannot lift weights with his hip. So, if you block him at the hip, you can push him all over the field. An old guy can do it with one hand, so imagine what a big, strong 300-pound guy can do if he really delivers a strong blow at the hip. He can devastate defenders. You do not have to be bigger than everybody you play against in order to devastate them. You can be a great blocker if you use great technique. This drill really starts to teach that technique.

As the season progresses, after you have mastered the first step, then you will just say, "Set," and do the whole block without holding on the first step. When the players get lined up, you want the bag between their legs and about arm's length away. You ask the players to reach out and touch the bag, and that length is about as far away as you want them. That spacing will put you in just about the right spot to take that first step, the power step, and then, on the second step, explode through the bag. The third step will then follow right behind.

When two players have executed this phase of the progression, you switch, and the other two players come over and take their chance. If you have 20 linemen to coach, then you are going to need 10 bags and will put 10 guys right on the line.

The final piece of the progression is called either hit and run or run and hit. These two drills are different. In one drill, you are in close to the bag. You can be at arm's distance away from the bag, the same as in step and hit. When the coach says, "Run and hit, right shoulder on sound," the players then step with their left foot, throw their right arm hard behind them, and drive the bag straight off the ball. To finish the block, they drive the bag for four yards and then drive it four more yards to the right. This drill is hit and run.

The opposite of that drill is run and hit. In run and hit, you want the blockers to be about four yards from the linebackers, or from the bags. You are going to simulate blocking linebackers in this drill. All the same fundamentals will still apply. If you call, "Run and hit, right shoulder," the blockers are going to take off with their left foot. On the fourth step, they will make contact. When you make contact, you are going to drive the bag back, then swing your tail, and drive the bag to one side or the other. That drill incorporates the final fundamental you are looking for. When you say swing the tail, you want to hit the bag so your tail turns toward the hole. You want to finish the block by moving the defender down the line of scrimmage, which is going to create horizontal openings when you run the offense. You want to drive the bags, or the defenders, in a lateral direction. You do not want to create linebackers when you block. If the defender is up close and the offensive lineman is blocking that defensive lineman right on his nose, then, when he makes a great hit and knocks the guy four yards straight off the ball and the defender falls off the block and makes the tackle, all you did was to create another linebacker to stop the play. It is far better to make the block, then swing your tail, and finish the block down the line of scrimmage. At this point, you have created a horizontal opening, a lateral opening, so the hole is much bigger. You are not only going to work run and hit as though you are blocking linebackers, but you are also going to work on finish, so you can now swing your tail and drive the bag in a lateral direction down the line of scrimmage, parallel with the line of scrimmage.

One major problem to avoid is, as the blocker swings his tail around, if his feet come outside the bag, then he is going to lose the defender. The defender will spin out of the block, or step out of the block, and you will have lost it. As you swing your tail, you must keep your feet apart, accelerate your feet on contact, and keep that defender between your legs. This coaching point is extremely important.

One of the things that you will find right in the middle of the playbook is a big section stating you do not teach the head as the initial point of contact. That type of contact is immoral; it is also illegal and causes neck injuries to players. You can rest very comfortably at night, knowing you are teaching a sound, moral, ethical, legal block. You still finish with the hands. You can be up-to-date in terms of hand usage, but, when you actually make contact with a defender, you would like to use the shoulder and really strike the man. The blow is much harder when you strike with your shoulder than when you lead with your hands. The other point is that people who teach lead with the hands are really trying to cover up the fact they are really leading with the face. That philosophy leads to the same problems the NCAA has tried to outlaw. Therefore, you should use the shoulder block, but do use hands to finish. This drill is a great time to demonstrate that.

That long explanation was really for only a five-minute drill once all the players learn how to execute. The first day of practice and the first day of spring ball, you plan 15 minutes so you can walk and talk through it, making sure all the new players learn. But, after the linemen have done this for a while, the drill is cut back to a 10-minute period, and then it goes down to a five-minute period. Once you really understand the drill, you can eliminate the surface phase and only use strike a blow, step and hit, and run and hit, and you can get all three drills done in three minutes. Everybody on the team is going to do this all at the same time.

Daily Routine

The second part of the offensive line practice plan is called the daily routine (Diagram 5.2). In routine period, you teach the stance and are also going to teach what is called bird-dog, which really is the first step you take when you strike or when you fire off the ball. You will teach takeoff in a couple of different ways and will also teach pulling.

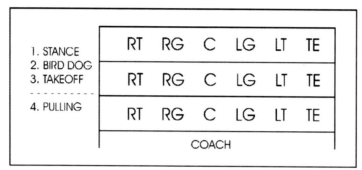

1. STANCE 2. BIRD DOG 3. TAKEOFF	RT	RG	C	LG	LT	TE
	RT	RG	C	LG	LT	TE
4. PULLING	RT	RG	C	LG	LT	TE
	COACH					

Diagram 5.2

If you had three offensive lines, you would take the offensive center and put him directly in front of the coach, facing the coach. You would take the right guard and put him five yards to the right of the center. The left guard would be five yards to the left of the center. The right tackle and left tackle would also align in their positions. Their backups would line up five yards directly behind them. Behind the offensive center, the second-team center aligns five yards away. If you have third- and fourth-team centers, they are each five yards farther away. The same thing holds true for the left guard, the backup, then the extra guys, all spaced five yards back. As a coach, you can stand out in the front of this drill where the center is and see all of your players, all at the same time. If you are doing this, then you are mass teaching. You are teaching everybody on your offense the same footwork, all at the same time. This method enables you to get through a lot of fundamentals in a really short period of time.

Stance

The first thing you are going to do in this progression is teach the stance. This point is very important. You want to teach a parallel stance. Some wing-T teams will put their dominant hand down and their dominant foot back. If you would like to have a perfectly balanced stance, you should not believe in that. You will instruct the offensive linemen to put their feet about armpit's width apart. The wider your stance, the less power you can generate on the first step. One of the things you will have to do as the season wears on is keep reining in your big offensive linemen. You should bring that stance back in, because they have a tendency to get really wide, and you want that stance fairly narrow. The next thing you tell the offensive linemen is to turn their toes in slightly. The reason is, as the linemen get down in their three-point stance, the power angles created in their legs will be locked in. As they get down in their stance and bend their knees, those power angles are locked in. On the other hand, if their toes are pointing out to the sideline and they get down in their stance, the power angles are not going straight ahead. If they turn their toes in slightly as they bend their knees, their feet will often straighten out and point north and south. You want those knees pointing straight ahead. You want to lock those power-producing angles in. You want to create some knee bend, and, as you get down, you are going to bend your knees and bring your heels to the top of the grass so you have a bend in the ankle, a bend in the knee, and a bend in the waist. You are going to allow your players to put their dominant hand down. It does not matter if their right hand is down or their left hand is down. The offensive linemen can have either hand down—whichever one is dominant.

For the tight end, you definitely dictate which hand is going to be down—always the inside arm. When the tight end is on the left side, he has a right-handed stance, with his right hand down; when he is on the right side, he has a left-handed stance, with his left hand down. This point is important because the tight end blocks down and gap blocks so much. You want that inside hand down to facilitate his gap step or his pull step, in order to block down inside more efficiently.

You have the linemen take their down hand and reach out as far in front as they can, without putting any weight on their fingertips. When the offensive linemen are down in their stance, the defense should never be able to identify who is pulling or pass blocking. The defense should never be able to read your stance. Linemen should look the same every time. When you get down in your stance, you want to make sure the defensive linemen cannot read you. In some programs, when the linemen are leaning way back, it is definitely pass or draw. When they are leaning way forward, it is definitely run. You would like to look the same all the time: feet narrow, toes pointed in, and an arm reached out in front as far as possible.

The non-dominant hand is going to lock in. You are going to wrap the wrist around the knee and lock in a power-producing angle. You do not want the off hand up on the thigh pad. You also do not want the off hand down on the knee, because that positioning starts to raise the body up. You want the off hand wrapped around the knee and want to lock a power-producing north and south angle into the knees. This type of stance allows you to make blocks with the chest on the thighs. From this perfectly balanced stance, the linemen can go in any direction.

You introduce this stance on the first day of training camp or on the first day of spring ball. You give quite a bit of time for teaching during this period. The offensive linemen will have the coach talking them through the stance drill for quite a while, until they fully understand what a good stance looks like and feels like.

Bird-Dog

In the first phase of daily routine, you just coach the stance, making sure the players are assuming their proper stance. You do not want to give up on any of these fundamentals throughout the entire season. The second phase is called bird-dog drill. In this drill, you work on exploding into the first step. It is only one step. You coach a bunch of different first steps for your players to take. As they take these steps, they will step and hold, just to see if they are taking the proper first step.

Straight-Ahead Step

The first step is called right foot straight ahead. When you step straight ahead, that step is used for an on block. When you take the first step, your heels will replace your toes. With the foot that steps, that same arm will throw hard behind you. As you step, you are going to step and hold it, so the coach can check all of his players. When they hold, each lineman should have a good base, butt over the heels, not overextended, and the chest should be down on their thighs. If you step with the right foot, you throw the right arm hard behind you. You throw the left arm hard in front of you and look like a bird-dog, out in the field, pointing to its prey.

Once the linemen know what the first step should look and feel like, you will rapid-fire this drill. Instead of stepping and holding, you are going to go three times faster and can hold it on the third repetition, if you want to. You simply practice the first straight step on command, then reset, step again, reset, and continue on command until you freeze the last repetition.

Fire Step

The next step is called a fire step. A fire step means as your feet move, you have your toes pointing north and south, and, on the first step, the toes will continue to point north and south, but the foot will step at a 45-degree angle. This step relates to what is called a fire block. You practice taking a fire step and hold it, bird-dog it. It does not take long for the coach to correct all of his guys once they actually know what they are doing. Players who have been in the program for four or five years really know what they are doing, so, at that point, the coach doesn't have to correct anybody.

Reach Step

The next step to work on is called a reach step. On the fire step, you went on a 45-degree angle and the toes stayed north and south. On the reach step, you step at a flat 90-degree angle, with the toes still pointing north and south, which keeps your shoulders also pointing north and south. During this drill, as each player steps to the right on a flat, lateral 90-degree angle, his toes are still north and south, and he still has his bird-dog position, with his chest on his thighs. Then, you will go reach step left on sound, step, and hold it. Obviously, a reach step ties into the reach block. When you get to teaching the reach block to your players, you will use the first step, which is called a reach step.

Pull Step

The next step is the pull step. The pull step relates to many of the blocks. You can be pulling on the trap or to lead on the sweep. You can be pulling to gap block a defender who is lined up inside of you. As you take a right pull step, the lineman steps with his right foot. He basically picks his right foot up and puts it back down again, but his toes will point directly to the sideline. The most important coaching point is that the backside foot must pivot at the same time. As you step with your right foot, the right arm throws hard behind you, in order to help the backside foot pivot and help generate momentum for the pull step. As the puller throws that arm hard behind him, he gets his shoulders turned, gets his backside foot pivoted, and gets his shoulders facing in the direction he needs to go.

When practicing the pull step, you are going to take the first step and hold it. One good way for a coach to check this footwork is to stand to the side. However, instead of running all the way over to the side to change positions, the coach can tell his players to face the sideline. What the players will have done, then, is turn around in their stance; you will have saved a lot of time, and the coach will not have to run all the way around the field over and over. The coach can check to see if the players' back foot pivots or not. He can check to see each player has his right arm hard behind him and is in the bird-dog position. The players' left foot should be pivoted all the way around. Both feet should be pointing to the sideline. When you take that step, instead of being right on the same yard line, the right foot can actually step back a little bit so, when the lineman pivots his right foot, he has a little distance between his feet and has a little bit better base between his feet and under his body.

Those four steps are worked on most often during bird-dog period: straight ahead, fire, reach and pull. If you can master those four steps, most of the blocks will come off those four steps for the first step of the block. During daily routine period, stance was the first phase and bird-dog footwork was the second. The third phase is called takeoff.

Takeoff

When you do takeoff, you can do it in any direction. You can go straight ahead, pull right, pull left, fire right, or fire left. When you do takeoff, the linemen, as you say the command, will sprint five yards as fast as they can. They will slow themselves down for the next five yards. They are going to run 10 total yards, but they are going to explode out of their stance for the initial five yards. As you do this, you always tell them to take off with either their right foot or their left foot. You want to see them explode out of their stance with the correct foot. If you do this enough, it becomes second nature. At first, you might have to think about it a little bit, but, as you do it and repeat it, it will become second nature to your players. These drills take a long time to explain, but, on the field, it is 10 minutes during the first practice, is five minutes during the second practice, and stays five minutes all the way through training camp. By the time the season rolls around, this period is only three minutes. Your coaches can go fast, checking the stance, bird-dogging the four types of footwork, taking off whichever way you need to take off, and doing the pulling drill.

You do takeoff drill two different ways. You can explode out of the stance and sprint or can have the linemen do a thing called duck walk, which simulates keeping your feet apart as you drive a man off the ball. The first thing you always do is just take off straight ahead on sound. All the linemen are in a good stance. All are going to take off with their right foot on sound straight ahead. After all the players have gone in one direction and have gone 10 yards, sprinting for five and decelerating for five, they are going to turn around and face the other direction. You, as the coach, have to move down to the other end of the field, and, at this point, they are going to take off with the left foot on sound. Then, you should be back in the original position you started in. Next, you repeat the drill, emphasizing the duck walk. The players have been taught to keep their feet apart as they make contact and drive the defender. All of them will be practically duck walking as they come out of their stance with their feet apart. This drill is necessary in order to keep the defender between the legs.

In the next portion of the same drill, you can work on another step. As you repeat the drill again, your first step now is going to be a pull right step. Again, sprint five yards and decelerate for five. Then, return using a pull left step. You can also work on taking off and using any kind of footwork you want—straight ahead, fire, reach, pull, whatever you need to see as a coach. You do it rapid-fire and do it fast, because, as a coach, all you have to do is be able to see the footwork you want to see each day.

11-Step Pulling Drill

The last thing done in daily routine is called an 11-step pulling drill (Diagram 5.3). When the players do this drill, they take 11 steps. Actually, they take 10 steps and, on their eleventh step, are getting back down in their original position. You walk the linemen through a pull technique where the linemen pull flat, work up the field as if they are going to wall off or log block, and then come back to the same spot they lined up in. You walk the linemen through it about one time, so they can see what you want. Then, you sprint through the complete sequence. You do not want to have the linemen walking through this and counting steps the whole year, because you can make robots out of them. You do not want to do that in the 11-step pull drill.

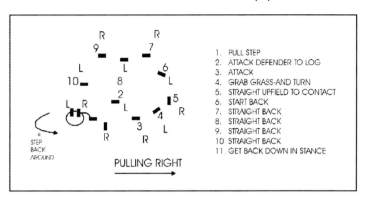

Diagram 5.3

If you are going to pull to the right, simulate a log block, and come back to the original position, with the eleventh step being nothing more than getting back down in your stance, it is a 10-step drill. The first step is a pull step to the right. Take the step and hold it. On the second step, you are going to attack the man you are logging. The third step continues along the same path. On the fourth step, you reach down, grab grass, and want to dip the shoulder. The fourth step is where contact occurs. It occurs with the inside foot and the inside shoulder making contact. Step five comes straight up the field. You simulate swinging your tail and starting to finish the block as the off arm comes into play. On step six, you bench press and start to turn the defender. Step six also starts each lineman back to his original position, followed by seven, eight, nine, and 10. Then, you simply turn around and get back down in your stance, which is the eleventh step. You do the 11-step pull drill to the right, then do the 11-step pull drill to the left. You are only going to count this for the player once; after that, you are going to run through all 11 steps at full speed. The first step will be the pull step on sound, two, three, four, grab grass, five turns vertically up the field, six starts you back from where you came from, seven, eight, nine, 10, and 11 is merely getting back down to your stance.

In summary, the daily routine period includes checking the stance, making sure the stance is good; bird-dog, firing out for the first step and holding it; takeoff with any step you need, sprint for five, decelerate for five, and turn around to go in the other direction; and the 11-step pulling drill, the final phase.

Blocking Technique Period

The next part of the practice for the linemen is called blocking technique period. You have two different types of blocks. The first type is called a single, or individual, block, and you have five of them. These blocks are 1-on-1 blocks performed by a single player. The second type of blocks is combination blocks performed by more than one player. Each of these different types of blocks begins with one of the first steps already taught and relates specifically to one or more particular plays in the wing-T offense.

Individual Blocks

On Block

The first block is called an on block (Diagram 5.4). This block simulates a defender lined up directly over the top of an offensive blocker. You are going to simulate the defender with one of the big bags at first and then a body after that. The first three days of camp, you use one of the big bags directly in front of one of the offensive blockers and on the line of scrimmage. When you say, "On right," you are blocking with the right shoulder. You are going to finish the block, the defender, or the bag flat down the line of scrimmage, parallel to the line of scrimmage to the right. Of course, the opposite is on left. The technique to emphasize is, if the blocker is going to strike with the right shoulder, then he must step with the left foot. As you strike the man, you begin to swing the tail, keep the man between your legs, and then take him in a flat direction to the right, down the line of scrimmage. On left means to strike with the left shoulder, drive the man in a left direction, and take your first step with your right foot.

Diagram 5.4

At first, you use the big bags. You will get two blockers, along with two linemen holding the bags. The blockers are all on one side, and the bag holders are all over on the other side. As a coach, you can be on either side. You want to be able to look at the blockers from behind and also be able to look at them from behind the defender. You can watch how the players come off, can see their eyes, and can see if their eyes are correct. The blockers will be down in a three-point stance. They are about an arm's distance from the bag. You begin by blocking on right, meaning you take your first step with the left foot, strike with the right shoulder, swing the tail to keep the man between your legs, and then drive them to the right. You ask both players to bring the bags back. The blocker and the bag holder pick the bag up and bring it back together. At this point, the man holding the bag gets a chance to come over and be the blocker. Once the blocker has finished on right and on left, he then goes over and holds the bag for the other man to block. When the blockers finish, they hold the position of their block so you can tell, as a coach, if they have the good blocking fundamentals that you taught during shoulder skill period. Once your players understand what is expected of them, they should be able to execute on block right and left. Once their partner executes it, they can go on to the next block. You can get a lot of blocks done in a relatively short period of time. Once training camp really gets going or the season gets going and you do not have to wear shorts and T-shirts anymore, then you won't block the bags anymore. You will bring the defensive people down and will actually block bodies that move. Blocking bodies is actually a much more realistic drill to do than blocking bags all the time. But, the bags are a great place to start because they allow you to emphasize the technique, and, if a blocker uses that same technique when he blocks a live body, then he is going to be a great blocker.

Gap Block

The second block you teach is called gap (Diagram 5.5). It is a very important block and is used to cut off penetration. In this drill, it is very important the man holding the bag lines up in the neutral zone. You want him even with the blocker, as if a defender just penetrated the line of scrimmage. You want him in the position he would be in if he were directly in the gap between the blocker and the next adjacent offensive lineman. It is important to have the bag in the neutral zone so the blocker has to pull step flat down the line, get his head across the front of the bag, and finish the block down the line of scrimmage. When you draw blocks, you draw the shoulder surface and draw where the head is, so the blockers know which shoulder to block with. You actually make contact with the right shoulder when gap block to the left. It is just the

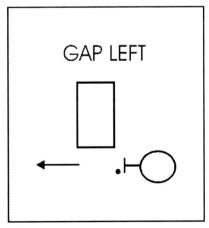

Diagram 5.5

opposite when you block gap right. In that maneuver, you pull step with the right foot, block flat down the line of scrimmage, and finish the block in the direction to the right. You teach the players to get their right ear across the front of the defender's belt buckle. Even though you are going to pull step and gap block, you still want the defender to stay between your legs. The gap block means you are going to be blocking with your head across the front of a defender and will be pulling inside, toward the line of scrimmage or toward the football. As a wing-T coach, you are going to see a lot of opponents try to penetrate the line of scrimmage against you, so this block is very important.

Down Block

The next individual block is called the down block (Diagram 5.6) and is used when blocking a man lined up inside of you. The defender is lined up over the adjacent blocker inside of you. This block could be a tight end blocking down on the man over the tackle or a tackle blocking down on a man over the guard. It could also be the center blocking back on a backside defensive lineman or the guard blocking down on a noseguard. You use down technique only when you know the defender will not be a penetrator. If any question exists as to whether or not the defender might penetrate, you use the pull step and a gap technique.

Diagram 5.6

When you are blocking down, your head goes behind. When you block down left, you are going to make contact with the left shoulder and your head will go behind. As you make contact, you swing your tail and finish the block right down the line of scrimmage, creating a lateral opening in the defense. On down right, the blocker would be on the left side of the bag, would block in the right direction, and finish the bag to the right, parallel to the line of scrimmage. One thing about the down technique is, if you are going to block with your left shoulder, in order to keep all of the fundamentals in place, you want to be able to step with the right foot and block with the left shoulder.

Therefore, when you down block, as you step with the right foot, you will get up on the ball of the left foot, and the left foot will actually pivot a little bit so you can take off and make contact with the left shoulder. Contact will occur on the second step. Notice that the fundamentals you learned in shoulder skill period are right in place and carry forward to technique period.

Fire Block

If you recall, the fire step is a 45-degree step with the toes pointed north and south. The fire step relates to the fire block (Diagram 5.7). This block is executed when you want to block a man who is lined up on your outside shoulder. On fire right, the defender is on the outside shoulder of the man blocking to the right. The first step is a 45-degree step, with toes still pointing north and south. On the second step, you are going to drive the inside knee and the left blocking surface—the forearm and the shoulder—through the inside of the man, right down the middle of the man. You are initially going to knock the defender back on a 45-degree angle, swing your tail, and take the man back to the inside, if you can. Most important, you would like to see a good, hard strike on this fire block. It is going to be a left shoulder block when you block fire right. The other important thing to emphasize is when you fire block, you are going to lower your strike point. Instead of the hip, you are now going to block on the thigh pad. You are going to bring the strike point down just a little. A lot of times, you will be firing out on a linebacker four yards away, and that strike point will lead to an opportunity to possibly cut the linebacker. You are allowed to do that in college football. As a high school coach, even if you block at the thigh pad, you should be okay. If not, use the hip as an aiming point.

Diagram 5.7

When blocking fire right, you will have the bag on the right shoulder of the blocker. The first step is a fire step. The second step is the contact step. On the second step, you want to drive the inside knee and blocking surface right through the middle of the man. You want to drive the knee right through the crotch area and drive the left shoulder right through the defender's outside thigh. Finish the block. Bring your third step, begin to swing the tail, and take the bag in the opposite direction.

Reach Block

The final individual block is called the reach block (Diagram 5.8). You have already taught the reach step during bird-dog drill. The reach block relates to the reach step. On a reach block right, you will reach step with the right foot. A reach step means you step at a 90-degree flat angle with your toes pointed north and south. After the first step, it becomes a fire block. Your first step is a reach step, and, after that, you are executing fire technique. The bag needs to be placed at least in the gap between the blocker and the next adjacent blocker. It really should be placed over the next adjacent man to the outside. If the blocker is a right guard, the bag should be placed over the right tackle. If the blocker is the right tackle, the bag should be placed over the tight end. If the blocker is a center, the bag should be placed over the right guard, when you reach right. If the blocker is good enough, he can take a reach step, execute fire technique, swing the tail, and take the defender back inside. But, if you can execute the reach block by getting squared up on the defender, getting the man between your legs, and driving him by maintaining contact, then you have done a heck of a job as an offensive lineman.

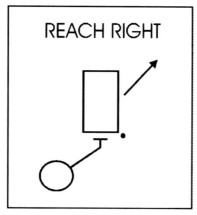

Diagram 5.8

The reach block concludes the five individual blocks. They are the 1-on-1 blocks. They are the first blocks that you teach. They are essential to everything you do. Other blocks exist, like trap and log, that you could teach as individual blocks, but you get those blocking techniques in the combination blocks.

Combination Blocks

Cross Block

The first combination block taught in the wing-T offense is called cross block (Diagram

5.9). You will notice when referring to combination blocks, the blocks are 2-on-2. You have a blocker, another blocker, a bag directly in front of the first blocker, and another bag directly in front of the second blocker. Cross block right means the man on the right is going to use down left blocking technique. He will block with his left shoulder, his head goes behind the defender, he swings his tail, and he takes the bag in the left direction. His first step is with his right foot. The blocker on the left, who is the inside blocker, is going to execute trap right. He is going to take a pull step to trap or can take a slight drop step, depending on how much width he needs in order to get this cross block executed. Then, he will work up into the line of scrimmage, inside out, with his head behind the defender. As you make contact, you swing your tail and take the block directly down the line of scrimmage. It is essential that the blocker blocking down left finishes his block parallel to the line of scrimmage, while the blocker blocking trap right also finishes his block parallel to the line of scrimmage. You are trying to create a lateral opening in the defense so you can run through a gaping hole with your offense. To execute this in practice, you are going to use four reps. You will cross block right. A blocker blocks down left, and the other blocker blocks trap right. Then, you come back, and the blockers switch sides. At this point, the man who was on the inside comes over and blocks down left. The man who blocked down left moves to the inside and blocks trap right. Both guys get to execute both techniques—the down and the trap. After the two blockers have had their turn to execute it, then the two players holding the bags come over and take two shots each at blocking the cross block.

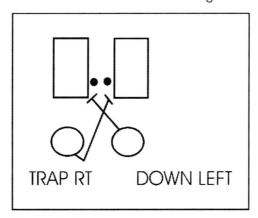

Diagram 5.9

The opposite of this block is cross block to the left and takes four more reps to get through. You are looking at a total of eight reps to get all the players to do each skill from both sides. If you cross block to the left, the man on the outside, or the man on the left, would block down right. The man on the inside would block trap left. In a cross block situation, if the linemen are split with a two- or three-foot split, the bags, or defenders, are directly in front of each of the blockers. The trap blocker has the responsibility, as the trapper, to adjust to the down blocker. If a collision happens between these two, it is the trapper's fault. The trapper must come as tight off the down blocker's tail as he can, without bumping into him.

Gut Block

Gut block is a combination block with two blockers (Diagram 5.10). It could be a center and a guard, a guard and a tackle, or a tackle and a tight end. When you execute the gut right technique, the man on the outside, the blocker on the right, blocks down left. He is going to hit with his left shoulder; therefore, he steps with his right foot. As he makes contact, he swings his tail and drives the defender flat down the line of scrimmage, perfectly parallel to the line of scrimmage. This block is used when blocking down on a defensive lineman and pulling around for a linebacker. The man on the left blocks gut right. He is going to put his head behind and is also going to block with his left shoulder. He will finish his block parallel to the line of scrimmage. Both blockers will do both skills and then switch, with the bag holders coming over, and both blocking gut right. After that, you work on gut left. Here, the blocking techniques switch. The man on the left blocks down to the right, finishing the block in the right direction, parallel to the line of scrimmage. The man on the right blocks gut left with his right shoulder and finishes his man in the right direction. When you execute this block, you would like the two blockers to line up as they do in a normal game situation where they have a two- or three-foot split between them. You want the first bag directly in the gap or over an adjacent blocker. The first bag will be on the line of scrimmage in the gap. The second defender, or bag, will be stacked behind the first defender, directly behind him. As they step through this block, you want no space between the blockers' tails.

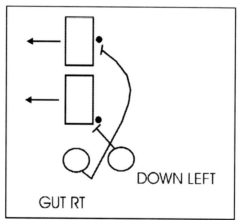

Diagram 5.10

Scoop Block

The next combination block is called scoop (Diagram 5.11). You can scoop to the right or to the left. In this block, you have two offensive blockers versus two defensive players. If you are using bags, the defender on the line of scrimmage will have one of the big bags. The defender who is off the line of scrimmage will have a smaller shield. What happens on a scoop block is one of the two blockers is going to block the defensive lineman on the line of scrimmage and the other blocker is going to come upfield and block what you simulate as a linebacker. When you do scoop, the two blockers are actually going to read and get a feel for the defensive lineman. The outside blocker takes a fire step, a 45-degree step, and his block is called fire right. The inside man is going to block reach right, so he takes a reach step. As they take their footwork, the rule is that the covered man takes a fire step and the uncovered man takes a reach step. These players could be a center and a guard against an even defense or could be a guard and a tackle against an odd defense. They could even be a tackle and a tight end against the 4-3 defense. On the scoop, the outside man takes a fire step. As he does so, the inside man takes a reach step. If the defensive player steps to the inside, then the guard reads his inside foot. If the defender steps to the inside on an angle, a slant, or a pinch, the guard knows he will now take that block over. If the defender works straight ahead, or works to the outside, as the guard takes the reach step, the guard will now climb on a 45-degree angle, right through the inside hip of the defensive player, and cut off the linebacker scraping through the playside. If the defensive lineman slants inside, the inside blocker takes the reach step and then becomes a fire blocker on the defensive lineman as he slants inside. Next, the lineman who took the fire step will climb and go block the linebacker scraping over the top. The fire blocker, as he fires on the way to the linebacker, is going to take his inside arm and punch the slanting defender into the offensive guard to help generate some momentum for the guard's reach technique. Scoop left is the opposite. Here, you have the man on the left block fire left, while the man on the right, on the inside, blocks reach left.

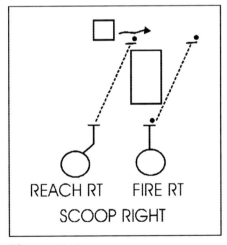

REACH RT   FIRE RT

SCOOP RIGHT

Diagram 5.11

Over Block

An over block is exactly the same as the scoop, except it is more predetermined (Diagram 5.12). This block is used on the backside of an option going away, wide to the flank. An example of this block has the left guard and the center using over block technique on the noseguard and the backside linebacker, with an option going to the right. The center, or the man on the right, is going to take a fire step with his right foot, just as he does on a fire block, except he is going to take his inside arm, rip through the outside arm of the defender, and just climb. If contact happens, you want him to rip through the defender so the defender turns his shoulders. The left guard, or man on the left, executes reach right. He will take the defender over with a little bit of contact help from the outside man, or the man on the right. It is just like a scoop, but it is predetermined that the blocker on the right, or to the outside, is going to go ahead and go to the backer every time. Obviously, the opposite would be over left, which is used backside when the play goes in the other direction. A great coaching point on this block is to make sure the man on the right gets good contact as he rips through the defender on the way to the linebacker. You do not want to avoid contact; rather, you want to make good contact. You want to rip through the defender and really turn his shoulders or open his shoulder for the reach blocker to come through.

Diagram 5.12

Lead Post Inside-Out Block

The last combination block you practice in the wing-T offense is called lead post inside-out (Diagram 5.13). This block is a 3-on-3 block. What you are simulating is a double-team down and trap out. The blocker in the middle will be the post blocker. Going to lead post inside-out to the right means you are going to be trapping to the right. The man furthest to the left is going to pull and trap to his right. He is going to use his right shoulder, his head will be inside as he makes contact, and he will finish his man down the line of scrimmage to the right. This block creates the lateral opening in the defense that the wing-T is trying to achieve. The middle man will be post left. He is going to post with his right shoulder, swing his tail, and then take his man in the left direction. The man on the right is going to block down left. The key coaching point here is the post blocker must not be so strong that he knocks the defensive man off the line of scrimmage. You do not want to do that. You want to create the lateral opening. The post should not be so strong that he knocks the defender back. The other thing is the post is going to step with his left foot; he is going to strike with his right shoulder. As he feels contact from the man to his outside, who is blocking down left, the two blockers, with their tails together, should swing their tails and take the defender down the line of scrimmage. If they get tight to each other, they should keep their tails together and should not get split. When the defensive man splits the double-team, it is because the blockers do not have their tails together. The trapper will pull inside out, trap his man with his right shoulder, and take him in the right direction. One additional point on the lead post: the post blocker and the lead blocker have to be able to pick up their two men on any kind of a stunt. Once in a while, you see a linebacker who steps up in the A gap. If that move happens, the center will come off his post or the inside man will come off his post. He will execute what you call gap technique on the penetrating linebacker. In that case, the offensive guard, or whoever the outside blocker to the right is, comes down on the nose and thus becomes the primary blocker on the nose. This post is known as conditional. You are going to post block the man all the way. You will come off that post only on one condition, and that condition is if the linebacker blitzes inside of you in the A gap. If the linebacker scrapes to the playside and the noseguard loops or angles away from the down blocker, the post should take his block over by himself. He has stepped with his left foot and blocked with his right shoulder. He should have his head inside of the nose. If the nose tries to go in that same direction, he will swing his tail and take the defender parallel to the line of scrimmage and down the line. When that move happens, the down blocker can come down, get a good punch on the nose, and then climb for the backside linebacker, who is scraping over the top. Often, the climbing angle will have to be vertically up the field, depending on the speed of the backside linebacker.

The man in the middle is going to block post with his right shoulder, so he is going to step with his left foot and block with his right shoulder. He is going to block a little bit higher because you want to elevate the defender. This time you will block up in the numbers. You want to elevate the defender so his hip is exposed. The man furthest to the right is going to block down to the left and should be right at the hip. The two of them should swing their tails and take the man straight down the line. The man furthest to the left will block trap to the right. He takes a pull step, adjusts tight off of their tails, and then traps, with his right shoulder inside out to the right.

As you practice this block against the many different looks you see from the defense, you rotate each lineman through each of the blocking positions. The man on

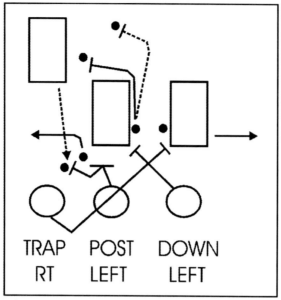

TRAP   POST   DOWN
RT   LEFT   LEFT

Diagram 5.13

the left moves around to the right and will now block lead. When each player has gone through the block three times, then the three players on defense get a chance to come back over on the offense, and they get to do it three times. You want to make sure you repeat this drill three times with each group so they all get to be trap blocker, post blocker, and lead blocker. When you finish, the next thing you want to do is switch the defense (e.g., a defensive lineman covering the man on the left, a defensive lineman on the man on the middle, and a linebacker on the man furthest to the right).

During the blocking technique period, you can practice any of six combination blocks and five individual blocks. Not enough time exists to work on every one of the blocks during every practice. The offensive line coach needs to pick out the blocks his players need the most work on, and those blocks are the ones he should repeat each week.

Pulling Drills

The offensive line practice plan starts each day with shoulder skills. The next thing you do is the routine period. Then, the linemen have a blocking technique period. Next, you work on pulling drills, which consist of a sweep drill, a waggle drill, a gut drill, and a trap drill. You teach all of the linemen to pull within these drills and will cross-train the linemen to play all the positions. A center learns the guard techniques, a tackle learns the guard techniques, and the guard learns how to do all the blocks. Everybody learns everything. You cross train everybody. By mass teaching, you have a chance to do that because you can get so many reps quickly. You teach all the linemen all the techniques for one big reason. You want to be able to play your best five, all the time, regardless of what position they may have started out in. You may go through part of the season with your five best linemen playing, and, then, all of a sudden, your right guard gets hurt. If your backup right tackle is the sixth best offensive lineman, then he has learned every technique a guard has ever had to learn from day one. As a result, your next best lineman can step right in there, and all you have to do is brush him up on assignments, because he has learned all the techniques.

Waggle Drill

In this particular drill, every lineman is a guard (Diagram 5.14). You use a spacing board, which is 16 feet long, one inch thick, and four inches wide. It marks the spaces in the offensive line. It has three dark spots representing the offensive linemen: the first dark spot is the guard, the second dark spot is the tackle, and the final dark spot is the tight end. The board also has light spots representing the amount of split between each position. All the linemen will line up on the first dark spot on the spacing board. You lay those spacing boards on the ground as wide as the center's feet. You have all the linemen in two lines, waiting to play the two guard positions. On each side, two players will be holding a bag or a shield, or just going live with pads. You want to have the first defender in a position where the first guard will pull and log on the waggle. You want to have the second defender in a position where he simulates a corner who has just blitzed off the edge and has started to penetrate the backfield. You can put the two defenders side by side either on the line of scrimmage or off the line of scrimmage, or else you can put them in tandem behind each other or can move them around, depending on what you are going to see by the defense and what defensive problems you are experiencing. Versus a 50 defense, you will have a defensive end on the tight end and a corner or a strong safety who has blitzed into the backfield.

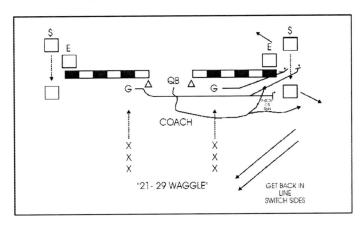

Diagram 5.14

You are going to do waggle drill to the right and to the left and do the drill rapid-fire, as fast as you can, in order to get as many reps as you can. In five minutes, the linemen get a ton of reps. The first way you do the drill is 29 waggle, which means you fake the sweep to the left, while the quarterback waggles to the right. You can do this drill with or without the quarterbacks. The first guard, the right guard, is going to take a pull step on his first step. He will then attack the first defensive player. You coach him that the kick-out angle and the log angle should be exactly the same. The kick-out is going to be with the head inside and with the right shoulder. The log will be with the head outside and with the left shoulder, when going to the right. However, the angle of approach, as you approach the defender, must look exactly the same so a log block appears to be a wrong-shoulder kick-out. As the guard takes a pull step, he adjusts. He is coming on a kick-out angle, but wants to execute log block technique on the defensive end. He will swing his tail and try to take the defensive end back into the line of scrimmage. The first guard is the log blocker. The backside guard is either going to kick out or lead the quarterback up the field. For the backside guard, who is the left guard on 29 waggle, his first step is also a pull step. On his second step, he crosses over for depth. If he is pulling to the right, his pull step will be with his right foot; he will cross over with his left foot to gain about a yard of ground into the backfield; and then he will flatten out and attack the flank. When he does that, he allows the fullback to go in front of him. The crossover step will allow the fullback to go in front of him and block the linebacker or become a receiver in the flat. As he crosses over, that step gives him about two yards of depth into the backfield, because he has already lined up off the ball in his stance. He should be about two yards from the back tip of the ball as he comes across the backfield. From there, he is reading the flank. If you have a corner who has blitzed into the backfield, the backside guard will trap him out, putting his head inside and finishing him on a 45-degree angle back into the backfield. This move is done because you do not want to try to outrun penetration. If the defense has had penetration, even if it is by the defensive end, the first guard will gut and let the penetration go, and the backside guard will kick the penetration out. The quarterback will take his two steps on the midline and begin to attack the flank. If the backside guard has kicked out, the quarterback will step underneath the kick-out and can either run or throw from there. If you get the flank logged, the quarterback can continue on his path, get around the end, and have a good end run. If no penetration happens, the backside guard will listen for a go call, lead the quarterback up the field, and block the next threat showing. That threat will either be a corner or a defensive back. If those defenders have dropped off, the guard can look to his inside for a linebacker scraping on second contain.

You can do the waggle drill with or without the quarterback. The guards pull, while the other offensive linemen are holding the shields. As they pull to the right, the second two guards go sprinting up to the line of scrimmage and get ready to go waggle in the other direction. The coach quickly makes the corrections he sees. The guards who were just blockers on the play at this point grab the shields. They hold the shields, and the two linemen who were holding the shields come to the back and get in line to play the guards next. After that exchange takes place, the next two guards have already sprinted up to the line. Here, the coach calls waggle to the left, or 21 waggle. The next two run 21 waggle, so they go to the left. The first guard pulls and logs, and the backside guard pulls, crosses over, and kicks out. You can rapid-fire the drill. It is 29 waggle, 21 waggle, 29 waggle, 21 waggle, 29 waggle, boom, boom, boom, boom, a lot of reps. If you do the drill this way, you can get tons of reps in five minutes. Every time your guards go, the next time they come to the back of the line, they switch sides so they can be the other guard. All of the pulling techniques are taught like this.

Sweep Drill

The sweep drill has the same type of set up as the waggle (Diagram 5.15). Every lineman is going to play guard. You are going to cross-train again. You have two guards up in position, in the guard spots, on the spacing boards. The cones are now placed two yards deep in the backfield and right on the inside leg of the tackle, which is marked by the second dark spot on the spacing boards. The coach is in a central location. The guards are down in their three-point stance, and the coach says, "21 sweep," or, "Sweep right," or whatever direction he chooses.

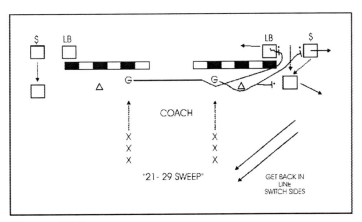

Diagram 5.15

The first guard is going to pull step on a 45-degree angle away from the line of scrimmage. On that step, his eyes go right to his target. You have two players holding shields in the positions where you are going to execute the sweep blocks. If you are playing against a penetrating strong safety or corner, you put the shield two yards deep in the backfield. The first guard is the kick-out guard. His first and second steps are at a 45-degree angle away from the line of scrimmage. His third step flattens out, and his fourth step starts downhill tight off the wingback's block. The wingback is blocking down on the defensive end. The guard is going to work inside out and wants his head inside, whether the defender has penetrated the backfield or he has to go up the field to kick him out. This block is with the right shoulder when you are going to the right, with the left shoulder when you are going to the left. This footwork will allow you to come downhill and get an inside-out path on the kick-out block. If you ever run sweep to a diveback side, it also allows the diveback to get out of the guard's way so no collision happens. If you pull the guard flat down the line of scrimmage and then try to run the sweep to the diveback side, the guard and back run into each other.

The backside guard takes a pull step with his right foot and sprints flat down the line of scrimmage until he gets to the other guard's position. When the backside guard gets to the right guard's position, he is going to gain a little bit of depth so he can step around any trash. The backside guard must not get knocked off by penetration. As he pulls, his eyes go immediately to the playside inside linebacker, and he needs to be ready for the linebacker to be scraping to the outside. The guard is going to come around the wingback's block, or through the first opening he can find in the line of scrimmage, enabling him to cut off the linebacker scraping. The guard is going to wall the scraping backer off, so his head will be upfield, and he will use a left-shoulder block. You want him to finish his block back toward the line of scrimmage.

On the coach's command, the first guards execute sweep right. As soon as they make contact, the coach makes any corrections he needs to make. The two guys who played defense will hand the shields to the two guys who just played offense, and the two guys on defense will, at this point, run to the back of the line and get lined up for their turn to play guard. While they do that, the next two guards have already sprinted up to the line of scrimmage, are in position, and ready to go. The coach says, "Sweep left," or, "29 sweep," and the first guard goes and kicks out; the second guard goes and walls off. While those two are doing that, the next guards run up to the line and get ready to go to the right on the next repetition. Every repetition is rapid-fire in order to get as many reps in as you can. You have taught all the linemen how to play guards on waggle and also on the sweep.

You can do the same thing with any trap play, any gut play, or any kind of play where you are pulling guards (Diagram 5.16). You do the exact same drill and just set the defense up the way you want it. If you were going to run 22 gut, the first guard is going to pull step. He is going to gut around the tight end's block and will be looking for the linebacker, who will be scraping into the off-tackle area. As the guard comes around, he blocks the linebacker with a wall-off technique, with his head upfield and blocking with his left shoulder. The defensive end is the penetrator, which is why you are calling this play. The backside guard pulls flat down the line as fast as he can and kicks the end out with his right shoulder. While the blockers are making the bag exchange, the next guards sprint up. The bag holders come to the back of the line and get ready to be guards. The next two guards run 28 gut to the left. You are alternating right, left, right, left, right, left. Every time the guards get a chance to come back and get lined up they switch sides so they can get a chance to do all the techniques.

Gut right, gut left, trap right, trap left—whatever kind of pulling technique you want to work on for that particular day—can be done in this fashion with this drill set up this way. You generally work on sweep and waggle drill all year long and add trap and gut drills as you need them.

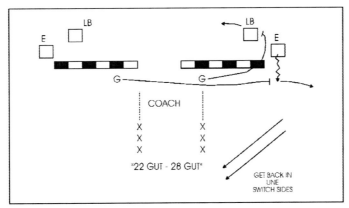

Diagram 5.16

Pass-Protection Drills

Mirror Drill

The next drills you are going to work on with the linemen are pass-protection drills (Diagram 5.17). The first drill is called mirror drill and is done with partners. The partners should be two or three yards apart. When you first do the drill, you have the linemen put their hands behind their back. You do not want the linemen using their hands in this drill yet, because you want them to learn to move their feet. You will start this drill with one blocker in a good pass-blocking position. You want good knee bend, head up, back arched, neck pulled, and the shoulders back. The other player, who is simulating the defense, is going to go back and forth, right and left, and make his partner move his feet and mirror him.

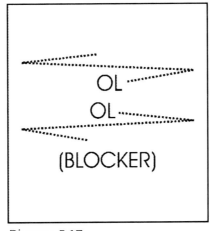

Diagram 5.17

On the coach's command, one partner starts moving right and left and the blocker will try to keep that man between his legs, just as he always does on any block, and slide with him, keeping his feet apart all the time. As they mirror, they slide their back foot first. This step allows them to always have space between their feet. What you do not want is for the blocker to open up and move his front foot first. This move would allow the defender escape avenues behind the blocker. You do the mirror drill with all the offensive linemen facing a partner. You do it with all the linemen at the same time. Then, you switch and the other man comes over, and he gets a chance to do the drill. This drill constitutes the first phase of the pass-blocking progression.

Jam Drill

The second part of the pass-protection progression is jam drill (Diagram 5.18). In this drill, the offensive pass blocker is going to assume a good pass-blocking position, with knees bent, shoulders back, neck pulled, and target with his hands. He is going to block through the picture window created by his hands at his target. The defensive partner will come forward. The blocker will jam one good shot, then recoil, and separate. The defensive man will keep coming. Then, the pass blocker will jam again, lock him out, and ride the defender upfield past the quarterback. You emphasize keeping a good body position, pass rusher between the legs, good knee bend, neck pulled back, all the proper fundamentals you have taught in the other drills.

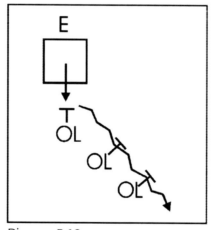

Diagram 5.18

Mirror and Jam

The next thing you want to do is incorporate both the mirror and the jam by combining the first two drills (Diagram 5.19). The offensive blocker is going to get into good position. The defensive man is going sideways and then attacks the blocker, forcing the blocker to jam him. The defensive man can go back and forth, left and right. Whenever he wants to, he can attack forward. Whatever simulates a pass rusher rushing an offensive lineman is what you want this defensive man to do. You will have the defensive man head fake to one side and then go to the other side, and you want the offensive blocker to execute a good jam on him.

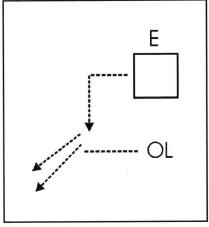

Diagram 5.19

Kick Step

The next part of this progression is called kick step (Diagram 5.20). On kick step, you are simulating blocking a wide rusher coming off the edge. The defender is going to come off the edge as if he is trying to get to the quarterback deep in the backfield. The offensive pass blocker already has the rusher quite a bit outside of him. The key is to intersect the pass rusher without the blocker opening himself up to getting beat inside. The one thing you do not want to do is turn the shoulders. If you turn the shoulders, you open up a clear path for the pass rusher to come inside of you. What you coach is to keep the shoulders square, cut the rusher off by taking an intersecting angle, and keeping inside-out position on him, so if the rusher does come back inside, you are in position to block him. You will do that with a technique called the kick step. The kick

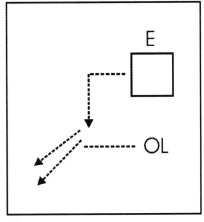

Diagram 5.20

step means you are going to step back and out with the outside foot, while trying to keep the shoulders square the whole time. You might have to kick step once, you might have to kick step again. The rhythm is kick step and slide, kick step and slide. The outside foot will kick step. The inside foot is called the post foot, and the post foot slides. You can kick and slide as many times as needed in order to get the amount of width you need to intersect the wide pass rusher. What you must not do is run way outside the rusher and open up the inside path to the quarterback. You want to keep inside-out leverage as you kick step backwards.

Stunt Pickup

The last part of the pass-blocking progression is called stunt pickup (Diagram 5.21). You use four players to do this drill. You usually teach the offensive linemen to do this against offensive linemen, and then you will do this against the defense live. The two pass rushers can do anything they want. One rusher can go inside, but you have to be able to block him. The other rusher can go outside, but you also have to be ready to block that rush. The two pass rushers can execute stunts or twists. The rusher on the outside, a defensive end, for example, may come crashing down inside; as he crashes, the inside man takes a step forward and then loops to the outside.

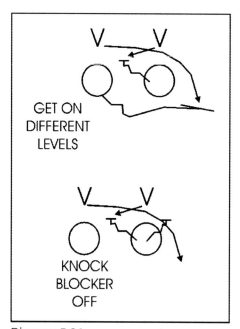

Diagram 5.21

You coach two ways to pick up these kinds of stunts. The first way is to man the stunt, which implies the blockers are going to block their man, regardless of where he goes. In order to do that, the pass blockers must be able to get on two different levels. The tackle has to step back a little bit on the snap and get a little bit more depth than the guard, or vice versa. You also have to be able to switch with your man and not run into each other. One way or another, you have to make sure that the two pass blockers do not knock each other down. If you are a man-to-man team and are going to block man-to-man all the way, then it is really important to get the pass blockers on different levels as they cross each other so they do not pick each other.

The other way to pass block stunts is with zone protection. When you zone, you are going to pass the stunt off. In order for two linemen to zone off a stunt, two things have to happen. First of all, the blocker who sees his man loop must yell the direction of the loop. As soon as he sees the looper go, he must yell, "Outside, outside, outside!" Next, both of the pass blockers are going to block their man until they hear the outside or inside call and until they feel the other blocker knock them off of their man. What happens is, as the penetrator comes down inside, the outside man keeps pass blocking him. As the inside man sees the loop, he yells, "Outside, outside!" and steps right through the hip of his adjacent blocker. He will knock him off and will take the block over, forcing the outside blocker to pick up the loop. Two things are important. One man must recognize and call the loop. Then, he must turn and knock the other blocker off the penetrator so that blocker will know he is to pick up the looper. You must be careful to stop the penetrator first, because you have plenty of time to come off on the loop. The defense does not have to run a stunt. They can pass-rush straight up the field. The pass blockers must always be prepared to block the man on them. They have to block the man on them and be honest about that block until they hear the call and feel the bump. The blockers must not anticipate and leave early.

Mixed Group Work

The final parts of the practice plan for the offensive linemen involve group work and team periods. You have a period called mixed group work, which is essential to the offensive line. Two parts make up mixed group work: running game drills and passing game drills.

Running Game

During the first part of mixed group work, you will run two running game drills (internal and perimeter) at the same time.

Internal Drill

This part of practice is where the offensive line—both guards, the center, both tackles, and sometimes the tight end—work on inside running plays (Diagram 5.22). A set of backs also participates in the drill. The defense has the front 7, or front 8, whatever the front is, with no defensive backs in the drill. What you work on are the internal run plays. You want to go off-tackle and up the middle, for the most part. You might throw a pass once in a while to keep the linebackers honest. You might, once in a while, run an outside play or an option to keep the defense from pitching down inside.

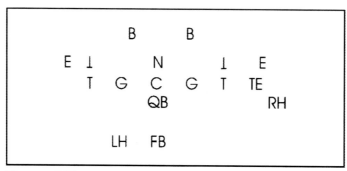

Diagram 5.22

You are going to take the same number of plays and run them over and over again until you get the inside game blocked the way you want. No matter what play you run, you are going to get the internal blocking scheme down, so you can block each front you will see. If you can move the ball inside in this kind of a drill, where the defense knows it is an inside run, then it will be much easier to run the ball once you start mixing it up with the flank and passing games and put 11 people out on the field, when the defense does not know if internal or perimeter plays are coming.

Perimeter Drill

While internal drill is going on, another drill, called perimeter drill, is happening (Diagram 5.23). Perimeter drill is the opposite of internal drill. It contains all of the outside running plays, flank passing, and plays where you want to protect the flank and the quarterback. You run bootlegs, waggles, sprint passes, and the perimeter running game. The defense in this drill has all their linebackers and defensive backs. If defensive ends drop into coverage or also force the run, then you have them in the drill. No defensive linemen take part in this drill, nor do any offensive tackles. Just as in internal drill, where no wide receivers and no defensive backs participate, this drill has no tackles and no defensive linemen. The center can be one of your good centers or not. You can put the noseguard in this drill and then have one of your good centers execute his blocking technique. Most of the time, you will use one of your substitutes to snap the ball.

This drill is going on at exactly the same time that internal drill is going on. Players can rotate every other day or can rotate halfway through the drill. If the drill is 10 minutes long, you can have the guards, the backs, and the tight end switch after five minutes and then do the same thing with the linebackers and the defensive ends.

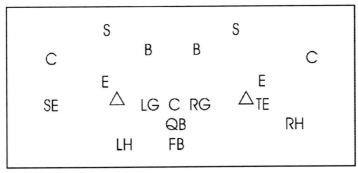

Diagram 5.23

Passing Game

During the second part of mixed group work, you work on the passing game, again with two different drills going on at the same time.

Pass Skeleton

At one end of the field, you will have a quarterback, a right half, a tight end, a fullback, a left half, and a split end (Diagram 5.24). They will be throwing pass routes against the defensive coverage people, including the defensive ends, if they are drop people; the linebackers; and the defensive backs, running whatever coverage you need to see. This drill is called pass skeleton or skelly. You are running routes against the coverages and executing your reads.

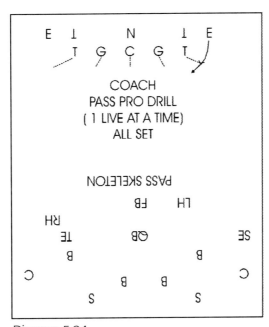

Diagram 5.24

Pass Pro

While skelly is going on, down at the offensive line end of the field, you have a drill in progress called pass pro. You have five interior offensive linemen, all down in their stance and ready to go. You put the defensive players across from them. You might use a noseguard, a defensive tackle, or a defensive end. The coach will stand back and indicate to one of the pass rushers that he is live on the play. Only one rusher is going at a time. However, the offense does not know which pass rusher is live, so they all have to take a good set. All the offensive linemen are working on exploding out of their stance, getting out of their stance quickly, and working on a good pass set. But, only one of them will actually end up blocking a live rusher. It is up to the offensive coach to decide which defender is live. You also incorporate the stunt pickup against the defense by having 2-on-2, 3-on-3, 3-on-2, or any combination you need to see from the defense.

Summary

This chapter detailed everything you do with the offensive line and every technique you teach the linemen throughout practices. You cannot teach them every technique, nor can you use every drill in every practice. What you do is to pick out a couple of single blocks, a couple of combination blocks, and then work those blocks until you feel as though your players have those blocks down pat and can execute them well. Then, the next day, you will go to other blocks you did not cover the first day and pick those up. It is the same thing with the waggle drills or any of the pulling drills—one day using waggle drill or sweep drill, the next day possibly gut drill. The teaching strategy is based on the week's game plan and whether or not you plan to run a lot of sweeps or a lot of waggles. In the pass pro drill, you try to get as much of that work in as you can each day. You are going to do skeleton almost every single day. Mixed group work is something you are certainly going to do all through training camp and spring football. As the season progresses, you do less and less of mixed group work and more and more of team work. Each practice, though, contains these basic elements, all of which clearly reinforce the fundamentals and techniques used in the wing-T offense.

6

Wing-T Game Planning

Coaches put too much pressure on themselves trying to come up with some magical game plan every week, which is not necessary. The plays in this offense have rules. If you block the rules, the plays will take care of themselves. The offensive staff should feel that the most important duty on game day is to make sure you have coaches who are disciplined and assigned to watch defenders. If you are going to run a play to the right, then you count defenders. For all the blocking rules described in the previous chapters, the foundation is counting defenders. You count defenders and then attack #3. If the #3 defender is penetrating up into the backfield, his reaction tells you to run inside him, off-tackle, or possibly farther inside—internal—depending on how #2 reacts. If the third defender is sealing down inside, then you should either be running at the fourth defender or throwing play-action in behind the fourth defender, depending on his reaction. The wing-T offense is a sequence-oriented offense. This offense allows you to say, "If they do this, we will do that." In order to be able to make those decisions, you must be disciplined as a coach and watch the defenders. You should have coaches on your staff who are responsible for watching #3, #4, and #2 all the time. If you have extra guys, you would like them to watch the free safety and the trail player from the backside. The whole basis for making game plan decisions is to watch the defensive players. From that point on, you don't have to be a magician. All you must do is be able to call the companion plays according to the defender's reactions. And, you can really torture a defense.

In this offense, you have three or four base series of plays. If you stick with those base series, watch the defenders, and call companion plays, you will not need anything else. You have the sweep, trap option, power, and belly series. You do not really need anything else. You just make it work. Some companion plays can help you break some keys now and then, but, for the most part, you should be able to make your offense work just by your coaches watching the defenders and their reactions.

Off-Season Film Study

The coaches on your staff do not talk about game plans at all until you have completed an exhaustive, off-season film study. This task involves at least three coaches and probably takes a good five to six hours just to cover the offense for one game film. Clearly, with that kind of effort and time put into it, it is not something you will necessarily do during each week of preparation for each game. As a coach running the wing-T, the other thing you will run into is you may be the only team in your league running the wing-T, which hinders you in trying to learn how your opponents will defend you. When I was the head coach at Edinborough, we were the only team in that league running the wing-T. I always try to be as unique as possible with what we do both offensively and defensively. If a lot of other teams are running wing-T in your league, then maybe the defensive people in your league are getting used to seeing the wing-T offense and also getting better at stopping it. However, your best film and scouting report are going to come from analyzing your own film from previous years. When you exchange films with your opponent, you get possibly three games. Maybe the first two are against I formation teams, and the third one is against a one-back passing team. What did your offense gain from that? You might not have gained anything. But, by studying your own film in the off-season and how the defenses react to you, you can get a good feel for how a particular team is going to try to defend the wing-T.

Play Charts

The off-season film study begins by reviewing and diagramming each play run the previous year (Diagram 6.1). You are going to use one piece of paper for every play run against your opponent in the previous game. Possibly, the first play called was 121, where the quarterback is going to reverse pivot, hand the ball off to the halfback on the sweep, then come on out, and fake the waggle. When breaking the film down in the off-season, you draw in your formation, which is 100. And, then, you draw in the defense you are facing, by jersey number. Do not put E's and T's and D's in the diagram, just jersey numbers. When you put the defense down by jersey number, this practice teaches you a lot of things. By putting down No. 80 on the diagram—representing possibly one of their outside linebackers or a defensive end—you can find out if he is flip-flopping to the wide side of the field or is going to the tight end all the time. You can determine whether he goes to the strength of your formation all the time or into the short side of the field. You can learn many different things before ever having the ball snapped, just by putting the defenders into jersey numbers. You obviously can learn who the starters are and who the backups are. Then, with your game program, you can pretty much figure out if seniors are at certain positions and, since they are graduating, who will be taking their place the following year. You also need to be able to study the individual defensive personnel and how good they are. You need to ask yourself the following: What can they do well? What can't they do well?

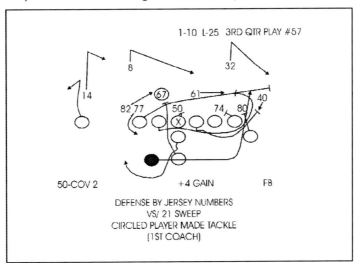

1-10 L-25 3RD QTR PLAY #57

50-COV 2   +4 GAIN   FB

DEFENSE BY JERSEY NUMBERS
VS/ 21 SWEEP
CIRCLED PLAYER MADE TACKLE
(1ST COACH)

Diagram 6.1

The next thing you should do differently from some staffs is not only assigning jersey numbers to all the defenders written down, but also noting every bit of their reaction to the play. You want to get as many reactions for these people drawn in as possible. You want to see who forces the sweep. You want to see if the free safety stays in the middle or not. You want to see how the linebackers key and how they react. You want to know what kinds of techniques the people play up front. This information is readily available to you; all you have to do is go through a game film. You may have to run the play back 22 times to do this. You should not have to, though, because you know who your own people were supposed to block. Consequently, at least, you should be able to begin to draw their blocks in and then start drawing the reaction from the defense. You draw the defensive player all the way to the play.

Just say, for instance, you ran 121 sweep to the right, and No. 67, the backside linebacker, was the guy who made the tackle, because your fullback was not able to get to him coming up through the line. Or, maybe your faking and ballhandling was not good enough to keep him from flowing. If No. 67 flew out of there and made the tackle, you put a circle around his number. That way, at the end of this exercise, you can keep track of how many tackles each player is making against you and who is the biggest nuisance. You can determine who you have to misdirect and who you have to make sure you get blocked. You learn a lot by taking time in the off-season to do this.

On each play chart, a lot of information is around the edges. For instance, you want to write down on the diagram the down and distance. Say that, for this play, it was first down and 10 yards to go; then, you would write, "1-10." If you were on the left offensive hash mark and the wide side of the field was to your right, then you would put an "L" or "LH" for the left hash mark. The next information you want to record is the yard line. If you were on your own end of the field, you would record that as minus (-25); if you were on the opponent's end and going in to score, you would record a plus (+25).

In the corner of the sheet, you put the quarter and the play number. Then, you are able to find plays by the number of the play. Clearly, if it is the third quarter and you have run only 26 plays, you might be in some trouble on the scoreboard. Conversely, if it is halftime and you have charted 38 plays, then you probably have been doing a great job at controlling the football and helping your defense out. At the bottom of the page, you are going to write in what the defense is. If you are seeing a 50 defense with a two-deep secondary, you write down, "50 cover 2." You also write down the result of the play. If this play gained four yards before you got tackled and you did get the play stopped for less than an efficient play, you write down what stopped the play. If the play was efficient, then you only record the result. If you make four yards or more on first or second down, then that play is considered efficient. If it is third down and one and you make two yards, that play is efficient, because you made the first down. If it is third down and eight, you only made six yards, and you had to punt, that play is not efficient. An efficient play makes the first down or the required yardage. For first and second down, the required yardage is four yards per play. If you gain four yards per play, that distance puts you in third-and-short. If you break a tackle, you gain more yards, and then you're down the field quickly.

That information is what you gather for just one play. It takes quite a while to do during the off-season. It usually takes about six to eight minutes per play, sometimes as long as 10 minutes, depending on how well the jersey numbers can be seen on the film. But, you will do that for every play of the game—every single play. One coach's job, while you are watching the film and running it back and forth, is to write this information on pre-made sheets used to record the plays. You can save yourself a lot of time if you can make sheets with the blocks already on them. Down and distance, hash mark, yard line, quarter, play, defense, and any comments you want to make are written on this sheet. You make a block for all those different information items. And, then, you have the center and the two guards and the two tackles drawn in pre-snap. You can immediately begin on each play and try to save yourself as much time as possible. It takes time to do this, and you have to be dedicated and committed to it. But, it is the very best thing you can do to garner information on your opponents. As mentioned earlier, before you ever start a game plan meeting, the first thing to do is this off-season film study, so you can gain as much information on your opponents as possible. This phase is the first of game planning, and it takes a while. You have one of your offensive coaches do this and, while he is busy, have other coaches doing other jobs.

Down and Distance, Field Position Tendency Chart

The second coach's job during off-season film study is to create a Down and Distance, Field Position Tendency Chart (Diagram 6.2). Across the top of the chart, you make a column for all the possible downs and distances you can have. You will have a column for first-and-ten, second down and 11-plus, and then all the second-down yardage situations. You do the same thing for third down. You have a column for third down and 11-plus and all the third-down yardage situations. You also will have a column for fourth downs. If any question ever exists about how many yards to go for a first down, for example, on second and 11-plus, you might put in parentheses that it was for 15 yards. What you have here is all the downs and distances across the top. You write all the field positions down the sides. You start from the opponent's five-yard line (+5) to the goal line, going in for a touchdown, which is called goal line. Say you get the ball first-and-five, and the defense is a 6-5. Then, you will write 6-5 in the box formed by the column for first down and the row for +5 to goal line. When you review this later, this entry reminds you the opponent is in a goal line defense at the five-yard line. You just mark down in each corresponding box whatever you see the opponent run. Obviously, you have no second-and-elevens from inside the five-yard line, so those boxes will be crossed out because it is not possible to do from the five-yard line.

DOWN & DISTANCE/ FIELD POSITION TENDENCY											
	1-10	2-11+	2-10	2-9	2-8	2-7	2-6	2-5	2-4	2-3	2-2
5 TO GOAL	65-1							65-1			GAP 8-1
20 TO 5 RED ZONE	44-1		BLITZ BLITZ	44-1			BLITZ				
50 TO 20 4 DOWN	44-3				44-3		44-3 44-3		44-3		44-1
-20 TO 50 3 DOWN	50-1 50-2 50-3	50-3			50-3 BLITZ	44-3		50-3	44-3		
-5 TO -20	44-3	BLITZ	50-3	44-3		50-3				50-3	50-3
GOAL TO 5 COMING OUT	44-3				50-3						

Diagram 6.2

As you progress down the chart, you have a row for the +20-yard line to the +5, which is called the red zone. You will chart opponents' red zone defenses and whatever they run in the red zone area. You write them in the corresponding blocks. The next area is called four-down territory, from the 50-yard line to the +20-yard line. It might be four-down territory for you, or it might not be. It depends on your field goal kicker's range. Some years, you make this area the +40-yard line to the +20-yard line, depending on your field goal kicker's range and what you want to consider four-down territory that year. The next area, working down the side of the page, is the three-down territory, from your own 20 (-20) out to midfield, or wherever four-down territory starts.

Continuing down the chart, you have the -5-yard line to the -20-yard line. That area is when you are really backed up and really need a first down. At the bottom of the page, the area from the goal line to the -5-yard line is called coming out. In this area of the field, you are talking about plays run from your own goal line to the -5-yard line. This area is when you really need to get off your own goal line, not get sacked in the end zone for safeties, and not have your ballcarrier stopped in the end zone for a safety. You try to run safe plays down here, so you do not turn it over and give the opponent an easy touchdown drive. Those things do happen once in a while, but, if you plan against it, you can minimize it.

What you want to know from this chart is which defenses your opponents were in with regard to all these different field positions and down-and-distance situations, represented by each of the blocks on the chart. When you game plan, you do not necessarily need to plan for all these downs and distances. For example, on second or third down, you may say anytime it is second down and nine-plus, anything higher than nine yards, you know they are going to be in some kind of man-to-man coverage and possibly some kind of a blitz. Maybe their percentage is really high, possibly 90 percent blitz or 90 percent man coverage, when it is second down and nine-plus yards to go. You will take out your game plan sheet, will list second down and nine-plus as an area or a down-and-distance grouping, and, here, can condense and combine the different defenses you see in there. The same thing holds true for second-and-short and third-down situations.

Every week, you may have a different set of guidelines for what constitutes short yardage and long yardage, based on how your opponent reacts. Being able to set up different guidelines is the beauty of doing it this way. You can get better tendencies. If you preprogram defensive tendencies into your own mind, sometimes, you will not be calling the best plays against those different defensive situations. You try to make these charts during off-season. You make 11 of them, one for each of your 11 opponents. You have these charts prepared in advance, and all you do is fill in the blocks as you are watching the films in the off-season.

As you are breaking down the film in the off-season, one coach is doing the play diagrams and one coach is doing the down and distance, field position tendency chart, filling in all the blocks. Here, you are finding out what the tendencies of the defense are. Maybe this week, they play short yardage on third-and-one, and, as soon as it's third-and-two, they don't play short yardage anymore. But, next week, you face an opponent playing short yardage all the way up to third-and-three. Every week, it might just be a little bit different, and this chart helps you tell exactly what the opponent's defensive tendencies are, not only by down and distance, but also by field position.

Personnel, Scheme, Attack, Comment Sheet

Say you have a quarterbacks coach, who also coaches the running backs, and you have a line coach and a receivers coach—those coaches are the minimum you need to coach the wing-T and do it well (Diagram 6.3). If so, you have three coaches working with your offense and have three things to do when you are conducting your off-season film breakdown. The third item you prepare during the off-season is a sheet for comments with regard to scheme of attack, personnel, or any points of emphasis you want to note for the following season. Three columns are on this sheet. The first column is for comments about the opponent's personnel. When you talk about their personnel, you are talking about their starters and backups—the comments you make about their personnel as you watch the film. For example, if you have observed No. 17 backs up the free safety, who is No. 14, you can make a list of all the backups, so you know who is going to take over for any seniors who might have been playing on defense the previous year. If you notice No. 60 was injured against a certain team, you can write that down. You may note that this player, if he has a serious injury, may not be as good next year or, perhaps, might be a defender you don't have to worry about attacking as much. Anything referring to the opponent's personnel you put in this first column.

PERSONNEL, SCHEME, ATTACK, COMMENT SHEET		
THEIR PERSONNEL	THEIR SCHEME	OUR ATTACK
#17 BACKUP FOR #14 FS #60 INJURED VS SDSU #58 BACKUP LB #7 SLOW TO CONTAIN	DE #75 PLAY TRAIL FOR REVERSE DE #77 DOES NOT TRAIL BLITZ IN RED ZONE 17 YD SLANT TO TE 1ST DOWN	BEGIN OFF TACKLE ATTACK LEFT DE WITH OFF TACKLE PLAY FS #10 NOT GOOD DEEP COVER, THROW PLAY ACTION POST

Diagram 6.3

The second column is reserved for comments on the opponent's defensive scheme. For instance, if their backside defensive end does stay home, trail the play, and look for reverses, that information is valuable and needs to be written down. If you see No. 75 on the backside does stay home and look for reverses, but also No. 77 on the other side does not stay home, then you know to run your reverse to No. 77. Another example is maybe your opponent blitzes only in the red zone. Maybe the only time you really have to worry about calling plays to beat the blitz is when they get to their red zone. Obviously, that tendency is another that you need to write down, and many more examples exist. Anything relating to their scheme and how they do things goes in this column. These notes provide wonderful references for the following year, when you once again make your game plans.

The last column is reserved for comments on your attack—in other words, what you want to do when attacking this team. Maybe, you are seeing an eight-man front and decide to begin off-tackle. You decide the left defensive end is the guy you should attack with the off-tackle power play because he is the guy who comes running up the field all the time and does not really squeeze or seal the off-tackle hole. Those items are what you want to know—where, who, and how you should be attacking. Possibly, you observe their free safety is not a good deep cover guy, so you can throw the post in behind him. Maybe, you notice he is a really strong run defender, so you make note of the fact you need to be throwing play-action and need to throw it early and often. Anything you say about the opponent's defensive scheme, your attack, or their personnel goes on this piece of paper. The third coach involved with the off-season film study is busy making notes in all these areas as you break down last year's film.

Along with the off-season film study, you want to compile as many statistics as you possibly can. You want to get as much information as possible about your opponent. You would like to make a preliminary game plan, even in the off-season, in terms of how (based on last year's defensive scheme) you are going to attack them in the upcoming season. You take all of this material, store it in a notebook, and file it away. You save it and keep film studies on your opponents from as long as five years back. When your opponent changes head coaches or a new scheme comes in, you simply empty out the notebook and start over again. Changes have happened quite a bit in our league, so we have had to start a number of new notebooks. At least four different teams in our league have changed coaches while I have been here. Each time, you prepare a different notebook, plus information on any new opponents you might have to play. You save those notebooks, because you never know when you are going to play those guys again down the road. You might meet them in a playoff game or in two years when your schedule changes. Who knows? You keep all that stuff filed. You get all the previous year's film study done in the off-season and keep it until the next year when you have to play them. Then, you can get the notebook out, watch the film again quickly, and refresh your memory from the notes previously made. You can see notes indicating exactly how you thought you should attack them, based on what you saw on film the year before. Obviously, you must now watch the film and see what they are doing differently this year. Have they changed their scheme? Maybe they are now a 4-4 team instead of a 50 team. If this change happens, it does not mean you wasted your off-season film study, because you can still learn a lot from it. You should really believe in it. You do not even consider talking about any game plans during the season unless you have first done this in the off-season. It is an extremely important exercise.

In-Season Film Study

The in-season film study is based upon the information you receive from film exchanges with your opponents for that particular year. The most important thing to look for is the statistical data you can get in terms of what defenses they play in certain downs and distances and key field positions. You use the same type of chart in which you can see the downs and distances across the top and the field positions down the side. You do another fully separate chart. If this year was the 1996 season and you obtained three films on each of your opponents this season, then the information from the three 1996 films you received gets plugged into separate charts. The one you do for yourself in the off-season is kept separate. Thus, you have two different charts. You are trying to accomplish what types of statistics you are going to find from putting all the defenses they currently use into the blocks, into the down-and-distance field position situations. Is it the same as what you saw against yourself in the previous off-season film study? That comparison is the first thing you look for from this year's game statistics. You want to get a true feel for this opponent. You want to know when they are going to blitz. You want to know what their short-yardage defense is. You want to know when they use those short-yardage defenses. You want to know what they do on first down. You want to know what they do on second down and long. These things are what you have to find out. What is their red zone defense? What is their coming out defense? You are trying to find out what types of tendencies they might have for each of these situations and whether they are the same as or different from the previous year's tendencies. You will find most of the really good teams you play against have a defensive package—a basic defense they believe in—and, most of the time, that package is what you see from year to year. But, change-ups are always going to occur. The opponents are going to change or add coverage. They might move their line on you, add a stunt, or add a new blitz once in a while. Thanks to your off-season and in-season film study, you should be able to nail them down. If they are not studying themselves, then you are going to have a tremendous advantage over them. If they are studying themselves and changing things up on you, again, it still goes back to how disciplined you are as a coaching staff to find out how their defenders react on game day and how adept you are at calling companion plays to account for those reactions.

Besides establishing what factors are the same about your opponents from year to year, you also look for differences this particular year. Therefore, you go back to your off-season film study, review it, watch the film quickly, read the comment pages, and look at the statistics you have previously seen. You want to know what is different, at this point. Have they made a new scheme? Are they using a new scheme? Are they blitzing more in the red zone, blitzing less in the red zone, blitzing more on first down, playing more man-to-man coverage? What things are different this year from last year? When an opponent changes from one year to the next, then you are probably going to see what you found in those films leading up to your game. You are going to see the new defense. Many teams go to new schemes and change-up their defense year by year. If they change it up, you are basically going to see that. In that case, your off-season film study was done in vain, except for personnel notes—and, then again, sometimes not. We have one particular opponent in our league who played a 4-3 defense. But, one year, we went up to play them, and, lo and behold, we faced a 6-1 defense the whole game. They beat us. We were caught a little flatfooted by their 6-1 defense, because they had never shown even one single snap of 6-1 defense. They beat us with it that particular day. We did not adjust quickly enough. We thought we could do some things by formation that we were prepared for. It just did not work out. The next year, we had a great game plan, thanks to our off-season film study for that 6-1 defense. When we got the film of this team the following year and started watching all their games, again, they were 4-3 on every snap. We did not see any 6-1 defense. We made our game plan in response to their 4-3 defense, but, just in case, we prepared a small package of plays we thought would hurt the 6-1 defense. We had that package of plays ready to go, if, in fact, they did the same thing to us they did a year before, which was to show 4-3 defense leading up to our game and then play 6-1 defense against us. We were ready for that the second time, and, of course, the second time we beat them, because what we saw is exactly what happened. We got 6-1 defense the whole game. We ended up using the smaller package of plays, but the key is we had that stuff practiced, had it thought out, and had it well conceived in advance. When we saw the 6-1 defense, we simply went to it, stayed with it, and actually had a fairly big day. Those things are what you can gain from your in-season and off-season film study. Again, gather up all the statistics. Find out what is different. Finally, if a new scheme appears, are you going to be ready for it?

Setting up Your Plan of Attack

Once you have all of the information gathered from both your in-season and off-season film study, you are going to figure out how to set up your plan of attack. A basic rule of thumb is used in establishing a game plan. The basic premise is, if the defense is a seven-man front, you want to begin by finding the flank. If it is an eight-man front, you begin off-tackle. How do you come to that conclusion? What you do is take the basic wing-T 100 formation and draw in a seven-man front (Diagram 6.4). You take an imaginary line and draw it through the outside foot of the tackles. Here, you want to count how many people are in the box—how many are between those tackles' outside feet, how many are in the front, and what is the offense's relationship to the defense. You need to know the ratio of defenders to offensive players. In most seven-man fronts, you have five offensive linemen inside the tackle box; with the ends removed, they have five defensive players. You call that equal strength. That equality does not mean any play between those tackles is not going to work. That thought is not true. But, what it does mean is you will begin the attack at the flank by attacking playside #3.

If it is a seven-man front, the defense has four defensive backs. They can either give you a two-deep shell and balance up their secondary, or a three-deep shell and overload their secondary to one side or another. Consequently, you begin the attack at the flank. In other words, find the flank and attack the third defender on the weakest side of their defense. For example, say they put the strong safety over to the defensive right, which is your offensive left. They are going to put that strong safety to the left because maybe the left is the wide side, or maybe the left is the strongside. You have

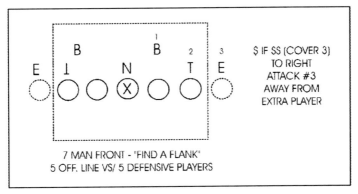

Diagram 6.4

to figure that out by film analysis and also by game-day observation. At that point, what they have done is to put an extra run defender with the front seven to make it like an eight-man front, except they have kept the three-deep secondary in the back row. Probably, your best flank attack is away from that rotated safety, especially if he is up close to the line of scrimmage, because he is an extra defender to that side. Therefore, you will begin the flank attack on the right, away from the strong safety. From that point, you begin to read the reactions of the defenders and adjust accordingly.

If it was a two-deep type of secondary and they were pretty well balanced, you do not necessarily have a strong safety you can attack to or away from, but what you do have at this time is that two-deep look. Versus the two-deep look, what you would like to do is attack where you have the flanking angles. If you had the wingback on the right in a position where he outflanked the third defender, you would probably begin the flank attack by attacking that third defender, whom you have outflanked with the wingback's blocking angles at the line of scrimmage.

The seven-man-front philosophy is, in either case, two deep or three deep, begun by attacking a flank. If you draw that imaginary line through the attackside A gap and count defenders, you can easily determine which defender is #3. You begin by attacking him and then want to see how he is reacting. If he is a penetrator up the field, you try to go off-tackle inside him and find out what #2 is doing. If this third defender is sealing down and is stopping the off-tackle play, then you want to come outside of him. Next, you want to know what the fourth defender does. If he is really aggressive on the run, obviously, the play-action passing behind him should be good. If the #4 defender is soft on the run or slow to react, then you just keep running right at him until you can force him to come up more aggressively. It is a continual cat-and-mouse game all the way through the game. It may look different in the first quarter than it does in the fourth. The third man may be a penetrator up the field. If so, you are going to run off-tackle. But, if #2 is penetrating as well, then you need to go inside of #2 also, with a play from the internal game. If #2 is not a penetrator and is going to seal down, then you will just stay right there, off-tackle, until something changes. In order to do that and not run the same play all the time, you need to have a couple of different plays hitting each area from a different series. As an example, 22, the buck off-tackle play, which can be blocked tag, gut, and power, conflicts with the sweep. The 82 down or 82 gut, in the 80 series, also hits right, off-tackle, and provides another look, another way to attack that same 2 hole, inside the #3 defender. Here, you are not merely running the same play all the time. Instead, you throw in different formations and run those two, three, or four plays—whatever you have—out of different formations. Next, you start using some motion and some shifting, and, before you know it, everything looks different to the defense, even though all you are doing is attacking their weakness inside #3 penetrating upfield every time. It is important to have play packages and have more than one way to attack defenders in a defense. That philosophy was discussed earlier. Begin the attack at the flank, then read the defenders, and find out what their reactions are.

For an eight-man front, you draw the imaginary line through the outside foot of the tackles and count the number of people inside the box (Diagram 6.5). In the eight-man-front game plan, you will split the tight ends a little extra, taking them out to five feet, sometimes six feet, and see how far the defensive ends will come out with you. If the defensive ends are a 7 technique, where they are assigned to play on the inside shoulder of the tight end, you can stretch them a little bit as the tight end comes out. At this point, the defensive end is no longer in the off-tackle box area, so, against an eight man front, you begin the attack off-tackle, because you have five blockers, and they have four defenders in that box. This 5-on-4 gives you a numerical edge, and so you begin in the off-tackle area and go from there. Again, if #3 begins to come back down and seal, even though he might be lined up wide, if he is going to seal hard, here, you can take the attack back to the flank and focus on what the fourth defender does. If #3 stays wide, but #2 starts working out or upfield, then you can go to your internal attack inside #2. It all works together. That basic premise is the beginning for the game plans against those two defensive fronts.

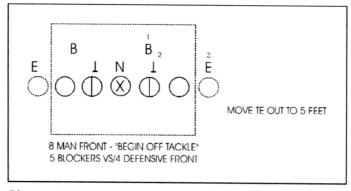

Diagram 6.5

Beginning the attack at the flank or at off-tackle means exactly that—you start there. But, the cat-and-mouse game, or the chess game, between the coaches continues throughout the game. As you get into your game, maybe #3 seals at the beginning of the game, but, by the second quarter, he is penetrating upfield because of how you have been attacking him. At this time, change your focus as a play caller, take advantage of his reaction, and run the ball off-tackle. If the guys on defense are watching them and your staff is disciplined, you will know exactly what plays to call. You just call the companion play and attack the other area, the void area, or the vulnerable area, however you describe it. You do not have to be a genius to make these play calls. You do not have to come up with some magical game plan every week. You can run your same offense from the first week of training camp, all the way through to the championship game, and not have to change anything. You just have to be ready to react to how those defensive people are reacting to you. Again, in order to do this, you need to have play packages, companion plays. If you block the tight end down, you should be able to hit outside of him, or inside of him. If you block the tackle down, you should be able to hit outside of him, or inside of him. Those choices are play packages and can be run with a number of different backfield actions, depending on how the linebackers are keying. You might want to use a certain action one week, rather than another. But, that method is basically how you call your plays: you just watch the defenders' reactions.

Coaches' Game-Day Responsibilities

The coaches' responsibilities on game day will be discussed briefly (Diagram 6.6). As you know, you number the defensive people in the defensive fronts. Consider a 50 defense, for example. Say you are going to run a play to your right. You draw an imaginary line through the attackside, right A gap (or the left A gap, if you were going to the left). Whoever the defenders are outside that imaginary line from the inside out are the defenders for whom you are going to set up your attack. You number them from inside out. The first guy is #1 (usually the linebacker over the guard in a 50 defense). The second guy from inside out is #2, usually a defensive tackle over your tackle. The third player from inside out, probably the defensive end or outside linebacker, is #3. The man closest to the flank, who is in a support position, will cover the pitch on the option, and take the flat or the curl zone in passing—the closest man to the line of scrimmage—is #4. The furthest man in the secondary, or the guy who is going to cover deep in their secondary, is #5.

Who watches these people? You assign #3 to the offensive coordinator. Your offensive coordinator should call the play, because he knows which direction the play is going; he sees the defense and finds out where #3 is aligned. He will watch #3 on this play rather than your own guys, because he wants to know what #3's reaction is. You will know what your own guys do by way of what happens out there on the field.

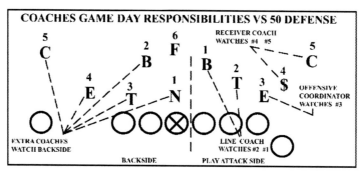

Diagram 6.6

You'll hear all the noise and ruckus. As a head coach, you are in control of the game, also, and are watching your players. But, your coaches cannot be. They must be watching their assigned defenders. Say this #3 is a seal guy who is going to seal down and take off-tackle away from you. You can bring the attack out to #4. Your receiver coach watches #4. You want him to know how hard this guy is attacking the flank. If you run to the flank, how hard is he coming at you? Is he soft, is he hard, is he quick to react, is he slow to react, what is his reaction? You want to know exactly what he is doing. You would also like your receiver coach to watch the fifth guy, as well. If he can see both of these guys, you get a little more information out of it and get a feel for the types of coverages and support systems the defense is giving you. It is important for the receivers coach to see #4, and, if he can, seeing #5 is great. If he can't see both, he must know what #4's doing. If you have extra coaches, then you can assign another extra one to #5 playside. The line coach is responsible for watching #2, so he has to know the second defender's reaction. All this information is being stored, and, between series, you feed all this information into the guy who is watching #3, your coordinator, who then analyzes the information. If the line coach tells him #2 is sealing and he also sees #3 is penetrating up into the backfield, then that information is all he needs to know. He knows you are going to take the attack and go right inside of #3 and run off-tackle. If #2 is sealing, then #3 is sealing, and you then know you must take the attack outside and either go right at #4 with the run or behind him with the play-action pass. As for the offensive line coach, he must see #2. If he can, also seeing #1 is great, because those observations will tell you if they are doing any blitzing, cross firing, or stunting.

The backside of the defense is counted as follows. The first guy is #1, not a zero. If they have a head-up nose, you do not count him or call him a zero; he is the first defender on the backside of the play. As you work toward the backside of the defense, the next defenders outside of the nose are #2, #3, #4, and #5.

As you look at the 4-3 defense, it is still a seven-man front (Diagram 6.7). Depending on whether or not you have a tight end in the game, the defense might show some eight-man-front looks, as well. However, again, say you are going to run to the right. Then, the attackside A gap is the right A gap, between the center and the guard on the right. Counting from inside out, the defensive tackle is #1, the defensive end is #2, the outside linebacker is #3 (or those two could possibly be reversed). If you have a tight end and a diveback in the backfield, the backer might stack in over the tackle and will thus become #2, and the end will become #3. You try to attack this defense a lot to the spread end side and will usually get the outside linebacker in a hip look to the spread end side. The man closest to the line of scrimmage in the secondary is usually the #4 player and the flat cover guy. The man who is deepest is usually the deep player or the halves or thirds cover player. Off the backside again, the first guy is #1, and then #2, #3, and #4, as you work your way out. Again, you begin by attacking #3. If you can put a tight end in the formation, then the defensive end will probably move out and the backer will come inside over the tackle. At that point, the end is #3, and you can watch his reactions so you will know whether to go inside or outside. Against a 4-3, you like to attack #1, the split end side. A 4-3 makes the outside linebacker #3, while the tackle and the end are #1 and #2, respectively, and the corner and safety are #4 and #5, respectively. Again, you begin by attacking #3 and finding out what his reaction is going to be and then continuing from there.

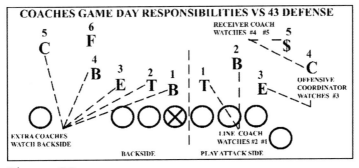

Diagram 6.7

In the 4-4 defense or eight-man front, say that the play is being called to the right (Diagram 6.8). Once you have drawn the imaginary line through the playside A gap on the right, you count from the inside out. Again, the backer and the defensive tackle can be reversed, but those two guys, depending on their positioning, are #1 and #2, however they sort themselves. The defensive end is the third guy. As for the outside linebacker or the strong safety, it does not matter which is #4. Remember, E's, T's, and B's are irrelevant. This player is #4. When you refer to the defenders, you say a defender is #4. You do not say that defender is a safety, a backer, or a corner. Outside, the thirds player is #5. Versus a 4-4, eight-man front, you begin your attack off-tackle. If you put a tight end wide and stretch his split, you will usually widen the defensive end a little bit. Here, you can begin your attack off-tackle. If the defensive end is not going to spread with the tight end's flex, then you get your flank game back, because the tight end and wing have outflanked the defense.

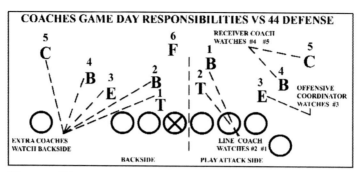

Diagram 6.8

Reviewing these three defenses, re-examine who on the defense each coach needs to watch. First, review the 50 defense. Your coordinator watches #3. He calls the play, watches #3, and knows how he is reacting. When the line coach hears the play, he makes sure to know what #2 is doing and attempts to find out what #1 is doing. The receivers coach makes sure he knows what #4 is doing and tries to find out about #5, as well. When you have a couple of graduate assistant coaches on your staff, then they are assigned to watch the backside guys, to see who trails, to see if any reverses can go, and also to watch the free safety in the middle and see if he is coming out of the middle in an attempt to be a ninth run defender. If he is, you know you can call post routes in behind him, if you can beat the corners.

Looking at the 4-3 defense and who is assigned to watch defenders, you start with #3. The backer to a split end side could be #3, or #3 could be the end to a tight end side. Regardless of which one it is, he is the guy who the quarterback coach, the coordinator, or the play caller will watch. The line coach watches #2. Again, you want your line coach to try to figure out what #1 does, as well. Your receivers coach is watching #4. If the corner is closest to the line, he is #4. Also, you want him to know what #5 does. If you see extra guys (e.g., free safety, trail player), find out how those guys are reacting and whether or not you can go for the post, the reverse, or whatever you might be looking for.

The final defense will be the eight-man front. Who watches whom? Again, the responsibilities are pretty simple. The line coach watches #2; if he can, seeing #1 is great. The coordinator calls the play and watches #3. The receivers coach watches #4 and #5, but especially #4.

Practicing Game Day

As coaches, one thing you ask your players to do is practice every day of the week for game day. How many times a week does your coaching staff practice what the coaches should do on game day? This focus is something you should insist your offensive staff work on every week. At the beginning of the week, you are busy breaking down the film, making the scouting report, compiling all the statistics, and making the game plan. You have many things to do at the beginning of each week. But, as the week winds down and the game day approaches, in those last two days before the game, most of the work—in terms of what the coaches have to do, of clerical things, and written things—is virtually finished. And so, at that point, they have a little extra time left. What you want them to do is practice game day. How do you do that? You take those guys in a room and put last year's game on or put on the game from the past Saturday that your opponent played. You would rather see the defense to the wing-T. Even though you are not seeing the previous week's game against the wing-T, it is still good to watch the defenders and how they react. You will know the next play is going to the right. The coordinator will watch #3 on the right side of your offense, the line coach will watch #2 and possibly #1, and the receivers coach will watch #4 and possibly #5. Maybe your two graduate assistants will watch the free safety and the trail player. Next, you turn on the film and run one play through, completely. After the play has run, you go around the room and ask, "What did #3 do?" "Line coach, what did #2 do?" "Receivers coach, what did #4 do?" Then, you turn the film back on, run the play back, and watch those three guys again. You are going to check yourselves. Did that defender really do what the coaches said he did? By going through the plays one at a time and stopping the action on film, you don't need to run it back and forth while the coaches are trying to find out what happened. Did #3 seal or did he penetrate? If a coach did not watch closely enough, or you missed it, you need more practice. If you, as the head coach, are the play caller, being in that position means you need to be watching #3. You need to practice this on game day, as well. And, if you assign that responsibility to somebody else, then he has to practice it in your place. You need to know those informational items and need to know them on game day in a hurry.

When the play is over, it sounds something like this. The line coach says, "#2 is penetrating." The receivers coach says, "#4 is real soft. We can run at him; he's backing up." Here, as an offensive play caller, you might see that #3 is sealing. If you know that #3 is sealing and that #4 is soft, then you also know your next play call should be at the flank. Or, say you just watched #3 penetrate and know that #2 is also penetrating because the line coach just told you that. In that case, you can run internal. But, seeing the defensive reactions that well is not going to happen on game day, and you will not get good at that unless you practice it. You've got to practice game day as coaches, just as your players have to practice game day as players. Practicing game day is something everyone does all the time after the game plans and all the scouting reports are done. It is exactly what you do on game day and is important for you to understand how those defenses work, how those defenses are numbered, and what you call. In order for everyone to be on the same page and call everything together, you practice your assignments on game day.

Writing the Game Plan

The next thing to discuss is exactly how you write the plan. When you do a game plan, what exactly is written on pieces of paper that you make up during that particular week? What exactly do you have with you on the field or in the press box on game day?

Summary Page

The first thing you do is put a summary page on the game plan (Diagram 6.9). On the summary page, you summarize the opponent's defense. This summary does not require a long explanation. You always keep in mind that your players will be more inclined to read something less cumbersome, less burdensome, less detailed, and less complicated. Keep in mind, then, that if you try to make it as simple as possible for your guys, they will read it and will study it, which is the ultimate goal. Your offensive scouting report could include hundreds of different details about your opponent's defense, but you don't want all that information in there. You want to know the base front spacing. You want to know the front change-ups. You want to know the base coverage. You want to know the primary change-up coverages. You want to know the goal-line and short-yardage defenses. You want to know the long-yardage defenses and whatever else you deem really important for that scouting report. You do not put a lot of information in the scouting report and also try not to put in too much information on the game plans, either.

```
                U.S.D. VS/ U.N.D.
                 OCT 22, 1996

   1. UND IS A 7 MAN FRONT. THEIR #1
      SPACING IS A 50 DEFENSE AND THEIR
      TOP CHANGE UPS ARE EAGLE STRONG AND
      WEAK. THEIR BASE COVERAGE IS COVER 3
      AND THEIR TOP CHANGE UP COVERAGE IS
      COVER 2.
   2. BEGIN YOUR ATTACK AT THE FLANK.
      USE SHIFTING TO GET MISMATCHES.
      YOUR PRIMARY FLANK PLAYS ARE:
      121-929          988 DOWN OPTION
      R21-BL29         LF 988-RT182 DOWN OPTION

   3. IF #3 SEALS YOUR PLAY ACTION GAME
      ATTACK #4 WITH:
      929-121 WAGGLE SOLID    989-181 KEEP PASS
      BL29-R21 WAGGLE SOLID   LF989-RT181 KEEP PASS

   4. IF #3 PENETRATES YOUR OFF TACKLE GAME
      WILL INCLUDE:
      182-988 DOWN        122-928 TAG
      RT182-LF988 DOWN   RT122-LF928 TAG

   5. IF BOTH #2 AND #3 BOTH PENETRATE
      YOUR INTERNAL GAME WILL INCLUDE:
      187-983 CT          124-926 G.T.
      RT187-LF183 CT     RT124-LF926 G.T.
```

Diagram 6.9

Following is a brief example of what a summary page on the game plan might contain. Just say you are getting ready to play the University of North Dakota. The first paragraph on this game plan, page one of the game plan sheet, would probably look like this: "UND is a 7-man front. Their number front is a 50 defense. Their front change-ups are eagle strong and weak. Their base coverage is cover 3, and their top change-up coverage is cover 2. They use a 6-5 goal line and eagle strong on short yardage. In long yardage situations, they play 2 man under coverage."

Notice, that first paragraph is a basic, brief description of what the opponent's defense is for that week. All the players need to know is this short description. You know they play a seven-man front and are basically a 50 package. You know what their change-ups are and know they use cover 3. You know what their goal-line, short-yardage, and long-down defensive packages are and the basic change-ups they use. That amount is plenty of information for your players in terms of what you need to summarize about your opponent's defense. Remember, this plan gets handed out to the quarterbacks and the coaches two days before game day. By then, they have already received the scouting report and practiced for two or three days against this defense. They already know these things, which are not something you need to hammer into them.

The second paragraph on page one, the summary page, is where you begin stating your plan of attack. In this case, you are going to begin your attack at the flank, because the defense is showing a seven-man front. You are going to use shifting to get mismatches or whatever else you might use shifting for. You are going to change formations on them. You might use shifting, use motion, or not do any of that. But, you begin your game plan at the flank. Your two base plays, the plays you think are going to best attack the flank, are listed in red. Here, red simply means something is hot. If it is in red, it is hot, and you are expecting to use it a lot in your next game. A play listed in blue is something not so hot, something you have in the game plan and have practiced, but not something you're planning on running as the focus for this particular game. It could become red listed as the game goes on, just as these red listed plays could become blue listed as the game goes on, depending on the reaction of the defense. Here, you describe your attack at the flank and list your primary plays. You might have a sweep, an option play, or whatever else you might want. You try to list all of those same plays from different formations. For example, if you decided on using 121 and 929, the sweep play, you might also choose to run it from red 21, blue 29, or any different formation from which you could plan on running that play for that particular week. You will also have an option listed. You try to list an option, a flank run, and a flank pass every week that you think you can make go. You are going to run them a number of times. For example, you might choose 988 and 182 down option, left 988, right 182 down option, which are the same play from different formations. You might have two, three, or four different formations you want to run that same play from.

The next part of the discussion will be the flank passing game. You have attacked #3 with the flank attack and, at this point, are anticipating #3 is sealing, trying to stop the off-tackle hole. You know you are going to keep attacking the flank. But, here, if #3 seals and you know #4 is also aggressive, then you focus on the play-action passing game. You're going to say, if #3 seals, your play-action passing game attacks #4 with the following plays. For example, you might run waggle solid and would list that play out of two different formations. You might select the keep pass, 989, 181, left 989, and right 181 keep pass. For this week, these plays might be the ones you selected to throw the ball in behind the fourth defender when he reacts hard to the run action. Those plays would listed in red. In other words, those plays are hot, they are primary. You plan on running those a lot. And, you plan on repeating those. Of course, they could become blue listed, depending on how the defensive reactions change during the game.

Next, if #3 penetrates and #2 is sealing, then you would need to package your off-tackle attack. You simply write what that package includes and, again, put a play down out of a couple of different formations. For example, you might use 88 down, 22, and 28 tag. Between the down play and the tag play, you have something to hit inside of #3, if he is penetrating, and outside of #2, if he is sealing. You list the hot-listed plays for each particular situation.

In the last paragraph of the summary, you deal with if #2 and #3 are both penetrating. Your internal game might include the halfback counter game and the fullback trap game up the middle. These examples are just hypothetical. You will want to fill these red plays in with anything you choose for that particular week. The complete summary tells you and your players how you are going to begin your attack and how you are going to evolve the attack in terms of the primary things you want to run and repeat frequently.

You can call a lot of things, and many things are going to be companion plays to your plan of attack, but may not be red listed. But, you are still going to practice them, anyway, because the reactions during the game may change, and what was red listed before may become blue listed at game time, and vice versa.

This description finishes page one of the game plan and how you write it up. The summary is five quick paragraphs. If you had a sixth one, it would include the drop-back passing attack. In terms of the wing-T, the four areas you want to attack in every game plan are internal, off-tackle, flank run, and flank pass if #4 is aggressive.

Hit Charts

Pages two and three include diagrams of the formations, as well as a list of the plays you are going to run from each formation (Diagram 6.10). Page three is identical to page two, except it contains the mirrors of the formations. You will have wing formation in every game plan—tight end and wing to one side and spread end and diveback to the other. Right after that, you will have what is called slots, or what looks like slots. You have a spread end and a wingback on the same side and a tight end and the diveback on the other side. To help you stay organized, you put the spread end to the right on one page and in all the formations and to the left on the next page. Then, you have double wing. In this, you have used wing, slot, and double wing. You write in the plays where they are going to hit out of each formation. Finally, you will have unbalanced. Wing, slot, double wing, and unbalanced will be addressed in every game plan, and the plays are written in where you are going to run them. You write the plan on pages two and three this way. You put the formations down, write the plays you are going to run out of each formation, and write in the areas where the plays will actually hit. You put run plays on the opposite side of the line of scrimmage. You put pass plays on your own side of the line of scrimmage in the backfield. You write the play in wherever the ball is going to be. If you have some plays you really like, ones you think you are going to repeat a lot, then they are listed in red. The ones you think are not going to get repeated a lot, but are ready, are listed in blue.

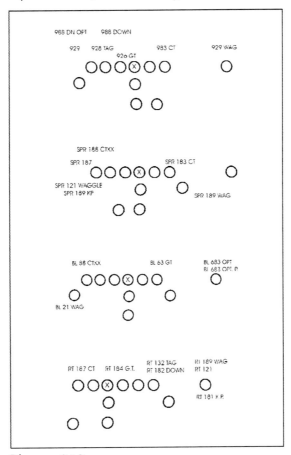

Diagram 6.10

Many college coaches fill in from flank to flank and have as many as 16, 18, and 20 plays from each formation. What you will notice is, if you are doing this right, in the wing-T, you will run many of the same plays from each different formation—wing, slot, double wing, and unbalanced. You are not just running different formations, but you are running the same plays out of those formations, and your kids are getting better at executing, and the defense has trouble recognizing. Throw in motions and shifts, and you have a double-edged sword. You get the best of all worlds in terms of the defense not being able to recognize what you are trying to do.

Both pages two and three are called hit charts. They are in cellophane, and your coordinator has them with him at all times. He will especially refer to those pages between series during the game. He can talk about the plays he has already run, can look over those play sheets, and can pick out all the plays he might need in any situation. If you got stopped on one particular series of downs, you do not want to waste too many possessions, so you have to address why you got stopped. If the defense is doing something different with their scheme—say you planned on #3 being a seal guy, and, at this point, he is penetrating, and you planned on #2 being a penetrator, and, at this point, he is sealing—you know you must adjust and go off-tackle. You go back to those play charts, start circling the plays which will hit the defense off-tackle, just to remind yourselves, then start using those plays, and keep the chess match going. Finding out how the defense is going to play over the course of four quarters is the key, as well as adjusting with the defense as they adjust to you. They may change it up on you once, but then go back to their base on the next play. Coaches must be disciplined to watch those players all the way through the game for this reason. If you get all the way through the second quarter and they have not once done anything differently, then you figure you do not have to watch those defenders anymore. You can watch your own guys and see how they are holding up against the players they are matched with. If the defense changes, then you are right back watching defenders so you can adjust your offense.

The coordinator does not look at any of that stuff while the offense is out on the field, running the offense. Those first three pages are basically pages he should be looking at between series, while he's talking to the other coaches and while they are gathering as much information as can possibly be accumulated by those three guys, or four, five, or whatever number you have.

Critical Call Sheet

The next page, page four of the game plan, consists of critical calls (Diagram 6.11). A critical call for you is any play, where, if you do not make the required yardage, you will lose possession of the ball, lose a direct opportunity to score some points, or give the opponent a direct opportunity to score points. In general, third and fourth downs are critical calls: goal line and red zone offense, two-point plays, specials, and coming-out calls. For example, third-and-one is critical in most field zones, but, if you are in four-down territory, then you have two downs in which to make the required yardage. You can then call the play on third down according to that. You try to make it on third down every time, so you keep yourselves out of those critical fourth-down situations. Sometimes, you can get third-and-long situations, and, if you just get half of it back and are in four-down territory, then you can go for the other half on fourth down. In that case, third-and-long may not be considered critical. Maybe, you are a little too far out for the field goal kicker, yet a little too close to be punting. That time is great to go on fourth down. A lot more teams go for fourth down than in the past.

```
                         U.N.D. CRITICAL CALLS
                             OCT 22, 1996

   3-1 OR LESS (DEF)              GOAL LINE DEFENSE (DEF)
   1.                             1.
   2.                             2.
   3-2 OR LESS (DEF)              3.
   1.                             4.
   2.                             5.
   3.                             6.
   3-3 TO 4 (DEF)                 COMING OUT OFFENSE (DEF)
   1.                             1.
   2.                             2.
   3.                             3.
   4.                             SPECIALS
   5.                             1.
   6.                             2.
   3-5 TO 8 (DEF)                 RED ZONE OFFENSE
   1.                             1.
   2.                             2.
   3.                             3.
   4.                             4.
   5.                             TWO POINT PLAYS
   6.                             1.
   3-9 PLUS (DEF)                 2.
   1.                             3.
   2.
   3.
   4.
   5.
```

Diagram 6.11

Third Downs

The first critical category is third down and one or less. You always have at least two choices in this situation, sometimes a third one. The next critical call is third down and two or less. These calls may be the same as on third-and-one or less, but they also may be different. Making two yards on third down is a lot different from making six inches. Therefore, you obviously put different kinds of choices in this category.

The next critical call is third down and three to four. If you are a good, solid run team, are running the ball, and are making yardage, you probably will have a lot of third down and three to four calls throughout the course of the game. You want your best plays in your game plan for this situation. When you get to this down and distance, you run your best football plays right here. What are your best football plays? Whatever is red-listed for you, basically, those plays are your best. They are the plays you felt you were going to use in this game plan a number of times and get a lot of repetitions on them. Many times in this situation, you like the waggle, bootleg, and keep pass plays, flank-pass oriented plays in nature, because the quarterback gets more options.

The next critical call is third down and five to eight. As a wing-T football team and as a run-oriented football team, you want to try to stay out of these kinds of situations as often as possible. These third downs are still attainable with parts of your package, if you have prepared for them. Sometimes, you will have a three-step-drop passing game, or maybe a five-step drop, or maybe your good play-action drop-back, and you can throw those easy-to-complete, short-to-intermediate routes and can get the required yardage. Or, possibly, you are just stubborn and think you can make eight yards anytime you want with the sweep play, the waggle play, or whatever. You fit it in here, depending on what you think you have to do or can do to gain five to eight yards and keep possession. One thing you always do is write down in parentheses what the expected defense is for that particular down and distance. What is the predominant defense you are probably going to see in that down and distance? For five to eight yards, you usually have about six choices, just as you do for three to four yards. It could be more, it could be less, depending on what you feel you need for that particular week.

The final category is third down and nine plus. You usually have five or six choices in this instance, but you also know, if you are in third down and nine or more all game, you are probably not going to win. In that case, you would be in trouble no matter what you're doing, but you have the best possible plays you can have for nine or more yards in this category. Obviously, you are either going to have to throw the ball down the field further, maybe hit a trap in a long-yardage situation, or use some kind of an option. For the most part, third down and nine plus is a pass, draw, or screen kind of a down. You do not necessarily like play-action in third and long because the defense does not honor it. But, sometimes, play-action might the best blocking scheme you have, so you have to go ahead and use it.

All of those situations discussed here require critical calls—third down and one or less, two or less, three to four, five to eight, and nine plus. The plays you use are all third-down yardage plays used over the years. As you look at the down and distance, field position chart from the off-season and in-season film study, you may find that one week it might be third down and three to four and the next week it might be third down and three to five. It is also possible that what is considered intermediate for some teams changes for others. One week it might be seven plus is all blitz; therefore, seven plus will be your long-yardage category for the week, instead of nine plus. Distances may change slightly, week by week, but, as a standard rule of thumb, these downs and distances will be used most of the time. Again, they are all critical calls. If it is fourth down and one and you are going for it, then that choice is the same—it is a critical call.

You have your coordinator refer to this list while the series is going on, in case you get in one of these situations. You may find that, all of a sudden, you are into a coming-out offense or are really backed up. You are only on your own one-yard line. What did you have planned for that? The beauty of page four in the game plan is all of these situations are thought out well in advance. They are planned for when you are in the staff room, and it is nice and cool. No pressure exists, no fans are yelling at you. You can take your time, be deliberate, and think about it. You can look at the defense, try to find the weaknesses in it, and mark down some calls to work in those particular situations. You do all this when you are nice and calm—not in the heat of battle, when the crowd is screaming and everybody is telling you, you don't know your butt from a hole in the ground and can't make a decent call. All those things can add up during the game and distract you. For that reason, you want to have these critical calls formulated well in advance, so all you do during the game, when that situation arises, is to look at your chart, which tells you what you need to do. For example, it's third down and one, you are expecting a double-eagle defense, and at that point is where you are going to attack because that point is the weakness of it. You know what you have planned for this team coming into the game in this situation.

You just look at the chart and call it. You are always going to keep track of yourselves. How well do you do on third down and one or less? You keep a running count, starting with game one; when game two comes, you add that to game one; when game three comes, you add that, so you have a running chart on yourselves. How are you doing on these critical calls? You are evaluating yourselves all the time. What is working? What is not working? What defenses are you seeing? What defenses are you not seeing? You are constantly updating, revising, and renovating this list on the basis of how these defenses are trying to play you.

Goal Line Offense

On the right-hand side of page four are other kinds of critical situations. The first one you write down is your goal line offense. You would like that goal line offense to be somewhere between four and eight plays. You would like to start spring ball with the plays you like to run down on the goal line, go all the way through training camp, games one, two, and three, and try to keep this as similar as possible from week to week, so you get good at executing this. You do not want to be changing up what you are doing down here in the most critical area on the whole field, by doing something you have never had a chance to execute. Coaches ask themselves how it is their offense can drive all the way down the field and then, when it gets to the goal line, can't score. Was it bad planning? Was it they didn't analyze thoroughly enough the defense they were going to see? Was it they did not get better at executing their package the way they should have? With your goal line offense, you try to keep it very much the same all the way through the year and just get better at it.

Coming Out

The next situation is called coming out. What is the defense going to do when you are backed up inside your own five-yard line? You are going to write the defense on the chart. Of course, it is there as a reminder to your play caller, so he knows, if he is not seeing that defense, then maybe he will have to change his calls. Coming out means you are backed up inside your own five-yard line. This case is where you do not want to be handing the ball off deep in the backfield. You do not want to be throwing late over the middle. You do not want deep drops where you could be sacked in the end zone. You want to be able to hand the ball off on direct teaming action if you can, make some yardage, and get the ball at least up to the four-yard line, where you can punt with the normal amount of room. You must be able to get off your own goal line. You make this plan very early in the week and practice it in your practices. You tell the kids you are going down to the other end and are going to practice coming out. Again, the key is well-thought-out calls prior to having to make those same calls under game pressure.

Specials

The next area on the sheet is for specials. Specials mean plays you do not normally run much of, but you have in the game plan for that week for a particular reason. Maybe, you have a reverse play in your plan. Maybe, you've seen on film that their trail player is undisciplined and does not look for the reverse. So, you put a reverse play in, practice it, and have it listed with your specials. A great time to call those kinds of plays is whenever you get a turnover in your opponent's end of the field. You can use these kinds of plays as momentum breakers. Other specials you can use are the halfback pass, any kind of new screen, a play requiring special personnel, anything special for the week—something you do not normally do a lot of, yet think that, at the right time, against this particular team, it is going to break on them.

Red Zone Offense

Next is the red zone offense. The red zone offense refers to when you are at the +20-yard line, going in to score a touchdown, all the way until the five. When you get around the five-yard line, the goal line attack starts to take over. What are you doing in the red zone? Are there special plays or patterns you want to use in the red zone? Maybe yes, maybe no. The other thing you can put in for a red zone attack is what you do not want to do. More than likely, you will continue doing whatever has worked best for you to get down the field in this category. You then list the things you do not want to do. As an example, maybe in their red zone, your opponent is a blitz team. In that case, you will not want to run certain plays, so you simply mark down you do not want to do this or that. This past year, I believe we scored in the red zone every time, except a couple. Only two times in the red zone happened when we did not score. I thought the coaches did a good job last winter. We studied it. We called up other schools and asked them the kinds of thing they tried to do in the red zone. Our offensive coordinator, Blair Hrovat, did a tremendous job on his study and found out a lot of interesting things. The most important thing we learned is to continue doing what has been successful for us in the past. That way, we won't screw ourselves up. The point is not to try to get too fancy down there. Do your bread-and-butter stuff and make it work. Keep in mind, the defense might change personality down there and, as a result, you might want to do some different things.

Two-Point Plays

Last, but not least, down in the bottom right-hand corner, are your two-point plays. This area is so important. If you study hard enough, you will find your opponent's defense defending the two-point play somewhere in your film library. Basically, you are going to write down what defense they run here. You are going to try and figure out what plays are going to beat that type of defense. You want this planned way in advance, because it is a lot of pressure when the game comes down to a two-point play, especially if it is right at the very end of the game. Over the years, the one at the end of the game is not always the deciding factor (e.g., those occasions when you went for two points two to three times earlier in the game and then the game ends up with a score indicating you would've won if you had made any one of those previous two-point plays). We had a situation this year when we got to the goal line on the last drive of the game and were nine points down. We had gone for two once before that and did not make it. If you figure that you get those two points back and are only down seven points, look at the potential difference those points make in the outcome of the game. Here, if you can score that last touchdown, you can go for the two-point conversion and win the game. Or, if you made the two and are only seven down, you can kick the single point and go into overtime. You never know when that two-point call written down on the game plan is going to make or break the difference in the game.

Every one of these categories on page four of your game plan sheet is critical. You are either going to give up possession of the ball or are going to lose a direct opportunity to score points right in that particular down and distance or area of the field. You do not want to be predictable. You do not want to necessarily do the same thing every time you get down there. But, you also want to be good enough to be able to execute your offense when you get down there and maybe do it from a different formation, a different shift, different motions, or whatever. Try to give the defense a different look, but also try to keep as much continuity in your attack as you possibly can.

Attacking Defenses

Next, some simple game planning that you should do will be explained, as well as how you might use the base series and base play packages to attack the three defenses discussed in this book.

Attacking the 50 Defense

Starting with the 20 package, the companion plays will be illustrated, and then how the companion plays work depending on the defensive reactions will be discussed (Diagram 6.12). If you are going to run to the right and attack the third defender, then the first play you are going to run is 121, the buck sweep to the right. You're attacking the flank because a 50 defense is a seven-man front and because you think by film study the third defender is going to seal when you block the tight end down and try to keep the off-tackle hole from opening up. As he seals, #4 is soft on the film you see, so, at this point, you know you can run the sweep right at #4. What is the companion play to that? If #3 is still sealing and #4 is coming hard against the run, you want to run 121 waggle solid. On that particular play, the quarterback fakes the sweep, starts his waggle footwork, gets #4 to react up to force the sweep, but then, as he drops back, throws the ball right in behind that fourth defender. That play is 121 waggle solid complementing 121 with regard to #4's reactions. If the third defender is not sealing anymore and begins to penetrate up the field to try and stop the 121 sweep play you have been running, you want to run the off-tackle play, which is 122 tag. Again, you can show buck action, hit the play off-tackle, and use a variety of blocking schemes, of which tag is the best, which means the tackle and guard both pull. This setup is nothing more than the old counter trey or counter gap blocking all the pros run. Everybody at every level runs this same thing: #3 is penetrating, and #2, who has been sealing to stop internal runs, here, wants to get up the field in order to stop this 122 tag by penetrating. You know your answer is to run 124 guard trap. You are going to come right back under the #2 defender and take advantage of his upfield penetration to stop 122 tag. If #2 seals, obviously, you will stay off-tackle. If #3 seals, you will go outside the flank. If #4 is soft, you will continue attacking the flank. And, if #4 comes hard, you will throw in behind him. Those four plays—121, 121 waggle solid, 122 tag, and 124 guard trap—comprise a play package taking care of all the reactions you are going to see from the people you have decided to attack on the playside. You might want to consider more complements to the four plays you already have selected. One of them is some kind of a counter coming backside, where the inside people are overpursuing. The 127 counter would be a great complement to any of the four calls as an inside play. That play would be inside to take advantage of quick inside linebacker flow. Then, the outside play you would use would be 121 waggle. At this point, you complement the sweep with the fake, come all the way backside with the quarterback, and attack the flank with a run-pass option. Those plays complement your 20 series, flank to flank. As you look at this game plan sheet, you have an answer for any reaction the defense can do to you from flank to flank, and each looks the same for the first two steps. Every single thing you do looks exactly the same for the first two steps. You could now expand these six plays to other formations or motion for different looks, yet still attack with the exact same thought processes.

You want to continue to do these same things, but you want to do them with a different backfield action. Exploring the belly package, you start with 182 down option.

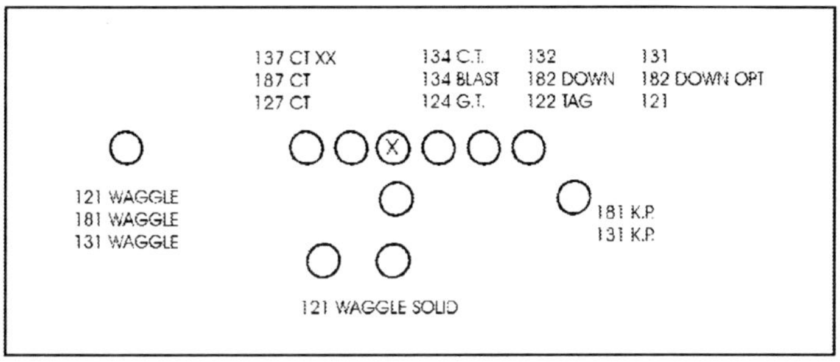
137 CT XX
187 CT
127 CT
134 C.T.
134 BLAST
124 G.T.
132
182 DOWN
122 TAG
131
182 DOWN OPT
121
121 WAGGLE
181 WAGGLE
131 WAGGLE
181 K.P.
131 K.P.
121 WAGGLE SOLID

Diagram 6.12

You are going to run option, faking the 82 down play, off-tackle, and the quarterback keeps the ball, comes on out, and options the fourth defender. You either block down on the third defender or log him. You can do other things, if he is a penetrator, but you start with the down option. You are running the down option because you can log and get the inside sealed, and you can get outside and attack #4. If #4 is fairly soft, you have a good play here. As soon as #4 becomes aggressive, then you want to go to 181 keep pass and throw the ball in behind him. Each play complements the other. If #3 decides he is going to penetrate rather than seal, you adjust with 182 down, trap #3 right out, and run the ball right off-tackle. You have taken advantage of that third defender's reaction and, again, are figuring #2 is still sealing. If #2 is coming up the field, a number of options exist that you can do. You can go with a counter trap. You can do anything hitting inside of #2 quickly. You can run 184, which is the quick belly. Certainly, you could run some kind of a 34 counter or 36 counter to the halfback on the 30 action. You could run 34 blast, which looks like the 80 package in some respects. But, you are going to have something hitting internal and hitting inside of #2 if he gives you that upfield penetrating reaction. Again, you want to build in some kind of counter in case they flow too hard. You have 187 counter, where the quarterback fakes the belly and hands the ball off to the wing coming back. You can use counter crisscross blocking; use counter tag blocking, where the tackle and the guard pull; or pull the tight end and the tackle. It just depends on what your defensive problems are. Also, off that 80 series, you would like to have something coming backside wide. You have an 80 waggle, so you say 181 waggle. You have basically been getting the same kinds of things done that you did with the 20 package, but with a different backfield action. It does not have to be 100 formation. You can go right 100, go red, or go spread 900. You can mix these formations up many different ways. All these packages just get the same things done. If you add the shifting in formations and have a couple different play packages from several formations, then you do not really need much else.

How about the 30 package? What can you do out of the 30s? You have 131, which is the power sweep. If #4 is soft, you have 131 keep pass. If #4 is aggressive, you have 132, which is the power off-tackle play. You again have 134 blast. You also have 134 counter or 136 counter, to take advantage of #2 being a penetrator. You have 137 counter or counter crisscross, where the halfbacks hand the ball to each other. You have 131 waggle to the backside. That combination completes another package of plays you can use, where you have flank-to-flank offense and have play packages built in such a way that, no matter what the defense does to react to you, you can go ahead and take advantage of that reaction with a companion play.

You should not run this offense unless you have at least two packages and can run every companion play in the package—and run them from all the formations and to both sides of each formation. Then, and only then, do you have a true wing-T offense. You have answers for what the defense gives you. You do not need zillions of plays. You can run the same plays, run them from different formations, use different motions, use different shifts, and look like a zillion different things to a defense. You are simply running the same four or six plays you have been running from the first day of training camp using the same attack concepts in every package. Your kids are getting better and better, and the defense is still trying to figure out what you are going to do to them next. That adaptability is the beauty of the wing-T offense. When I was a football player in college, we had the splitback veer as our offense, and the coaches used to brag about how they loved it so much because it was an offense where, if the defense did this, then we did that. We took advantage of their reaction. The wing-T does the same thing for you.

2H Attacking the 4-3 Defense

Against the 4-3 defense, run your base offense (Diagram 6.13). You know the 4-3 defense is a seven-man front, but, because of the even spacing, it retains some of the properties of an eight-man front. One thing you do is split the tight end five to six feet. You might get a defense where the defensive end is on the tight end in a 9 technique, the defensive tackle is in a 3 technique over the guard, and what you have done is really spread and opened up the off-tackle hole, putting a great deal of pressure on the Sam backer, the man playing on the outside shoulder of the tackle. You have created a lot of space for him to step up and plug. As soon as the 9-technique defensive end starts to move down inside, of course, you can recognize it right away, and then your flank game is going to be good. You would probably start this attack off-tackle. If you go back to the 20 series, you would probably start this package with 122 and block it with either tag, power, or whatever blocking scheme you wanted to use. As soon as you could get #3 to close down some or move his alignment, then you would go to the 121 sweep, but would probably begin off-tackle. Then, you have 124 guard trap for when #2 becomes a penetrator. Again, you have 121 waggle solid in case the fourth defender comes really hard and want to throw the ball in behind him. You have 121 waggle, which hits backside, away from the flow at the flank, and 127 or 167 counter backside on the inside. So, at this point, you have inside, internal, off-tackle, and flank. You have flank passing, so you have a way to get in behind #4. You have counter and something to counter flow back to the flank. You have flank-to-flank offense, with the first two steps looking exactly the same, and the ball can be in any one of six different points. But, the play looks the same to the defense. Blocking schemes look the same; so does the backfield action. You would begin with 182 down, if you were going to go to the 80 package. Then, when #3 became conscious of off-tackle, you would go 182 down option, get the down option play, and use those two as complements. If #4 is soft, you continue to run option, and, if he's not and is aggressive, 181 keep pass in behind him should be good. You have 184 inside and could use the quick belly package or counter flow. You have 187 counter, which counters the flow back to the weakside. Obviously, you have 181 waggle, which counters flow back to the outside. As you see, these plays are the same ones you just attacked the 50 defense with, only with a different starting point and with adjustments in your blockings. Your rules and attack concepts will hold up versus all the defenses.

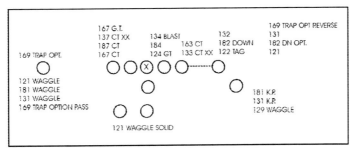

Diagram 6.13

If you want to go with the same type of setup and want to run your 30 package, then 132 is the off-tackle play out of the 30 series and is what you would start with, and then you judge how #3 is reacting. Then, you might go to 131 as a companion play. Next, you could go to 131 keep pass, if #4 is really aggressive, where the quarterback fakes the sweep, keeps the ball in the same direction, and has a run or pass option to throw in behind the corner or the #4 defender. The 134 blast is the internal play to go with that. The 137 counter crisscross would be the inside counter, and then you have 131 waggle for a play-action pass to counter the flow to the outside. At the outset, when the defense overcommits, you can go inside of them or outside of them, depending on how that backside trail player runs and how fast the whole defense pursues to the football.

Also, against the 4-3 defense, you want to attack to the spread end side. You would like to run 100 formation, but you can choose spread 900 and run to the left as well, or red formation, or unbalanced. But, you want to attack the spread end against this defense. You are going to go with guard trap a little bit wider and trap the #2 defender, the contain defensive end. You would use 167 guard trap and judge the defender's (defensive end's) reaction. If the end is going to seal on the trap, then you want to be able to log him and go outside with trap option, which would be 169 trap option, crack, or however you want to block it. You run trap option, especially if #4 is soft and #3 is aggressive, or you can go trap-option pass, if #4 is really aggressive. Then, the complementary play would be 169 trap-option pass. At this point, you have inside, outside, and outside pass. You could run some gut plays and some internal guard traps to give you an internal game. The 67 guard trap would almost be considered off-tackle, depending on how #2 is reacting. Of course, you can run the counter crisscross, the trap-option reverse, and the waggle plays back away from the spread end. You could run the 133 counter crisscross, which would give you an inside counter, or could run 163 counter, depending on whether or not you want to have the halfbacks hand the ball to each other. You have 169 trap option reverse, where you can bring the spread end back across and pitch him the ball off the trap-option series. Of course, 129 waggle is a good complement to all of this. You can see by looking back, even with the right halfback in three-step motion and flow beginning to the spread end side, that you have flank-to-flank offense. That offensive look is going to look exactly the same to the defense as the first two steps, regardless of where the ball attacks. The first two steps are going to look exactly the same, no matter where the ball ends up attacking. That fact is the beauty of this offense. It's flank to flank, with motion, without motion, and you can have direct hitting plays, counter plays, whatever you need.

Attacking the 4-4 Defense

Against the 4-4 defense, start with your base football plays (Diagram 6.14). Begin there and adjust your blocking schemes to fit the 4-4 defense. All the rules are in the book for you, so you can just take them and start to create. Since the 4-4 defense shows an even front and the tackle is uncovered, you would take the tight end and split him five to six feet to see how far the defensive end will widen out with him. If you can create a big bubble between the defensive end and the defensive tackle, that space will give you a vulnerable off-tackle area, and that area is where you would begin your attack. Starting with the 20s, you would start with 122, since you are starting off-tackle to attack an eight-man front. You will select tag as the basic blocking scheme. Once the third defender becomes conscious of stopping the off-tackle area, 121, the sweep play, would serve as the companion play. Once #4 becomes really aggressive in his attempt to stop the sweep play, then 121 waggle solid enables you to show the same look, with the quarterback faking the sweep to the left half, starting his waggle, then dropping straight back, and throwing the ball in behind #4. You show the sweep look and throw the ball right in behind him. If #2 is a big penetrator, then you can go 124 guard trap, gut, guard-trap gut, or whatever it is you favor as an internal blocking scheme. Again, you have four plays that attack the playside of the defense, and you can go inside, off-tackle, outside, or throw a play-action pass in behind the fourth defender. You also have the same look for two steps with the counter game, where you could run 127 or 167 counter and hand the ball off to the right halfback, who is the wingback coming back, countering the flow. Then, you add 121 waggle, which counters the flow to the outside, with the quarterback having the run-pass option.

A different backfield action, with the same kind of conflicts for the defense, would be the 80s, or belly action. You would start with 182 down, because it gives you a

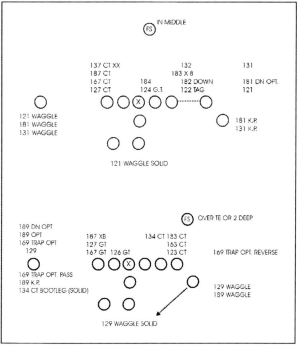

Diagram 6.14

direct shot at an off-tackle play, and, as soon as #3 becomes a seal-conscious guy, you would adjust with 181 down option as the companion play. One other thing to do against the 4-4 defense is to use the 83 cross-block influence, which is kind of a companion play to 82 down. You can go 83 cross block and influence the right halfback. He steps at #3, as if he is going to come down on him, and then turns out, and the tight end goes across on the linebacker, and you cross block. You use the 83 footwork, as opposed to 82, for the fullback, and, at this point, you have a little bit more of a deliberate path, allowing him more of a cutback opportunity than a direct path, as 82 down would. That play would be something you might use in conjunction with 82 down. You have an internal play. You can go quick belly, 184. You can use some kind of a counter tackle trap play to get you inside of #2, such as 187 counter, to counter the flow back inside. You have 181 waggle, which again counters the flow back to the outside.

Using the 30 series against eight-man fronts isn't great unless your opponent is one of those teams using all four guys inside and always doing A or B-gap stunts. One guy stunts A, the other guy goes B, and they keep mixing that stuff up on you. The 30s will offer a better sweep, because you can fire block everybody; instead of pulling guards, you can let the fullback be the lead blocker and kick out. At this point, you can pick up all the internal blitzing and still get the sweep run correctly. You would start with 132, the off-tackle play—double-team down, kick-out, good old-fashioned power football. The 131 is the sweep you use when #3 becomes seal conscious. You use the 131 keep pass to the flank, when #3 is soft. The 181 keep pass would be the same thing within the 80 series to attack to #3's side, if #4 is really aggressive. If you get the fourth defender coming hard for down option, 181 keep pass should hurt him. They cannot stop everything. For counter plays, you have 137 counter or counter crisscross, and the halfbacks can hand the ball to each other; in that case, 121 waggle or 131 waggle would be fine as well.

Against the 4-4 defense, if the free safety likes to stay in the middle and be a middle third defender, the following is how you should run the package. Once that free safety becomes strong conscious, comes over in a two-deep alignment, or comes over, lines up, and plays man-to-man on the tight end, then you would like to run the entire package of plays by putting the back in motion across the backfield and running the same packages of plays back to the weakside. Then, back to the weakside, start with the internal play. The internal play would be 126 guard trap, gut, or guard trap gut. You can also use 167 or 127 guard trap, which is a little bit wider. You can go outside with the 129 sweep, which would be the sweep outside to the left. Then, off of that, you would have 129 waggle solid, if #4 is really aggressive, so you can throw the ball in behind him. That play completes the plays to the playside. You can also attack back to the weakside. You can run 123 counter or 163 counter and hand the ball off to the halfback coming back through. You have 129 waggle, which is part of this package. You can then add the other dimension of the trap option. You can use 169 trap option with crack, for example, or 169 trap option pass. At this point, you have a flank-to-flank offense with the 20 series, but you are also including the trap option, as well. Because, again, for the first few steps, it all looks the same to the defense, and they do not know where the ball is going to hit. You can even add 169 trap option reverse back to the left side. You are attacking the defense at all points, and the look is exactly the same to the defense for the first two steps.

If you wanted to get into the 80 package, you could run 187 cross block. You could run 189 option or 188 down option, some kind of option play to the wide side, and attack #4. You can go 189 keep pass, if #4's really aggressive. That play gives you a chance to throw the ball in behind him. You have 134 tackle trap counter, which looks just like the cross block series and provides you with a counter. You could add 134 counter bootleg, or solid, with the tackle staying home, either way, fake the tackle trap counter, and keep coming outside to the flank. All those things are good. You also have 189 waggle, which allows you to attack outside to the weakside against flow. You could also have 183 counter, which gives you a counter inside from the 80 series. As you can see, you can build a heck of an attack. Look at all this football you have to attack the 4-4 defense with only one formation. All you are doing is running the same plays, either strongside or weakside. That combination is enough right there for 10 game plans. You can simply add your series in on the basis of how the defense is playing or can use the best series for your kids.

7

The Jet Sweep Series

One of the most exciting new developments in the wing-T offense in recent years has been the addition of the jet sweep or speed sweep series. This series is another way to run the buck sweep series but with a faster tempo. Many teams at all levels, including pro football, are running some form of speed sweep. The speed sweep series is based on creating assignment conflicts for the defense in the same manner as all of the other series in the wing-T. The major difference is the type of motion used by the running backs. Rather than using the traditional three-step, wingback motion, this series incorporates extended motion by one of the two halfbacks crossing the backfield. The speed of the motion places the defense in conflict, since the flank can be attacked with extreme suddenness. This series also incorporates some zone blocking principles rather than a block in at the hole, a block out at the hole, and a block through the hole, like most other traditional series. Once the ball has been snapped, most of the traditional wing-T plays can still be executed. Many ways exist to complement this series with the ability to add plays to fit anyone's offense.

The speed sweep is a tremendous complement to the triple option for those coaches who have chosen to incorporate the triple option into their package. In fact, a defense must employ the exact opposite strategies to stop the two packages. Against the triple option, the defense must tighten down the alignments of their defensive linemen so they can prevent their release to the linebacker level. Most defenses will align their defensive linemen over the offensive linemen in techniques so tight they approach being head-up. They are coached to jam and squeeze the release of the offensive blockers to not only keep the linebackers free but also to come off on the first threat in the option. At this point, the scraping linebackers will flow over the top of the defensive lineman to attack the next threat in the option. This tightening of techniques is necessary for stopping the triple option but will be costly to the defense against the speed sweep.

To stop the speed sweep from attacking the flank before the defense can react, the defense will need to widen out on the line of scrimmage enabling them to defeat the reach blocks at the point of attack. By widening their alignments, they now permit the offensive linemen to freely release to the linebacker level, which allows the offense to run the triple option at will.

One of the most important coaching points is the speed of the motions in the wing-T. It is vital that the offense uses both three-step motion by the wingback and speed sweep (extended) motion. It is also vital that these motions look as similar as possible for the first three steps. If the fullback is aligned with his heels at four yards from the back tip of the football and the wingback is aligned correctly, then this timing has a chance. The wingback must be aligned with his toes two yards from the back tip of the football and his outside foot 3.5 yards from the outside foot of the offensive tackle. When he takes off in three-step motion, he must run at full speed. This point cannot be emphasized enough; he must run at full speed. The wingback aims for the toes of the inside foot of an imaginary diveback if he is a pitchback or a blocker at the opposite flank. He aims for the heel of the outside foot of an imaginary diveback if he is a ballcarrier. When he uses jet motion, he aims for the tail of the quarterback, and, again, he runs full speed. Coaches will always know if the wingbacks are doing a good job with their motions when the defensive coaches comment after practices that the defensive players are having a hard time telling the difference between three-step motion and extended motion. When a coach gets those types of comments, he can sit back and smile because he knows that he is doing a good job coaching the backfield techniques. When your own defense, who sees you in practice every day, cannot tell the difference between the two types of motion, then you know that the opponent's defense, who only has three days to practice for this motion, has no chance of being able to tell the difference.

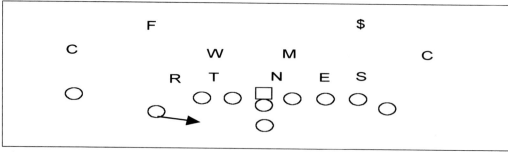

Diagram 7.1. Three-step motion

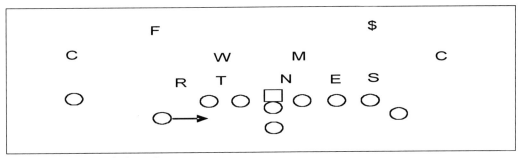

Diagram 7.2. Extended motion

Cadence

This motion can be timed with the quarterback's cadence, or it can be signaled with the nod of the head or the lifting of a heel. In the past, I have used three different cadences for extended motion. In the first cadence, the quarterback calls the play in the huddle and then says, "On red," which means the ball will be snapped on the "R" in red. When the quarterback is under the center and has determined everyone is ready, he yells, "Set," at which time, the wingback takes off. When the wingback has reached the prescribed landmark, the quarterback yells, "Red," and the ball is snapped.

The second cadence we have used for extended motion is when the quarterback says, "On second red," which means the ball will be snapped on the "R" in the second red. When the quarterback is under the center and has determined everyone is ready, he again yells, "Set," at which time the wingback takes off. When the wingback has almost reached the prescribed landmark, the quarterback yells, "Red, red," and the ball is snapped. This second red will cause any defenders, who think they know the cadence, to jump into the neutral zone just before the ball is snapped.

The third cadence we have used for extended motion is when the quarterback says, "On double set red," which means the ball will again be snapped on the "R" in red. We would use this cadence if we wanted to shift the formation first and then go in extended motion. When the quarterback is under the center and has determined everyone is ready, he again yells, "Set," at which time the offense will shift into a new formation. After all of the offensive players are set for one second, the quarterback yells, "Set," again, and the wingback takes off in motion. When the wingback has reached the prescribed landmark, the quarterback yells, "Red," and the ball is snapped. Any defenders who might want to react to cadence will now have the additional burden of recognizing the new formation. The shifting of formations will destroy defensive recognition.

The offense can also use a silent signal to start the motion and then snap the ball on the first sound, which is completely non-rhythmic for the defense. The quarterback, making some sort of signal to the wingback to start him in motion, would do this. Common signals are the nodding of the head or the lifting of a heel. When the wingback reaches the prescribed landmark, the quarterback yells, "Set," and the ball is snapped on the "S" in set. In the huddle, the quarterback would have told the offense that the cadence is on sound, meaning the first sound that they hear.

Landmarks

For most of the plays in the speed sweep series and especially for the speed sweep itself, the ball should be snapped when the wingback reaches the gap between the near guard and tackle. However, the quarterback must get a feel for the timing of the play and the speed of his backs. This knowledge enables him to adjust the timing and snap the ball at the most optimal time for each halfback. If the wingback is running at full speed, it should take approximately three or three and one half steps for him to reach his landmark. If your three-step motion is also flat and fast, then the defense will not be able to make any quick adjustments for either type of motion.

Many types of plays can take advantage of extended motion, and many of them will have different landmarks. For instance, one favorite play is the full sprint-out play, where the quarterback has a run-pass option at the flank. In this play, the wingback is coached to take off in full speed motion and get all the way to the opposite hash mark before the ball is snapped. Extended motion is also used to throw the belly keep pass with flood routes. In these plays, the ball is snapped just as the wingback passes the quarterback. As with all phases of the wing-T, you are only limited by your own imagination when it comes to this offense.

The Offensive Line in the Speed Sweep

The first priority for all offensive football is the offensive line. The speed sweep series requires a combination of traditional wing-T blocking and zone blocking. The speed sweep will make your offensive linemen better players because it will expose them to both types of techniques.

Rules for the speed sweep are as follows. This example is for 21 jet, which is run to the right.

- 2 – Tight: reach, on, backer
  Spread: release, stalk 5 (could crack 4, if called)
- 3 – Reach, on, backer (pull with 3 call)
- 4 – Pull, wall off

5 – Reach, on, backer
6 – Reach, on, backer
7 – Cutoff
8 – Tight: cutoff
    Spread: cutoff

The frontside tight end will use a reach block technique taking a flat, 90-degree step with his outside foot. This step should be parallel, with the toes pointing straight ahead. He will block with his inside shoulder and his head to the outside. If the defender aligned on the tight end slants inside, then the tight end lets him go and climbs to the linebacker level. A good change-up here is to use cut technique. The tight end uses the same footwork but will drive his inside shoulder through the outside thigh pad of the defender. It is imperative that the tight end does not allow penetration at the point of attack.

When running this play to a split end side, the split end will release to the outside shoulder of the corner and stalk the defender responsible for the deep outside zone to that side. This play can also be called with a crack call. This call requires the split end to crack the fourth defender, who is usually the strong safety. At this point, the pulling guard would block the corner.

The frontside tackle blocks the first man on or outside of his alignment. He does not block the B gap defender, but he is assigned to block the first man on the line of scrimmage outside the B gap defender. He will also take a reach step with his outside foot to block the man aligned on or outside. If the defender aligned on the playside tackle slants to the inside, then he lets him go and climbs to the linebacker level. It is imperative for the frontside tackle to not allow penetration at the point of attack, so he may want to use cut technique to keep penetration from happening.

When running this play to a split end-wingback flank, times will exist when the defender on the playside tackle is aligned too wide. If the defender is too wide, then the wingback and tackle can make a 3 call, causing the wingback to block down and the tackle to pull and block the wingback's man. In this case, you have the defense beat if you are mixing the triple option with the speed sweep.

The frontside guard will pull flat, keying the wingback's block. The wingback is assigned to block the defender who is aligned over him. The guard should key that block as he pulls. If the wingback has blocked his man to the inside, then the guard will pull around that block and wall off from the linebacker level to the safety level. As the guard walls off, he will look to his inside for the first threat scraping inside out from the linebacker level. If no threat exists from the linebacker level, then he should climb to the safety level and block the first defender to show.

If the wingback's block is being stretched to the outside, then the pulling guard should wall off inside that block. Again, the guard should then look to block the linebacker level first or to the safety level next.

The offensive center's rule is reach, on, backer, which is a new concept to a wing-T center. His rule tells him that he will reach to the playside guard and cut any defender in the A gap area. If no defender is aligned in the A gap, then the center will climb to the linebacker level. Against a 50 defense, the center should look for a blitzing inside linebacker.

The backside guard is much like the center, he will reach to the backside A gap area and cut any defender in that area. That defender includes a nose aligned head-up on the offensive center. If no defenders are in those areas, then the backside guard climbs to the linebacker level.

The backside tackle and tight end have the same rule, which is to release to the cutoff point. They will release through the backside B and C gaps and climb from the linebacker level to the safety level. No chance exists that any defender on the backside of this play can stop the play, if he is aligned on the line of scrimmage. This concept will enable the backside linemen to release down the field immediately.

The Backfield Techniques

The backfield techniques for the speed sweep are based on precision and timing, like all of the other series in the wing-T. However, this package will actually take less precision and allow them to use their speed more than most wing-T offensive series. The motion is full speed, and the play is full speed, which allows the halfbacks to use their speed to outrun the defense.

Most wing-T teams using the speed sweep are running it as part of their 20 series. This choice gives them an additional sweep play to complement the buck sweep and keeps the companion plays the same. The buck sweep uses the fullback up the middle and the waggle as two of the basic companion plays. The speed sweep can also use the fullback up the middle and the waggle as companions; however, the down series is also a great companion to the speed sweep to the tight end side.

The package you will see in this chapter shows some of both packages but starts with the buck series as the companion plays to the speed sweep. The backfield techniques explained here reflect the buck sweep series, since the fullback will be faking up the middle and the quarterback will be faking the waggle.

The Quarterback

On the snap of the football, the quarterback will bring the ball to his belt and pivot off of his playside foot almost 180 degrees. He should be about 12 inches from being completely turned around. His back should be almost parallel to the line of scrimmage, and his tail should be in the playside A gap (the ball will be snapped when the wingback is approximately in the backside B gap). This distance is approximately four feet or one big step away from the quarterback. As the quarterback pivots, it is best not to be completely flat. The wingback will be running for a point about one foot behind the tail of the quarterback, so very little space exists as the quarterback pivots. If he is about 12 inches from being parallel, then the rest of the 20 series will be easier to execute. The handoff to the wingback will be made in the playside A gap and will be made when the wingback is directly behind the quarterback. As with all other wing-T handoffs, the quarterback should not reach the ball but hand it off at forearm's length. The quarterback will feather the ball into the wingback's pocket by laying the ball on the table hand. It is the quarterback's responsibility to get the ball to the wingback. After faking the handoff to the wingback, the quarterback will push off his playside foot and step straight back into the backfield. He will not be on the midline, but he should step as if he were on a new midline behind the frontside A gap. The fullback will be attacking the tail of the center and faking over an imaginary ball, in what is called a proximity fake. He should stay tight to the quarterback as he winds his path into and beyond the line of scrimmage to block the linebacker level. The quarterback does not actually fake to the fullback, but the proximity of their shoulders and the action of the fullback faking over an imaginary ball creates the proximity fake. After the handoff, the quarterback takes two steps straight back into the backfield behind the frontside A gap and then attacks the opposite flank, faking the waggle play.

The Ballcarrier (Backside Wingback)

The wingback carrying the ball will take off in extended motion, running full speed and aiming for a point about one foot behind the tail of the quarterback. The ball will be snapped when the wingback is about four feet from the quarterback. As the quarterback places the ball on the wingback's table hand, he will secure the handoff by sliding the ball into a secure position and covering the ball with four points of pressure. After securing the handoff, the wingback should belly his path to about one yard of depth into the backfield, to allow himself an opportunity to read the block of the pulling guard and either cut up the field or continue to outrun the flank. As the wingback attacks the flank, he is reading the block of the opposite halfback. He cuts up the field, if penetration is at the flank or if the play is being stretched. Use your speed and outrun the flank, if not. The ballcarrier should outrun the flank, if he can. To set up the blocks, he can bounce from the hash, to the alley, to the numbers, and to the sideline.

The Fullback

The fullback should use the same techniques he would use if he were running the 20 series versus an odd defense. It is extremely important that he align with his heels four yards from the back tip of the football. His first step should be with his playside foot for the tail of the offensive center. He will own the midline, since the quarterback will reverse pivot to the A gap and beyond the midline. On his second step, he will fake over an imaginary football, creating the proximity fake with the quarterback. He will then wind his path to the playside foot of the offensive center and climb to the linebacker level to block the first defender to show.

The Blocker (Frontside Wingback)

The frontside wingback takes his normal alignment from the tackle but may need to cheat inside at times depending on the defense. His basic assignment is to block the defender aligned over him, but, if the playside tackle's man is too wide, then the wingback and the tackle make a 3 call, which switches their assignments. At this point, the wingback would block down and the tackle will pull to block the defender aligned over the wingback. Start for a point one yard outside the defender and try to hook the defender to the inside. Cut his outside leg, if he stretches or runs to the outside. If you do not use cut technique, then maintain contact with the defender and stay squared up on him. If the defender is off the line of scrimmage and running to the outside, always try to cut him. Do not allow the defender to penetrate into the backfield, since this penetration will not allow the pulling guard to attack the flank. It is easier to cut the defender, if he is off the line of scrimmage, but, if he is on the line of scrimmage, then stretch him to the outside.

Examples of the Speed Sweep Play

The first example is Liz red 21 jet, which is the speed sweep to a tight end-wingback flank with Liz motion (meaning the left-hand inside). Refer to Diagrams 7.3 through 7.6. The next example is Liz blue 21 jet, which is the speed sweep to a split end-wingback flank with Liz motion. Refer to Diagrams 7.7 through 7.10.

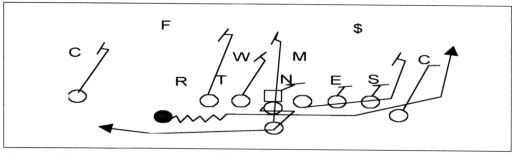

Diagram 7.3. Liz red 21 jet versus overshift

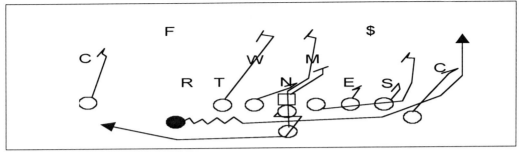

Diagram 7.4. Liz red 21 jet versus 50

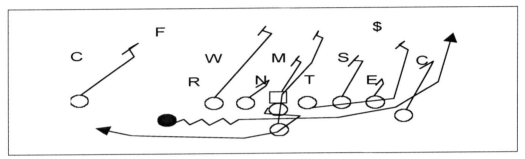

Diagram 7.5. Liz red 21 jet versus 4-3

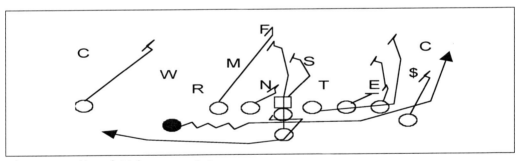

Diagram 7.6. Liz red 21 jet versus 4-4

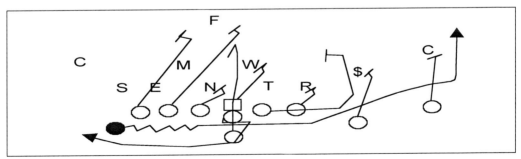

Diagram 7.7. Liz blue 21 jet versus overshift

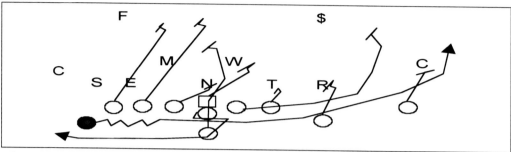

Diagram 7.8. Liz blue 21 jet versus 50

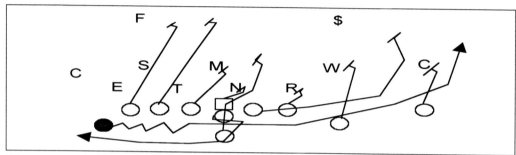

Diagram 7.9. Liz blue 21 jet versus 4-3

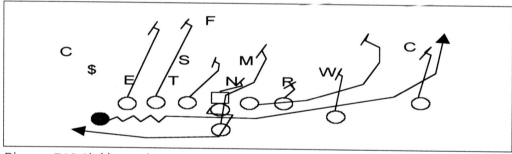

Diagram 7.10. Liz blue 21 jet versus 4-4

So far, you have seen how to run the speed sweep to a tight end-wingback flank and to a split end-wingback flank versus all of the most common defenses you will probably go against. If another defense is not covered in these diagrams, then just simply follow the blocking rules as previously described. You will most likely see a variety of defenses against the wing-T offense, but the speed sweep and the triple option will limit the number of fronts and coverages you will see.

Diagrams 7.11 through 7.14 will illustrate the speed sweep from different formation variables and will only be diagrammed against one defensive front. The blocking does not change, so the defensive front is not important. What is important is the amount of imagination possible with this offense. Many more variations exist than the ones shown in these diagrams.

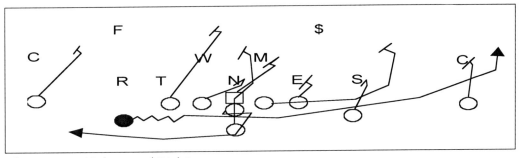

Diagram 7.11. Liz loose red 21 jet

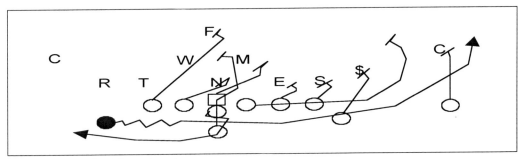

Diagram 7.12. Liz right red 21 jet

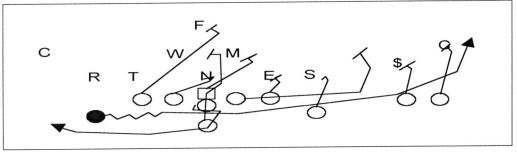

Diagram 7.13. Liz loose right red 21 jet

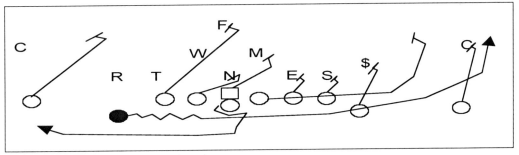

Diagram 7.14. Liz empty pro red 21 jet

Companion Plays

Two packages can be used to complement the speed sweep. The first and most obvious is the 20 (buck) series. The second complementary package is the down series, when you are running the speed sweep package to a tight end-wingback flank. Diagrams 7.15 through 7.18 illustrate the two packages of complementary plays. The first package (Diagrams 7.15 and 7.16) complements the speed sweep to the tight end-wingback flank. The next package (Diagrams 7.17 and 7.18) complements the speed sweep to the split end-wingback flank.

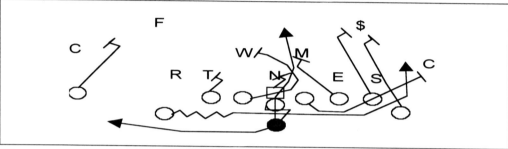

Diagram 7.15. Liz red 24 gut

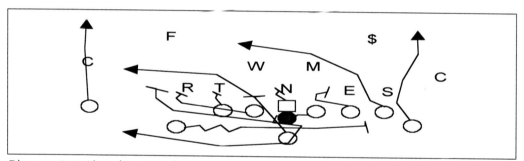

Diagram 7.16. Liz red 21 waggle

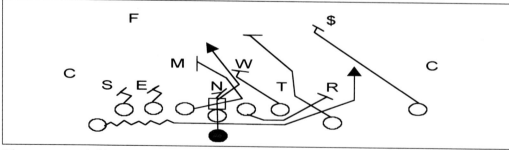

Diagram 7.17. Liz blue 24 gut

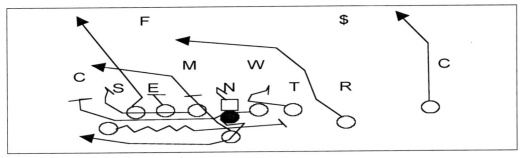

Diagram 7.18. Liz blue 21 waggle

The next package (Diagrams 7.19 through 7.21) illustrates the use of the down series to complement the speed sweep to the tight end-wingback flank. The keep pass from this package opens up the possibility of bunch routes, since three receivers will be in a confined space. Additionally, the speed of the motion will not allow the defense the required time to adjust to the bunch formation.

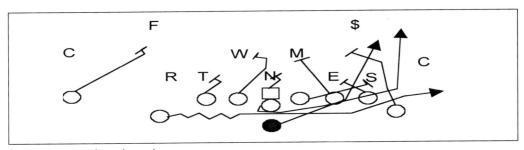

Diagram 7.19. Liz red 82 down

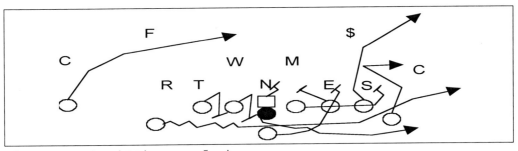

Diagram 7.20. Liz red 81 keep pass flood

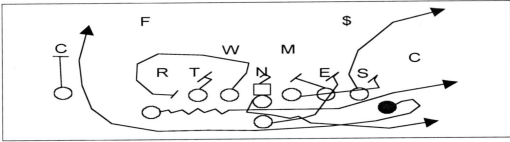

Diagram 7.21. Liz red 81 keep pass reverse at 9

About the Author

Dennis Creehan is the defensive coordinator for the Calgary Stampeders of the Canadian Football League, a position he assumed in 2004. One of the most respected coaches in the game, his more than three decades of coaching experience includes successful stints at the high school, collegiate, and professional levels.

Creehan began his coaching career (1971-'74) at Keystone Oaks High School in Pittsburgh, Pennsylvania, after a stellar playing career as a strong safety at Edinboro University. A three-year starter for the Scots, Creehan served as team captain in his senior season, earned first-team all-ECAC accolades, and helped lead Edinboro to Lambert Bowl honors. At Keystone Oaks, he served as offensive coordinator and also coached wrestling and baseball.

In 1974, Creehan joined Johnny Majors' staff at the University of Pittsburgh, where he spent one year as a graduate assistant. He then served as the offensive coordinator at Carnegie-Mellon for a single season, before returning to his alma mater as defensive coordinator prior to the 1976 season. Three years later, in 1979, Creehan was elevated to the position of head football coach at Edinboro. During his six years at the helm of the Fighting Scots' gridiron program, his teams won two league titles and were nationally ranked four times. During his tenure at Edinboro, his teams posted a 39-20-1 record (.658)—a winning percentage that continues to rank as the highest in Edinboro football history. For his efforts with the Fighting Scots, he received three conference coach-of-the-year honors.

From 1985 to 1987 and 1991 to 1992, he served as the defensive line coach and special teams coordinator for the Edmonton Eskimos of the Canadian Football League. During his tenure with the Eskimos, Edmonton was 35-16, won two conference titles (1986 and 1991), and appeared in the Grey Cup (1986).

From 1987 to 1989, Creehan was the outside linebackers' coach at the University of California, Berkeley. He then moved to San Francisco State in 1990, where he served as the head football coach and assistant athletic director for the Gators for a year.

In 1992, Creehan was named head football coach at South Dakota. During his five years at the helm of the Coyotes, Creehan resuscitated a struggling program, leading his teams to 28 wins, including 26 in his last three years. In 1997, Creehan moved to Arkansas State, where he served as defensive coordinator for a season, before joining the staff at Rutgers University as the Scarlet Knights' defensive coordinator—a position he held for three years.

Creehan then served as the special teams coordinator at Duke University for two seasons (2001-2002), where he also worked with the Blue Devils' inside and outside linebackers. In 2003, he joined the staff at the United States Military Academy as the Black Knights' special teams coordinator.

Creehan is widely considered as one of the most knowledgeable coaches in the game on the Wing-T offense. He has written several books on the Wing-T and has been featured on more than a dozen well-received instructional videos on his popular offensive system.

A Hall of Fame member at both Bethel Park (PA) High School and Edinboro University, Creehan earned master's degrees from both Duquesne University in 1973 and Pittsburgh in 1977. He and his wife, Linda, have two sons: Kevin, a professor at Virginia Tech University, and Casey, an assistant football coach at James Madison University.